God Moments

D1383660

God Moments

*Why Faith Really Matters
to a New Generation*

Jeremy Langford

ORBIS BOOKS

Maryknoll, New York 10545

Copyright © 2001 by Jeremy W. Langford

Published by Orbis Books, Maryknoll, New York, U.S.A.

Manufactured in the United States of America

Some of the selections in this work were originally published by the author in the following and are gratefully used with permission: "You're from a Broken Home," "Navigating the River of Life," and selections on Immanuel Kant and C. S. Lewis originally appeared in "Odyssey of a Young Adult Catholic," *New Theology Review* 11, no. 1 (1998): 41–52; material on the great question and the great invitation of Christianity, Saint Augustine's legacy, and *praxis* originally appeared in "Welcome Generation X!?!" *Church* 14, no. 4 (1998): 13–18; portions of "Accepting the Gift of Peace" originally appeared in *The Works* 1, no. 1 (fall 1999): 23–25; portions of "The Courage to Be" originally appeared in *The Works* 2, no. 2 (winter 2000): 22; material on common good, citizenship, friendship, and community originally appeared in *The Works* 2, nos. 4 (summer 2000): 34 and 5 (fall 2000): 25, and vol. 3, no. 1 (winter 2001): 23. "The Road to Emmaus: A Challenge to Our Generation and Those Who Minister to Us" originally appeared in slightly different form as "Ministering to Gen-X Catholics, Jesus Style," *America* 182, no. 14 (April 22, 2000): 6–10.

Terry Anderson's poem "Faith" can be found in *Den of Lions* (New York: Random House, Ballantine Books, 1993), 117–118, and is used with permission of the author.

Scripture quotations are from the New Revised Standard Version of the Bible, copyright © 1989 by the Division of Christian Education of the National Council of Churches of Christ in the USA. Used by permission. All rights reserved.

Library of Congress Cataloging-in-Publication Data

Langford, Jeremy.
    God moments : why faith really matters to a new generation / Jeremy Langford.
      p. cm.
    Includes bibliographical references (p.).
    ISBN 1-57075-390-3 (pbk.)
      1. Christian life—Catholic authors. I. Title.

BX2350.2 .L29 2001
248.4'82—dc21

                          2001036363

for Liz, my companion in all

for Josh, my brother and best friend

and
for my family—

my mother, Margaret
and
my father, Jim, stepmother, Jill,
and my adopted siblings, Trevor and Emily

"Let all that you do be done in love"

—1 Corinthians 16:14

CONTENTS

PART THREE
SEEING: BEING TRANSFORMED AND PERCEIVING IN A NEW WAY

PART FOUR
ACTING: FAITH WITHOUT WORKS IS DEAD

PROLOGUE

"You're from a Broken Home"

When I was ten years old and my younger brother, Josh, was eight, our parents got divorced. In what seemed a flash, my brother and I said good-bye to all that we had known in South Bend, Indiana; packed everything we owned into a truck; loaded our German Shepherd, Kira, into the station wagon; and moved with our mother to her hometown of Minneapolis.

As the new "man of the house" by a mere seventeen months, I felt a keen sense of responsibility for my brother and mother. I also felt a deep sense of loss in being so far away from my father. The whole notion of "visitation" was just sinking in and it made no sense—what did it mean to "visit" one of my parents? Why couldn't I just *live* with *both* of my parents and be a "normal" family?

Over time, though I did not accept it, I learned to deal with the reality of our family situation. My mother worked hard to make ends meet and to be very involved in our lives—especially when it came to ensuring that we received a good education and were involved in sports—while my father did the same from afar. As I got back to the business of being a kid, I started to relax a bit. Once school began I worked hard to meet people and develop friendships and move forward.

Just as I was beginning to feel at home, one of my classmates from the neighborhood caught up with me after school and asked if we could walk home together. As we approached the modest townhouse my mother was renting, my acquaintance asked if he could meet my family sometime. "Well," I said rather matter of factly, "my parents are divorced and my dad lives in Indiana, where I'm from. But sometime you can meet my mom, brother, and our dog if you want."

"Oh," he replied before running off, "you're from a broken home."

I stood there stunned. *Broken home?* What could that possibly mean?

Perhaps this neighbor kid—and even the whole world—knew something I was too dumb or naïve to understand: children from broken homes don't make it. How could they? The very foundation of their lives gets shattered right under their feet, right before their very eyes. *Broken home, broken heart, broken dreams, broken future.*

I immediately hated the whole concept of broken home. Josh and I had been told that our parents loved us and that we would be assured good relationships with them both. What was broken about that? Sure, my parents were no longer together, and there were many difficult times, but in the end we were not broken, were we?

As I walked up the steps of our townhouse, the words *broken home* made their way into the recesses of my wounded psyche. My brother was not yet home from school and my mother was still at work, so when I opened the door and heard its creak echo in the empty hallway, I got clobbered with the weight of my own existence. Closing the door behind me as if to shut out the whole world, I dragged myself slowly up the stairs to my bedroom, threw myself on my bed, and started to cry. Uncontrollably.

On that lonely afternoon I stared out onto the parking lot just beneath my window. The sun was high in the sky as my eyes traced the outlines of the cracked blacktop surface and then focused on each object that littered its surface: broken bottles, rusty cans, old newspapers, discarded toys. When that became too much, I followed the useless rain gutter along the side of the leaky garage up to the roof. More litter, including a shattered mirror to reflect my shattered feelings.

I must have studied the parking lot for hours, because I snapped out of my quandary only when I noticed the sun was setting. At that moment I felt an incredible sense of peace. Beautiful hues of orange, red, and yellow filled the sky and bathed everything in a majestic light. My mind turned back to the idea that I was from a broken home. In that instant, in my ten-year-old way, I recognized that my home, my family, and my life would be broken only if I allowed them to be. Somehow I realized that I was more than I seemed, bigger than my situation.

Refixing my gaze on the garage roof, I once again caught sight of the shards of the broken mirror, now glowing in the sun's light. Suddenly everything outside and inside me seemed brighter.

Looking back now I see that, as lonely and broken as I felt at that crucial juncture in my young life, I was anything but alone.[1]

Introduction

Where in the World Is God?

For reasons that belong to the realm of mystery, our glimpses of God, or "God moments," come and go. Like a cosmic game of hide-and-go-seek, now we see God, now we don't. Sometimes we find God right where we figured we would—in long conversations with close friends, at the dinner table with family, in hugs from loved ones, at weddings, funerals, and baptisms. Other times we are surprised to find God, as Catholic novelist Flannery O'Connor once wrote, "flitting from tree to tree in the back of our minds," calling us to look more deeply into who we are, daring us to drop our baggage and run free. And sometimes God finds us just when we least expect it, when we turn our backs and give up.

We may not be able to describe God, exactly, but we know when we have God moments. We know it in our souls.

The trouble with God moments is that we forget them so easily. We go right back to playing hide-and-go-seek with God. Sometimes God hides and we find her. Sometimes we hide and he finds us. But the eternal question "Where in the world is God?" echoes in the marrow of our bones.

Having grown up Catholic, I had a pretty good idea that I could find God in the churches I knew as a kid. The church building was God's "house" on earth, and the Roman Catholic Church was the second in command to God as head of the household.

But somewhere along the way I got to thinking that God had too many houses to be in them all at the same time. And if he could be in them all simultaneously, I wondered, why would God limit himself to just Catholic churches? Why wouldn't he fill every space that groaned with emptiness or claimed to be his home? And, by that logic, why would he confine himself to bricks and mortar at all—why wouldn't God just set himself loose in the world?

My response to these questions was to stop going to Mass on a regular basis. After all, if God is loose in the world, did I really need to go to church to find him?

Much to my surprise, the answer has turned out to be yes, I do need to go to church in addition to seeking God in every other corner of the world.

Five years ago, while in my mid-twenties, I decided to find a church I liked and start going regularly if I was to find God, if God was to find me, and if I was to find me. It sounds irreverent and even shallow to talk about "shopping" for the right church, but that is what I did. I had been living in the city of Chicago for a couple of years and had "tried" a few of the popular churches that attracted young people. Some I liked better than others, and all the while I kept hearing from friends and acquaintances that I really should check out Old Saint Patrick's Church in the downtown area. "It's a cool place that makes faith relevant without being uncomfortable," one friend said in the midst of telling me its history as the oldest public building in the city and describing its emphasis on good preaching, music, liturgy, community, and outreach programs. "Besides," another buddy joked, "Old St. Pat's hosts the 'World's Largest Block Party' summer fundraiser that gathers hundreds of thousands of people for killer parties, so why not check it out?" At that time in my life I needed to party, pray, worship, and serve with seekers who were in the same rickety boat as I was. So I finally got myself to St. Pat's.

Having made my way to the church one Sunday morning, I was struck by the beauty of the building and the feel of the place. But I quickly became painfully aware that as I listened to the readings, concentrated on the homily, and mouthed the prayers, I did not find God as easily as I had hoped. Instead, I was overcome by questions: What is all of this faith stuff about? What are we doing here? Is the Bible fact or fiction? Does the priest believe all that he has said? Do we?

By the time we reached the profession of faith, the familiar words suddenly hit me like bullets: "*We believe* in one God, the Father, the Almighty, maker of heaven and earth, of all that is, seen and unseen. ...*We believe* in one Lord, Jesus Christ, the only Son of God eternally begotten of the Father.... *We believe* in the Holy Spirit, the Lord, the giver of life, who proceeds from the Father and the Son.... *We believe* in one holy catholic and apostolic Church.... We look for the resurrection of the dead, and the life of the world to come. Amen."

While my mind swirled with questions, I rattled off the Creed, as I had throughout my childhood and young adult years, without knowing if I really believed or even understood what I was saying. But I vowed that no matter how frustrated I was, I would keep going to church and working on my faith life.

As a restless seeker loaded with doubt and famished with spiritual hunger, I spent the next year as a not-so-infrequent Mass-goer at Old St. Pat's. Eventually I came to know Father John Cusick, a popular preacher at the church and the director of Young Adult Ministry for the Archdiocese of Chicago. At first I did not want to reveal my true identity as a bewildered, unsure, and uneasy young Catholic. Somehow I had it in my head that priests and religious are not the kinds of people who understand real doubt and spiritual struggle. But over time—as I asked questions, attended Mass, met other seekers, asked more questions, and vented frustrations—Fr. Cusick ("please, call me John") hung with me at every turn as he listened, shared his own struggles, and offered his hard-won insights.

Not too long into our friendship, John asked me to be a speaker in a program called Theology-on-Tap. Sponsored by the Archdiocese of Chicago, Theology-on-Tap is an annual summer forum for young adults that combines lecture and discussion, food and beer. It is the largest Catholic young adult speaker program in the country, and at the time was in its fifteenth year and reaching nearly fifty parishes and over two thousand young people a night! Today it reaches over sixty parishes and nearly three thousand young people a night.

I immediately said no to John's invitation—absolutely not. But he signed me up anyway, arguing that while I might not recognize it at the time, the experience would be good for me. I had never been to a Theology-on-Tap talk, so I had no idea who the speakers were, who would go to such talks, or what I could possibly offer people. And I dreaded speaking to my peers, because I feared they would call my bluff, challenge my points, or simply laugh at me. But John would not hear excuses, so out of desperation I outlined a talk called "Seeking: A Way of Life" and for three nights met with my peers in different parishes throughout the city.

I will never forget those first few talks. Each night I was profoundly moved by my peers—members of the infamous Generation X—who took time out of their busy schedules to attend a talk on faith issues, asked great questions, shared their own struggles, laughed about the ups and downs of life, and pointed to times in their lives when God's presence was either overwhelmingly obvious or mysteriously obscure.

As John suspected, what happened those nights and in so many other talks I've given and conversations I've had with my peers is that we broke through many of the stereotypes that others hold about us and that we hold about others and got down to basics. We got down to being human. We got down to sharing our God moments.

This book is about God moments—those that are as brief and beautiful as a sunset or as lasting and profound as being in love. God moments come to us all. They are moments of recognition when we know what is true, realize what is real, and experience what is good. God moments are rare glimpses into eternity that happen in time. They are moments pregnant with love and life that help us give birth to our best selves and encourage others to find their best selves. They are moments that fill us with thanksgiving, overwhelm us with joy, offer us hope. They are moments that teach us that faith really matters.

In reflecting on our generation, the art of seeking, the Christian call to see with eyes of faith, and the importance of serving those in need, I hope to inspire and encourage you to dig deep into life and think about your faith. In sharing some God moments from my life and experience, I hope to prompt you to recognize and remember your own God moments. In all honesty, I never imagined that I would be writing a book for my peers about God, faith, or Catholicism. Perhaps you never imagined that you'd be reading one. And therein lies the beauty of our relationship through these pages. We are bound together by the mere fact that we are seekers—seeking truth, life, love, friendship, meaning, understanding, fulfillment, peace, happiness. We may seek different things in different ways. We may find different answers to our radically different questions. But let's enjoy this journey together, for life is one big God moment waiting to be embraced—and we have a much better chance of embracing life in all its fullness if we do it together.

PART ONE

TALKIN' 'BOUT MY GENERATION . . . *X*

"To what then will I compare the people of this generation, and what are they like?"

—Luke 7:31

Introduction

"Can You Please Explain Generation X to Me?"

A few years ago I was speaking in a parish basement to a group of over a hundred of my peers. In the back of the room a few "older" people were huddled together, looking somewhat uncomfortable and whispering whenever a point struck them.

After the talk, as with most talks about such personal issues as faith, various people got in line to ask follow-up questions, share an insight of their own, challenge a point I had made, or just say hello. At the end of the line stood two of the older adults, obviously a married couple, who had been sitting in the back of the room. They were holding hands and looked concerned. Once the line had thinned and they did not have to worry about being overheard, the woman began speaking while her husband drifted off to the side: "I am a concerned parent," she began, "and I am wondering if you can *please* explain *Generation X* to me?"

"The term?" I asked in return.

"Well, yes, the term and what it can tell me about my son," she responded with a pained look on her face. "You see, he's about your age and is lost, anxious, cynical, depressed. I don't know what I did wrong in raising him or how to reach him. When I try to talk to him, he just shuts me out, especially when I bring up faith, and tells me I will never understand him or his generation. Please help me."

In trying to offer a response, two things became painfully clear: first, I realized that I really dislike the term *Generation X*, and second, offering insight into my generation is no easy task—not even for one smack dab in the middle of it. As a single, white, middle-income, Catholic male from the Midwest, my understanding of Generation X (because this term is so widely used to describe our peer group, I will use it despite its negative connotations) is clearly limited. Therefore, I make no claim to know everything about or to speak for *all* of our generation. What I do claim is that, as the nation's most ethnically, racially, culturally, economically, politically, academically, and religiously diverse group, we are beyond easy stereotypes and deserve to be taken seriously, even in our irreverent, untraditional ways.

Though we ended up talking for more than an hour, this concerned mother and I parted ways with more questions than answers. But we had reached across generations and generalizations and talked honestly about our lives, families, faith, and hopes.

When I asked some friends how they would have answered the distressed woman's question or would explain the who, what, where, when, why, and how of our generation, their answers were immediate and heartfelt. My friend Terrence dismissed the name and all talk about *Generation X* as being hype created by advertisers who tell us what to believe about ourselves and then sell us stuff to help us maintain our manufactured identity. Another friend, Karen, said she feels there are many things to lament about our generation—to paraphrase her words, that we grew up in a culture of divorce, did not learn traditional values, pay more attention to movies and music than government and public policy, are scared to form our own families, find happiness in Prozac pills when all else fails, don't trust institutions, and revel in leading busy lives that deter us from thinking about deeper things. But she also shared her belief that we are ironically aware of our fragmented existence and could very well prove to be a generation devoted to healing rifts, redefining government, promoting service, and even bringing the spiritual back into daily life.

The question, "Can you please explain Generation X to me?" has plagued me since the troubled mother first asked it. But rather than get caught up in technical analyses, I want to briefly reflect on the origin of the term and the forces that have shaped us as necessary steps toward the heart of the matter—a deeper discussion of our spiritual hungers and the life of faith.

1

X Marks What Spot?

Ifirst heard the term *Generation X* in 1992. Having recently graduated from the University of Notre Dame, I was twenty-two years old, out of school, out of work, and full of untapped passion. With my bachelor's degree in English and philosophy firmly in hand, I appeared to be what the media had begun to describe as the typical Gen Xer—clueless about what to do with my life.

The discussions about my generation were just heating up, but I was only vaguely interested in what people were saying. On one hand, I took comfort in knowing that, like me, many of my peers were struggling with their futures. On the other hand, I resented the way my generation was being stereotyped. I knew many people who, rather than being aimless, were aiming for dreams of rewarding lives that not only captured the best and made up for the worst of our parents' lives and our upbringing but also grew from our own original creativity.

Defending my dreams was nothing new. Throughout my undergraduate years when people discovered what I was studying, they would usually ask with condescending bewilderment, "What are you going to do with *that*?" Since I loved my studies and was determined to earn a Ph.D. in American literature so that I could someday teach college, I would gladly offer long-winded discourses on the value and virtue of a liberal arts education, on "learning how to learn." But as time went on and I grew increasingly tired of the question and more fearful of the future, I eventually whittled my answer down to a simple and hopeful, "I'm going to be happy."

Again, people were quick to point out, "happy doesn't pay the bills." So I crossed my fingers and even prayed that I would be accepted into a good Ph.D. program with funding enough to live, study, and reach my dreams. After spending the fall of my senior year preparing for and taking the Graduate Records Examination (GRE), I was rewarded by having to spend my Christmas break filling out applications to my top five choices of graduate schools. I then spent the next few months waiting impatiently for at least one "yes" that would justify my idealism and validate my future.

By March, at the beginning of spring break and just two months away from my graduation, the fifth and final rejection letter came in the mail literally as I was heading out the door to pile into a car full of friends bound for Florida. I had made a quick detour into the mail room to see if any good news had come from the one school that I thought for certain would accept me. Sure enough, an envelope from the school sat all alone in my box. But it was thin, so I knew immediately that it was a rejection—no welcome materials or brochures that day.

I opened the envelope with a sigh and read the opening lines that said something like: "Thank you for your application for graduate studies in American literature. While your grade point average, GRE scores, and letters of recommendation are highly competitive, we regret to inform you that due to unprecedented numbers of applicants and limited funding we cannot offer you a place in the upcoming class of graduate students. . . ."

My disappointment was only compounded by the fact that this same school had written me a week earlier saying that I had been accepted as a dormitory resident assistant to help defray some of the cost of my graduate education. For a moment I thought about moving into the dorm the next fall and leaving it to Student Housing to kick me out!—at least that way I'd have a place to live for a while as I figured out what my next move would be. But I cleared the daydream from my mind, stuffed the letter back into the mailbox, slinked down the stairs to the parking lot behind the dorm, got into the car with my friends, and took off for Florida. I thought seriously about my life on the trip, but my friends were great about helping me lighten up, have fun, and savor these last spring break moments.

When I returned from spring break, however, reality sank in: I had no idea what I was going to do with my life! My family was very supportive and offered such assurances as "things will work out," "you did not study so hard for nothing," and—crazy as it sounded to me—"God has a plan for you."

I rejected all such comforts but did accept a job with my father and stepmother's small sports publishing company, Diamond Communications. The deal was that for room, board, and a small monthly salary, I could learn the business of publishing from the bottom up. From the time I was twelve years old I had done odd jobs for the company, which included loading and unloading books at the warehouse, packing orders, answering phones, and helping out at trade shows. Now I would learn everything from editing and proofreading to marketing and running author tours to handling the finances.

Though I remain deeply grateful for the several months I worked at Diamond, I could not help feeling back then that I had somehow blown it: four years of independence at college only to end up back at home! My lofty goals of teaching American literature had been reduced to meaningless distractions from the more "realistic" pursuits of finding a job, making money, and getting on with life. No matter what was in my head or in my heart, all the facts added up to one thing: I was a typical aimless "Gen Xer."

Even when I decided to leave my job with Diamond, move out of my family's house and into an apartment with a friend, and take a job at a bookstore, I had to face the stereotype of being just another clueless Xer. My friends and I found it deliciously ironic and funny that instead of being a professor of literature and writing books, I was selling other people's books at the Little Professor Book Center. But all kidding aside, I remember one day in particular with a mixture of anger and sadness. I was shelving books in the philosophy section at the bookstore when a professor I recognized from Notre Dame walked over to me to ask a question about a book. In the course of answering his question I asked him how things were at Notre Dame.

"Did you go there?" he asked.

"Yes," I said proudly.

"Then what the hell are you doing working *here?*" he asked. Without waiting for an answer, he added, "I mean you have a degree from Notre Dame, for God's sake, and you're shelving books!"

I tried to explain that I loved working at the bookstore and that I was looking at jobs in publishing. He didn't care; all he could say was, "I don't understand your generation" before he bought a book on human nature and went his way.

Understanding our generation has literally become a job. In a recent television special on how car manufacturers develop new models and styles for different age groups, one of the young hot shots from Chrysler identified himself as a "Gen X Marketing Expert," which in sales lingo translates to "GenXpert." He said his job is to keep his finger on the pulse of Generation X so that he can help engineers design cars that are cool. I guess he means cars that are at once original and mass produced!

During recent years, many attempts have been made to define and describe our generation. Much of the discussion has been sociological, revolving around determining ranges of birth dates, corresponding numbers of births during those years, and general attributes that differentiate us from other generations. For example, in their national bestseller *The Fourth Turning*, historians and generational theorists William Strauss and Neil Howe describe today's young adults as the "13er" generation (because we are literally the thirteenth generation to call ourselves Americans) and they place our birth years from 1961 to 1981, giving us a total of 80 million members. Others like George Barna and William Dunn have delineated narrower birth boundaries; both begin with the year 1965 but Barna argues that the era ends in 1983 (making our generation's population 70 million) while Dunn holds that it ends in 1976 (making us 44 million in number).[1]

While there is debate over the specific birth years that define our generation, it seems reasonable to say that the members of our generation were born between 1960—when the G. D. Searle Drug Company marketed the first commercially produced birth control pill—and 1980—when Ronald Reagan was elected president and the nation moved away from experimentation and back toward tradition.[2] The bottom line is that there are a lot of us. And we cannot be ignored or cast aside under a pile of stereotypes.

Unfortunately, much of the discussion about our generation outside of birth boundaries boils down to mindless labels: *Slackers, Twenty/Thirty-somethings, Grunge Kids, 13ers, Busters, Tweeners, Late Bloomers, Post Boomers, Boomlets, Atari Wavers, Nintendo Wavers, Repair Generation, MTV Generation,* and *Generation X.*[3] Of these equally annoying options, *Generation X* has become the most common. The origin of the term is unclear—it may have been a slogan for corporate advertising strategies aimed at American youth, a 1960s term for British adolescents, or the enigmatic name of a 1970s English punk band.[4]

No matter where the term came from, author Douglas Coupland made it famous in his 1991 novel *Generation X*[5] and wed it to the restless, middle-class young adult characters who form the plot of this and his other books. If art imitates reality, then Coupland's fictional characters tell us something about ourselves. But fiction, as Coupland admits by his reluctance to serve as the spokesperson of his generation, is not enough to explain exactly what the Generation X epithet signifies.

Generally speaking, the X in Generation X has stood for "superficial, easily distracted, rootless, inscrutable, self-centered, unfocused, pathetic, plucky, [and] merely confused."[6] Further descriptions of Generation X include "the whiny generation," "a generation of gripers," "a generation adrift," "the tuned-out generation," "slackers," and the "numb generation."[7]

While most of us simply reject being labeled and move on, a twenty-something Melissa Shirk spoke for many of us when she told *Sojourners* magazine:

> I have grown weary of the stereotypes and false representations of my generation—a generation that (believe it or not) gives me great hope. Let me introduce you to some of my twenty-something friends: Analisa teaches on a Navajo reservation. Kathy teaches learning disabled children...and Michael is studying for his doctorate in American history and gay studies. Amy, a full-time volunteer for Bread for the City and Zacchaeus Free Clinic in Washington, DC, loved it so much she extended her one-year term for another year of (yes) *service*. Andrea is in medical school and Mike is a stellar graphic artist. Angela has a golden voice and a passion for AIDS education; Karen was so inspired by Mother Teresa that she traveled to India to meet and work with her.[8]

In the years since the term *Generation X* and its negative definitions took hold, some observers have been inspired by young people like Melissa and have looked for more positive data to help describe us. According to Margot Hornblower in her 1997 *Time* magazine cover story, "Great Xpectations": "Slapped with the label Generation X, [Xers have] turned the tag into a badge of honor. They are X-citing, X-igent, X-pansive. They're the next big thing."[9] The good news is that many of us balance earning a living while getting an education with pursuing our dreams; we develop justice-oriented programs, start our own entrepreneurial businesses, help lead the way in technology and other areas, and engage institutions like government, religion, and marriage in new and challenging ways.

Of course, neither extreme is entirely accurate—we are neither entirely sinners nor entirely saints. But the facts suggest that we Gen Xers are much more than people originally thought we were.

Rather than looking at our generation through the monocle of dates or labels or stereotypes, it makes much more sense for us to look at our generation through a prism that offers a multi-faceted perspective on our origins, our parents and their generation, the culture and milieu into which we were born and reared, the world we live in as young adults, and our own very real hungers and yearnings.

2

Generation eX

Growing Up Divorced in More Ways than One

Some of my earliest memories include seeing my mother and father glued to the television and having very serious and involved conversations at the dinner table. It was 1973–74 and, as a three- and four-year-old, I had no idea about what was going on in the world or in the conversation between my parents. My younger brother was of no help. All I knew was that during the days, among more nurturing endeavors, my mother would put my brother and me on her lap and park us in front of the television as she reacted to what she was witnessing. Then she would talk hurriedly with my father in the evenings as he joined us on the couch and watched more of the same thing for himself.

As I later came to understand, what was being played out on the small screen and on the national stage were not only the Watergate scandal and subsequent impeachment proceedings of President Richard M. Nixon but also public debates about whether to pull U. S. troops out of Vietnam.

When I asked my mother—an avid historian—to confirm my memories and help me better understand what she and my dad had been talking about, what it had been like to be young parents raising kids at that time in American history, and how she thought such events had affected me and my generation as a whole, she paused and said, "Those events affected us all." Then she explained that it meant a lot to her that we could talk about our generations and try to make sense of our experiences.

She explained that her generation had come of age in the sixties, a time of radical change and revolution in this country. Young Boomers were fighting corrupt institutions and trying to find ways of planting their ideals and dreams so that they might bear fruit in the future. Those were exciting but difficult times. They saw both ends of the spectrum—love, peace, freedom, and civil rights on the one end and the assassinations of John F. Kennedy, Martin Luther King, Jr., and Robert Kennedy as well as the horrible rioting and police action at the 1968 Democratic National Convention in Chicago on the other end. While Xers were born at a time when the country was in great pain, we share in common with Boomers and all generations a desire to make sense of things as well as find and create meaning that we can cling to.

The Baby Boomers

For most of us twenty- and thirty-somethings, at least one (and more likely both) of our parents is a member of the so-called Baby Boomer generation. As the children of the Baby Boomers, we have been called the Baby Busters. Immediately these labels give off different connotations and prompt deeper questions. The term *Baby Boomer* makes that generation sound prosperous, fulfilled, strong in number. In contrast, the term *Baby Buster* makes our generation sound bankrupt, unfulfilled, weak in number. Moreover, these monikers immediately make us wonder: What shaped our parents' experiences? What did our generation bust? And, if things are broken, who is responsible and what, if anything, can be done to "fix" them?

Generally speaking, the Baby Boomers are so named because they were born in record numbers during the prosperous years following the triumphant end to the Second World War. As their parents helped re-build post-war America, they set their sights on getting married, having kids, finding good jobs, and buying homes. Boomers were born during a time of great enthusiasm and hope. This era is captured in movies, songs, books, and the memories of many Americans as an era

> when large institutions were regarded as effective, government as powerful, science as benign, schools as good, careers as reliable, families as strong, and crimes as under control. Government could afford to do almost anything it wanted while still balancing its budget. From year to year the middle class grew, and the gap between rich and poor narrowed. Worker

productivity and family incomes grew at the fastest pace ever measured, with no end in sight.... The wealthier and more community-minded America grew, the nicer (if blander) it became. Crime and divorce rates declined, ushering in an era of unlocked front doors, of nicely groomed youths, of President Eisenhower celebrating the well-being of the American family.[1]

As kids, Boomers were seen as the first generation of Americans capable of having the best of everything, knowing their inner selves, and creating a utopia not only within their own national borders but reaching as far as third-world countries. The first generation of children to experience the then-new invention of television, they were exposed to programming that was rich with "simple plots of competent parents, smart scientists, honest leaders, and happy endings."[2] And children onscreen and in real life had the run of things—*they* were the center of attention, not only their parents' but also, for the first time, advertisers'. Without glorifying the past, we can say that the cumulative effect of parental and pop culture influences for Boomer children, more or less, was that they felt safe, welcomed, and loved. Their problems and those of society at large seemed fixable by competent parents and institutions.

But all that was to change as Boomer children grew into their young adult years. Some call Boomers' young adult years a time of rebellion; others call them a time of awakening. In either case, Boomers felt that the mores and message of their childhood years that had provided safety through institutions, community rooted in self-knowledge and mutual benefit, and opportunity made possible through education and a booming economy smacked of mind-numbing uniformity. Boomers had been "raised to ask fundamental questions and apply fundamental principles" while being taught to hold their individuality in the highest esteem. The result was that Boomers revolted against their parents' ways of doing things.[3]

Across the country, students turned college campuses into hotbeds of social unrest. What caused the strongest youth reaction was the Vietnam War, which lasted from 1960 to 1975. In backing the South Vietnamese with arms and troops against attacks by the Communist North Vietnamese, the United States became embroiled in a bloody battle on foreign soil that many argue never should have happened or at the least never should have lasted as long as it did. While one of every sixteen male Boomers saw combat, ten times as many committed draft felonies as were killed in the war. By 1970, following the shooting by police of four Kent State students during a protest against the war, Boomers were more fully engaged in opposing the war.

Yet, even though prior to the 1972 election eighteen-year-olds were awarded the right to vote and by 1972 there were twenty-five million newly eligible voters, half of the Boomers failed to vote. They had made it clear that by and large they did not support Richard M. Nixon. Nevertheless, the future scandalous leader still won the election over George McGovern. Some argue that the Boomers did not vote because they had turned away from institutions, marriage, family, and professions and toward self-discovery through such routes as psychic phenomena and experiments in communal living as well as through the "Jesus Freak," New Age, born-again, and Human Potential movements.[4] In many aspects of their daily lives, young-adult Boomers reshaped the way America went about work (meaningful careers over productivity), image (independence over conformity), play (inner reward over communal achievement), consumerism (unique over mainstream), progress (feeling over doing), and beliefs and values (pick-and-choose over tradition).

Now that they have reached midlife, Boomers have become the focus of many interesting studies and commentaries that examine what their early rebellions and awakenings have translated into and how their vision of the way things ought to be has affected the country and future generations. Books like Phyllis Tickle's *Re-Discovering the Sacred: Spirituality in America*, Wade Clark Roof's *A Generation of Seekers: The Spiritual Journeys of the Baby Boom Generation*, and David Brooks's *Bobos in Paradise: The New Upper Class and How They Got There* have all sold well (the latter two enjoyed long-lasting national bestseller status), proving that Boomers like to read about themselves while trying to gain insight into their pasts, presents, and futures.

Because the Boomer generation is so large and established, it has set the course for American culture. Of the many influences this generation has had on modern life, two stand out. First, Boomers have been able to merge free-spirit idealism with money-making entrepreneurism and have blurred the lines between social consciousness and personal gain. Second, while Boomers have sparked a spiritual reawakening, their distrust of institutions has carried over to other generations and has often promoted an individualistic style of seeking.

To the first point, as many of the Boomers became more established in the work world, they brought with them the idealistic values of the 1960s and created a new way of living that allows people to achieve financial success while at the same time remaining free-spirit rebels. David Brooks describes this new culture as a mix between bourgeois mainstream culture and bohemian counterculture. He has coined the term "Bobos" (bourgeois bohemians) for Boomers, giving the following reasons:

> Founding design firms, they find a way to be an artist and still qualify for stock options. Building gourmet companies like Ben & Jerry's or Nantucket Nectars, they've found a way to be dippy hippies and multinational corporate fat cats. Using William S. Burroughs in ads for Nike sneakers and incorporating Rolling Stones anthems into their marketing campaigns, they've reconciled the antiestablishment style with the corporate imperative. Listening to management gurus who tell them to thrive on chaos and unleash their creative potential, they've reconciled the spirit of the imagination with service to the bottom line. Turning university towns like Princeton and Palo Alto into entrepreneurial centers, they have reconciled the highbrow with the high tax bracket. Dressing like Bill Gates in worn chinos on his way to a stockholders' meeting, they've reconciled undergraduate fashion with upper-crust occupations. Going on eco-adventure vacations, they've reconciled aristocratic thrill-seeking with social concern. Shopping at Benetton or the Body Shop, they've brought together consciousness-raising and cost control.[5]

Many Boomers do not fit this description and rightly take offense at such portrayals. But the popular culture has so embraced the kind of Boomer/Bobo mentioned above that the prevailing values of our time cater to people who wish to build a life that defies easy categorization and allows them to get what they can for themselves while maintaining at least a modicum of concern for others.

To the second point, as the Boomers have moved into their forties and fifties, they have exhibited a strong interest in spirituality but have shied away from institutional religion in favor of a more personalized faith life. In her book *Re-Discovering the Sacred*, Phyllis Tickle cites three main events or causes for both the Boomers' profound interest in the sacred and their deep distrust of institutions: (1) the atomic bombings of Hiroshima on August 6, 1945 and Nagasaki on August 9, 1945;

(2) the period of 1960–1975, which included the Vietnam War, the assassinations of the Kennedy brothers and Martin Luther King Jr., and
the Watergate scandal that led to the resignation of President Nixon;
and (3) the closing of the American frontier through territorial expan-
sion westward and a successful space program that sent man to the
moon. These three events, argues Tickle, caused, respectively, a rift between God and humankind, between institutions and those they were
meant to serve, and between the conscious world and the as-yet undis-
covered unconscious world. The result is that Boomers have relied on
themselves to identify and feed their profound spiritual hungers: "The
one clear lesson that we as a citizenry got out of Vietnam was pervasive
as well as central: Never trust authority—not its morals or its integrity
or (God help us) its edicts, directions, and explanations.... No authority, ever. Period. After Nam, Nixon, and that string of assassinations at
home and abroad, the individual's perception of right and wrong, do
and don't do, believe and don't believe became the litmus test for commitment and...also for moral responsibility and judgment."[6]

In many ways the Boomers' turning away from institutions and toward the self deeply affected America's attitude toward external authority, including the authority of religious institutions. The result has been
a privatized quest for the sacred. Statistics show that only 1 percent of
Boomers say they definitely do not believe in God, but 80 percent believe that attending church is unnecessary.[7]

At the same time, Boomers have been busy "respiritualizing American culture and resacralizing its institutions. Even as they wreck old
notions of teamwork, loyalty, and fraternal association...they are trying
to restore a new foundation for public virtue."[8] Talk of values, family,
family values, God, faith, spirituality, morals, sin, shame, forgiveness,
and redemption fills the airwaves and dominates conversations as
Boomers pass judgment on just about everything. Books on heaven,
hell, angels, Satan, spiritual lessons on everything from running a business to raising a family, and healing are national bestsellers. As corporate loyalty wanes, Boomers are looking for simpler careers and home-
based work so they can spend more time with their children or just slow
down. Many Boomer women are becoming primary breadwinners and
are running for office, while more Boomer men are focusing on being
good fathers and are joining men's movements like Promise Keepers to
call males to loftier ideals. All of this is interesting, writes Evan Thomas,
because "the people who seem most desperate to create a new civil

society are baby boomers, the generation that was largely responsible for trashing the old one."⁹

The Baby Busters?

As the descendants of the Baby Boomers, our generation has been called the "Baby Busters." Originally, the moniker referred to the declining birth rate as young adult Boomers decided not to have as many children as their parents did. With the introduction of the first commercially produced birth control pill Enovid 10 and the 1973 Supreme Court's *Roe v. Wade* ruling that made abortion legal, it became easier for parents to avoid having children, even by mistake.

Nonetheless—despite Boomers' decision not to have kids or to limit the size of their families, combined with the Pill and legalized abortion—the number of so-called Busters still rivals that of their immediate predecessors. Even though Boomers were limiting the size of their families, making the rate of births in the late sixties and early seventies much lower than that of the late forties and fifties, the number of women of childbearing age was much higher than ever before.

Therefore, as time has passed, the label "Baby Busters" has come to say less about the number of people in our generation and something much more ominous about *what we inherited.*

In many respects, we were being born into a "busted" culture marked by the "breakdown of political leadership, a troubling dissolution of family structures, and a chaotic education in schools with confusing, directionless objectives."¹⁰ The era in which we grew up—the sixties, seventies, and eighties—saw unprecedented changes in the political, social, and economic environment that, for the first time in American history, have made the future of society's young members uncertain. These changes include increasing costs for higher education, fewer job and income prospects, less of a chance to own a home, less of a chance that we will surpass our parents' standards of living, and the dubious title of being the most incarcerated generation ever.¹¹

When our parents got divorced in 1980, my brother and I felt firsthand the effects of being separated from an institution we had come to count on. Our once-familiar lives suddenly seemed foreign. Our vocabularies grew to include words like *separation, lawyer, divorce, ex-husband/wife, broken home, custody, "for the good of the children," single parent, visitation, alimony, annulment, re-married, step-parent.* In what seemed a flash we lost our rights to childhood and were told that the "courts" and the "adults" would be looking out for our "real rights" and our "best interests." Fortunately for us, Josh and I had each other, and together we processed all that was going on and tried to make sense of things as we moved forward in life.

But, as we came to discover, we were not alone. *Nor was divorce limited to the dissolution of marriages and the breakup of families.* We grew up in a culture of divorce that ranged from the breakdown of the family to the breakdown of just about everything else.

In 1961 America saw 375,000 divorces involving 500,000 children. Ten years later the yearly divorce rate had risen to 650,000 divorces, affecting 1 million children. By 1975 there were 1 million divorces affecting more than 1.1 million children.[12] A similar number of our generation saw their parents' marriage dissolve *each year* from that point on, making us what I call "Generation eX." Today estimates indicate that more than 40 percent of the members of our generation are children of divorce, compared to only 11 percent of those born during the fifties. In addition, the number of unwed mothers also doubled in only two decades, making the chances about fifty-fifty that today's young adults spent at least some time living with a single parent.[13] Today the statistics remain staggering: more than 40 percent of marriages end in divorce; the total number of divorced adults has grown from 4.3 million in 1970 to 20 million today; the married population has dropped from 72 percent in 1970 to 60 percent today; and the average duration of first marriages is eight years, though the chances of divorce are the highest in the third year of marriage.[14]

Since the early seventies, studies on the effects of divorce on the parties involved have come a long way. Early studies focused on the parents and assumed that if they felt better off, then their kids must feel the same way. But as divorce became more of an epidemic, studies began to show that while divorced parents felt free and independent, their kids hungered for stability, constancy, harmony, and permanence in family life.[15] All too often children of divorce had to face their problems without the help of their parents—who were busy focusing on their own problems—and lived hurried childhoods.

To make matters worse, children of divorce are often forced to relocate their place of residence and change schools as many as three or four times on average. Typically such changes are prompted by economic needs such as cheaper housing, job opportunities, better child-care, and extended family support. In our case, after our parents got divorced my brother and I moved and changed schools three times in as many years. At a time when friendships, mentors, family, and stability are crucial for development, self-esteem, and the experience of childhood, children of divorce are faced with simply trying to survive and make sense of their experience no matter how loving or well-intentioned their parents may be. Statistics constantly show that divorce makes it harder for kids to be kids and for them to succeed in the long run. Children of divorce often have trouble managing hostility, trusting friends, concentrating in school, and, later in life, making long-term commitments in relationships let alone to institutions.

In a provocative feature article entitled "What Divorce Does to Kids," *Time* magazine shared the story of a forty-year-old woman named Joanne whose parents divorced when she was nine. One day she came home from school and was told by her mother, "Daddy's moved out." Like horrors emerging from a Pandora's box, her fears flew out of her—fears of abandonment, of loss, of coming home one day and having her world shattered. Though it is said that time heals all wounds, as time went on Joanne noticed that her fears had turned into bursts of bitterness, jealousy, and doubt. Her relationships fell apart one after the other because she preordained them to fail, as if there was a void inside her, or as she says, "unfinished business that I couldn't get to." Eventually Joanne found herself in psychotherapy and finally was able to fall in love and marry. But, thirty-one years after her parents' divorce, she still feels its effects.

As *Time* writer Walter Kirn points out in the article, "For America's children of divorce—a million new ones every year—unfinished business is a way of life. For adults divorce is a conclusion, but for children it's the beginning of uncertainty. Where will I live? Will I see my friends again? Will my mom's new boyfriend leave her too?" According to Judith Wallerstein, clinical psychologist and expert on the effects divorce has on kids, children take a long time to get over divorce. In fact, the effects of divorce tend to show up as these children reach maturity and struggle to form their own adult relationships. There are two ends of the spectrum: Some see themselves as doomed to repeat their parents' errors. Others take a hard line and vow that once married they will never be divorced, no matter what. And many live somewhere in between.[16]

There is of course another side to the story. While divorce elevates the risk for kids to have certain kinds of problems, it does not automatically mark them for failure. Plenty of kids from intact families have deeper problems than kids from divorced families. Likewise, plenty of kids from both types of families are well-integrated, successful people. And, as my brother and I can attest, divorce has a way of challenging kids to rise above their situations and often calls them to focus more clearly on their personal goals and to enjoy life in new ways at an earlier age.

Nevertheless, for those from intact or split families, divorce as a matter of cultural fact is one of the major forces affecting Generation eX.

But Generation eX has faced divorce in many more ways than the dissolution of marriages and the breakdown of the family. Throughout the sixties, seventies, and eighties America underwent a series of divorces that injured or dissolved the bond between the past and the present, institutions and those they were supposed to serve, companies and their employees, education systems and their students, federal structures such as welfare and social security and both the tax-payers who fund them and the beneficiaries intended to receive them.

In 1974, Generation eX earned the dubious title of being the most impoverished generation in America. As Senator Daniel Patrick Moynihan put it, the United States had become "the first society in history in which a person is more likely to be poor if young rather than old" (that is, poorest in relation to the affluence of the rest of the society).[17] Among other cuts, government spending on financial aid for disadvantaged families was dramatically reduced, leaving many families without the food stamps, school lunch programs, health care assistance, and federal housing help they had come to rely on.[18]

As parents, especially single parents, worked harder to pay the bills, they spent less and less time with their children. This was true for low-income and middle-income families. In parents' stead, television served as a surrogate parent, for better or for worse. Friendships also took on a new importance, as peers worked through the complexities of growing up.

When I was in seventh grade, my brother and I went to live with our dad. Brian, my best friend through junior high and early high school, and I both came from divorced families, only at that time my dad was remarried and his mom was not. But our parents worked, so we hung out at his house every day after school and listened to music and watched countless hours of MTV, Nickelodeon, HBO, and sports. We also hung out at the mall and played video games until we had spent our small allowances and had to wait for the next installment. We did everything together. Statistics indicate that the more time kids spend unsupervised alone or with each other after school, the greater the chance of their abusing drugs and alcohol, breaking the law, or simply acting in ways their parents would not have allowed had they been there. While we certainly did many things we shouldn't have, Brian and I had good parents and generally lived up to their expectations. We were the lucky ones. We knew plenty of kids whose home lives taught them little about values, respect, or responsibility and whose after-school time was anything but "wholesome."

During our growing up years, Generation eX faced the escalation of many negative forces such as child abductions, nuclear threat, drug and alcohol use, teenage sex and pregnancies, anorexia, AIDS, cynicism, and suicide. As we entered high school, budgets were being cut and schools were literally and figuratively falling apart. All the while the cost of college was soaring, the job market was shrinking, the cost of homes was rising, and the institutions of health care and social security were ailing.[19]

Of course, many of the issues listed in this chapter are of great concern to people outside generation eX. And many, like Senator Moynihan, have worked to improve everything from health care to social security. But the fact remains that our generation came of age in a culture of divorce that, while not the same kind of bonding force as war, helped define how we see ourselves and the world we inhabit.

3

Life at the Speed of Time

Whether or not we grew up as latchkey kids in single- or two-parent homes, there is no denying that we were deeply affected by television, radio, and eventually the merging of the two in MTV. And the more we tuned in, the more we were fed regular doses of products and pop culture.

One of the most popular fashion crazes of our junior high and high school years was the Swatch Watch. Remember those? Like the Fat Boys who plugged them, they came in all shapes, sizes, and colors. And we wore them not so much to keep time (though Morris Day and the Time told us we must always know *what time it is*) as to look cool.

But little did we realize that our Swatch watches signified more than the power of advertising and fashion fads. They were a shining symbol of our culture's obsession with time, technology, and progress. As slogans like "time is money" became more and more popular, so did the need for counter-slogans encouraging families and friends to spend more "quality time" with each other. The faster the world moved, the more people got left behind in the whirlwind.

Life today could not be any more different from the days when people lived by raising crops and herding animals. Back then people set their lives according to the rhythms of nature, the passing of the seasons, changes in temperature, and the length of light in a day. There was not much need for measuring small units of time.

But being restless humans, we could not resist the temptation to set time to the beat of our drums, and then to set our lives to the mechanical tick-tock of time. Though the ancient Egyptians had invented enormous sundials that the Greeks and Romans eventually modified into pocket sundials, these were useless for telling time on overcast days or at night. Ancient inventors tried to remedy this by creating water clocks and hourglasses filled with sand that would measure the passing minutes more or less accurately. But it was not until the fourteenth century that Europeans finally devised mechanical timepieces.

The first real steps toward the mechanical measurement of time, however, came not from farmers or merchants but from religious people anxious to perform promptly and regularly their duties to God. These early clocks were really alarms that sounded rather than showed the time. In monasteries a chamber clock would sound off in the wee hours of the morning and awaken a sleeping monk who in turn would climb a tower and ring a bell to summon the other monks to prayer. Eventually the towers were equipped with clocks that would automatically ring the bell according to the seven canonical hours of the Church. In between the designated prayer times, the clock was silent.

But it was not long before bell towers cropped up in cities and were equipped with clocks that ticked off the seconds, minutes, and hours in the day. Like grand conductors, tower clocks directed the activities of busy townspeople racing in the streets below. By the early eighteenth century clocks had become portable, and not much later people rushed from here to there with smaller spring-loaded watches strapped to their wrists.[1]

When Swatch watches came along, they were millions of miles away from their predecessors. Rather than ringing off hours to pray to God, these watches with their electronic sounds honored the god of the marketplace. I remember as a teenager looking at my Swatch to see how long before I could get out of school and race to the mall to play video games or to a friend's house to plop down in front of the television and watch music videos or HBO movies.

If my experience of childhood and the teen years is anything like yours, then we are bonded in no small way in and through the pop culture that flickered its way into our psyches through tubes, metal, and glass. As GenX theologian Tom Beaudoin explains in his book *Virtual Faith: The Irreverent Spiritual Quest of Generation X:*

> During our lifetimes, especially during the critical period of the 1980s, pop culture was the amniotic fluid that sustained us. ... This shared generational experience of popular culture "events" produced an actively and potentially shared constellation of cultural meanings. By *events* I mean a host of different

pop culture phenomena, including bodily costuming, music videos, and cyberspace, as well as movies, popular songs, television shows, board games, and countless other popularly engaged "products," "trends," or the like. All of these, for better or worse, have stamped a generation. Pop culture provides the matrix that contains much of what counts as "meaning" for our generation.[2]

Our shared experience of such pop culture referents includes, as Beaudoin points out, games like Dungeons and Dragons, Rubik's Cube, Atari, Space Invader, Pac Man, Frogger, Dig Dug, and Tron; television shows like *Knight Rider, Gilligan's Island, The Brady Bunch, The Partridge Family, Friday Night Videos, Miami Vice, Love Boat, Three's Company, Mork and Mindy,* and *Dallas;* movies like *Flashdance, Star Wars, E.T., Tron, Ghostbusters, Footloose,* and *Reality Bites;* music groups and performers like The Go Gos, Duran Duran, Hall and Oates, REO Speedwagon, Madonna, Kurt Cobain, and Pearl Jam; political events like Iran-Contra, Live Aid, Grenada, Lebanon; and pop culture creations/ fashions like Baby on Board signs, parachute pants, Jordache jeans, Gap, friendship bracelets, and Birkenstock. The list goes on and on.

Because we embrace and express ourselves through popular culture, we are also bonded by experiencing and, in many cases, driving the constant evolution of technology that in the blink of an eye has brought us from hand-held video games to Palm Pilots, from VCRs to DVD home theaters, from home computers to the Internet and Web TV.

Remember when *Star Wars* and *E.T.* were light years ahead of their time? Remember how those special effects and storylines hurled us into new dimensions and made us think about the big picture of life? When we were kids, Josh and I went to see *E.T.* with our Aunt Lois. As the three of us welcomed the lonesome extraterrestrial into our hearts, we felt closer to each other. We laughed with him as he dressed in women's clothing, loved with him as he healed people with his glowing finger, cried with him as his life force nearly slipped out of his body, and longed with him as he tried to phone home. If God moments come in all packages, *E.T.* was a wonderful early experience of the sacred that dwells in friendship, family, and love. What was being played out on screen was being written into our souls and we left the theater more willing to see the sacred in everyday life.

We also left the theater with the paradoxical desire for peaceful communion with the transcendent *and* a craving for mind-blowing special effects and technology. We could hardly wait for the next close en-counter with aliens and other heartwarming extraterrestrials. With each new movie, producers and directors were forced to top their previous achievements in everything from special effects to box office records to Academy awards.

We barely had to wait for one blockbuster to run its course before another took its place. Technology just kept getting more and more so-phisticated. In 1965 the semiconductor pioneer Gordon Moore pre-dicted that chip density—and thus all kinds of computing power—would double every eighteen months or so. He has turned out to be right and the result has been that the acceleration of technology has grown expo-nentially, allowing us to not only create better special effects but also to do more of everything in less time. Our lives have been changed right to the core. James Gleick, author of *Faster: The Acceleration of Just About Everything*, makes us face the reality that we have created:

> We are in a rush. We are making haste.... Airport gates are minor intensifiers of the lose-not-a-minute anguish of our age. There are other intensifiers—places and objects that signify im-patience. Certain notorious intersections and tollbooths. Doctors' anterooms ("waiting" rooms). The DOOR CLOSE button in elevators, so often a placebo, with no function but to distract for a moment those riders to whom ten seconds seems an eternity. Speed-dial buttons on telephones.... Remote controls.... We are awash in things, in information, in news, in the old rubble and shiny new toys of our complex civilization, and—strange, perhaps—stuff means speed.... We live in a buzz.[3]

We cannot help but wonder, now that we can do more in less time, are we really better off?

Unlike our agrarian ancestors and the monks who invented the bell tower to help them pray regularly, we feel unraveled and inefficient without our day planners—which offer us inspiring quotes, lessons in prioritizing, and endless columns for our to-do lists. But are we really more balanced because we can jam more into our days? We feel lost without our watches—which not only record hundredths of seconds but also gauge our heart rates, miles walked, and the direction in which we are going. But are we any more at home in the world with mini naviga-tional systems on our arms? We feel isolated without our cell phones—

which now report the news, track stock quotes, and send and receive e-mail. But are we really any more connected to other people when we talk to them from our cars?

For all the entertainment, advertising, information, pop culture, and noise we take in, how much of it feeds us at the soul level? As we make our way in the world, what do we really want out of life? And where does God fit into the picture, if at all?

When I moved to Chicago in 1993, it was the first time in my life that I felt truly free. Free *from* my parents' divorce, *from* the anxiety of hunting for a job and a place to live, and *from* the ambiguity of life right after college. Free *to* be who I was at the time, *to* dive headfirst into adulthood, and *to* set my sights on the person I wanted to become in the midst of our ever-increasingly fast-paced world.

Though I had lived on campus at Notre Dame and with a friend in an apartment after graduation, it was not the same as being on my own. My parents had always told me that there is nothing quite as liberating and wonderful as the day you hang your first picture on the wall of your first apartment. They turned out to be right. Even before I had finished unpacking my modest belongings in my tiny studio apartment, I unrolled my favorite poster—Picasso's *Don Quixote*—and hung it on the wall above my desk. Like Cervantes's dreamy, passionate seeker, I was ready to chase my own windmills.

Ever since I can remember I have loved books, stories, far-away lands, and characters whose lives give life to others. Having come from a family of educators and avid readers, I had grown up believing that books can change the world and put us in touch with the most significant questions and most enduring answers. I still believe it.

As I mentioned earlier, following graduation from college, I worked briefly for my family's publishing company and briefly in a bookstore. As if hawking books at the Little Professor were not ironic enough, I lived with my friend Bill in an apartment on Enchanted Forest Way. Instead of using my liberal arts education to build a career, I lived like one of Robin Hood's merry dreamers in the Enchanted Forest as Bill, then a graduate student in Spanish languages and literature, and I hung out, watched movies, went to the bars, and wondered where our lives would lead.

But I held out hope that somehow God really did have a plan for me. Each week I sent out a few resumes to various publishing houses specializing in literature, philosophy, and even religion, and held my breath.

After a number of "we'd-love-to-have-you-but-we-are-not-hiring-right-now" letters, I finally got a call from Fr. George Lane, S.J., director of the Chicago-based Catholic publishing house Loyola Press, asking me to interview for an editorial position. The pay was low and I was not sure I wanted to edit religious books, but I had grown up a Cubs fan and loved the idea of living near Wrigley Field, catching ball games, and getting paid to read. So I went for the interview, they made an offer, and I accepted right on the spot.

After my first few months, my boss, a wonderful Jesuit named Joseph Downey (who was seventy-seven years old at the time), walked into my office and said, "Langford, I've got an important project for you. It's a book called *The Catholic Tradition Before and After Vatican II: 1878–1993*, and I think you're ready for it." At that point I had only taken an editing class at the University of Chicago, assisted other editors with their work, and handled just one project on my own. But Fr. Downey had been paying close attention to me and felt I was ready. My fear at the time was that he would figure out that I did not know much about the Catholic tradition and had no right editing this book!

Throughout that fall and winter I devoted most of my time and energy to working on that project. I was determined to learn about the Catholic tradition while making the book letter perfect. I also became good friends with the author, Tim McCarthy, and together we got the book into tip-top shape.

The day before the book was due to the printer, I took the galley pages home for one last review. I ended up pulling an all-nighter.

The next morning, as I stood waiting for the 152 Addison bus to pick me up for work, I watched dime-sized snowflakes gently cover the icy Chicago sidewalk. I was feeling a little grumpy at having traded cozy for cold. Despite being overly tired, I had somehow willed myself to the bus stop earlier than usual—I was running ahead of schedule. Deadlines and schedules punctuate my life as a book editor; this day was no exception. Getting that book out on time was consuming my gray-dawn thoughts.

As the snow fell with increasing intensity, I retreated deeper inside myself. My body was standing out there in the cold, but the rest of me was trapped somewhere in the timeline of the day. Eventually the groan of an approaching bus startled me back to the moment at hand, and I

squinted to make out the number "152" on the front of the bus. Soon
I'd be on my way to work, and soon after that I'd be mailing the manuscript and diskette to the printer.

The bus finally pulled up to my corner and the doors opened.
Peering in, I saw a middle-aged man coming forward with an elderly
woman clutching his arm. I thought about shoving my way past them,
but decided that my kind act for the day would be getting out of the
way so this other man could perform his kind act for the day. Within a
few seconds, the man had deposited his delicate cargo on the corner
and reboarded the bus. I started to follow in his path when I heard the
elderly woman say, as if to herself (but loud enough for me to hear),
"Oh my, it's so icy today, I don't know if I'll be able to make it to the
hospital *just down the street.*"

It was one of those moments when you want to pretend that you
did not hear a plea for help so that you can just go about your business.

But I had heard it.

With one foot on the first step of the bus and the other on the
curb, I looked at the half-smiling driver, then my watch, and finally the
gray-haired woman.

In my bag sat the typeset pages of *The Catholic Tradition.* Chapters
on peace and justice seemed to be whispering to me, "What are you
going to do?" As if being the only person at the bus stop—and probably
the whole city—with the guilt complex of the Catholic tradition in a
book bag were not enough, the bus driver became my moral judge. His
expression said it all, "What are you going to do?"

In a great John Wayne–style moment, I looked at the bus driver
and said, "Go on without me." He smiled, shut the door, and took off. I
turned back and offered the woman my arm as the exhaust fumes engulfed us.

"Thank you so much, young man," the elderly woman said in a
half-fake tone of surprise. "Normally I make this walk by myself, but
today it's too dangerous."

"No problem," I said, forcing a smile.

Saint Joseph's Hospital was just down the street from my apartment
in Lincoln Park. I'd passed it many times. But that day it felt miles away
as measured by our cautious steps on the snow-hidden glaze of ice.
Gradually, I gave up trying to sneak peeks at my watch and fantasizing
about throwing the woman over my shoulder and running her to her
destination. I simply resolved to enjoy my time with this seemingly

fragile soul, who politely reminded me that introductions were in order by offering, "My name is Frances."

I told her my name, and then Frances and I chatted a little about the weather, my job as an editor, and our mutual love of Chicago. We shared stories of our adventures downtown, and she recounted happy memories of city life when she was my age.

About halfway to the hospital, Frances asked, "Can we stop here a minute so I can catch my breath?" Though I wanted to say sarcastically, "God, I'm glad you said it first because we've really been hauling ass," I thought it better to hold onto her arm and tell her to take her time.

Without warning, she looked at me and asked, "Are you Catholic?" The question caught me off guard, though I might have mentioned where I went to college or where I worked. Nonetheless, I couldn't answer immediately. I'd been privately asking myself the same question for such a long time that it sounded foreign coming from somebody else, especially from somebody I'd just met. As I watched her breath vaporize in the chilly air, I felt my canned answer making its way to my lips—"Yes, I am," I finally responded.

"I can tell," replied Frances with a firm nod.

From the back of my mind sprang a haunting question I once heard at an Easter Mass: *If you were on trial for being a Christian, would there be enough evidence to convict you?* The answer has continually eluded me. Ironically, on this random winter morning, a piece of evidence was surfacing. Maybe my being Catholic did matter. Maybe Frances's "I can tell" was pointing to some truth about myself I don't ordinarily acknowledge.

We continued our trek, but my mind felt frozen and numb as I pondered what I mean when I say I am Catholic.

When we finally reached the hospital doors, I wished my new friend well—"I hope it's nothing serious and that you're going to be okay."

"Oh," she answered delightedly, "I'm fine. I just come down here once a week to volunteer—you know, cheer the patients up."

I was hit hard again. My assumptions about this woman had been all wrong, and I stood awkwardly in awe of her as she read the surprise on my face.

I couldn't help but ask her, "Are *you* Catholic?" to which she happily answered, "Yes, I am." Somehow her answer sounded different from mine—stronger, more confident.

After leaning down to hug Frances good-bye, I headed back to my bus stop. It hadn't been terribly long since I had last been there, but everything about my morning had changed. And still buried in my book bag was that manuscript on the Catholic tradition.

I caught the next bus and, as I watched people getting on and off, I replayed Frances's question: "Are you Catholic?" It was no longer a theoretical matter; that day the answer counted. It certainly counted to Frances as she made her way out into the freezing cold to comfort those who were in pain. In a powerful way, Frances was challenging me to think about what I *really* mean when I say I'm Catholic.

My interest in church history and theology stems from a personal quest to get at the essence of Catholicism, of Christianity, of faith. Yet, the more I study, the more I get lost in rhetoric and ritual and lose sight of application and practice. Religion itself runs the risk of replacing the God it points toward. For some, Catholicism is nice and neat—questions have answers. I've often wished it were so for me. But Frances was calling me to dispense with niceties in favor of getting down to the nitty-gritty. Through her words and her actions, she challenged me to examine how my being Catholic meshes with the all-too-often sloppy details of my daily life.

Initially, I wouldn't have thought that walking Frances to the hospital had much to do with my being Catholic. I saw a chance to help, and, no matter how reluctantly, I did. It was not as if I heard a damsel in distress and, like a spiritual superman, made a quick change into *Catholicman* and sprang into action. So how do I explain my answer to the question "Are you Catholic?"

Perhaps my Catholic upbringing is so ingrained in me that I cannot separate it from other forces that motivate me to be the person I am. Calling myself Catholic is automatic. But such an explanation no longer suffices, for I cannot be a passive recipient of my faith. I've worked too hard. Therefore, the crucial question at this stage in my life has become: Do I *choose* to be Catholic, and if so, what does my choice mean?

Within my search to discover who I am, what I believe, and how it all mixes together, I have come to realize that embracing the search itself is as important as what the search reveals. By accepting my search as an ongoing process, I meet people like Frances who spark thoughts and insights I might otherwise miss. And by taking the time, by stopping in the middle of a fast-paced world, I catch glimpses of truth and beauty that would otherwise remain hidden. I catch God in the moment.

The point of my journey, then, is not that I succeed at being a perfect person or a perfect Catholic, but that I embrace the *process* of becoming myself and becoming Catholic. The quiet hours I spend contemplating who I am and what I believe are complemented with active hours of being out in the world. Consequently, my life and my Catholicism are constantly evolving—sometimes together, sometimes apart.

On that cold winter day I felt a powerful warmth that had been stoked by the humanity and Catholic conviction embodied in my unexpected companion Frances. And as I mailed *The Catholic Tradition* in time to meet the printer's deadline, I smiled to think that I'd come a few steps closer to understanding the message contained in its pages. I haven't seen Frances since that day, but her challenge continues to take on deeper meanings and nuances, and therefore becomes more crucial, each step of the way: Are you Catholic?

4

Our Spiritual Hungers

A few years before the Smashing Pumpkins broke up as a band, my friend Matt and I scored tickets to a surprise concert they performed at a tiny Chicago bar called the Double Door. Matt had heard that the Double Door often booked top-rated bands for special gigs but would release fake information about who the band was until the last minute. We had heard radio spots announcing that a band called the Frogs was coming to the Double Door, but rumors were circulating as to who the Frogs really were. Matt got the lowdown from someone who knew someone at the Double Door that the surprise band was really the Pumpkins, and he spent hours trying to get tickets. His efforts paid off and we got four tickets for something like $7 a piece.

On the night of the concert Matt, two of our friends, and I were out of our heads with excitement. We all loved the Pumpkins and could not wait to see them up close. After a couple of beers we grabbed a cab to the Double Door and made our way into the crowded bar. The anticipation in the room was palpable as people swapped guesses as to who the band was going to be. Being a tall guy, Matt helped us plow our way through the crowd up to the front of the bar. Soon enough a warm-up band came out and played some serious thrasher music. It was loud, out of tune, and even obnoxious, but we didn't care as long as the Pumpkins were next.

After the warm-up band finished, the stagehands set up for the next band. In the interim, we sent someone from our group for more beer and held our places. All of a sudden out came Billy Corgan and the other Smashing Pumpkins band members. The small crowd went absolutely nuts.

As the Pumpkins played hit after hit, the crowd got more and more into the concert. None of us could believe that the Pumpkins would play such a small venue and that we were there to see it. But the band seemed to love it as much as we did. They played as hard as they do at stadium concerts.

Toward the end of the concert I looked over to see what Matt was doing. Like the rest of us, he was sweating and dancing to the music. But his eyes were closed and he seemed to be off somewhere else, almost in a trance. When he opened his eyes, he yelled to me, "I'm gonna get out of here and go home. I feel amazing and I want it to last."

"But the concert isn't over," I yelled in astonishment.

"I don't care, I'm perfect right now and I gotta get outta here."

The next day I asked Matt why he had left before the final set. He said he really couldn't explain it, but he was on such a high from the music and the experience that he was literally overwhelmed. "You know I'm not a religious guy, but that was like a religious experience," he explained. "I felt as good as I have in years, just living in the moment. It was awesome."

There is no doubt that music is one art form that can transport us into transcendence. In Matt's case, connecting with the band, their words, and their performance gave him a feeling of being alive. Though he made the common disclaimer that he is not religious, he still likened his experience to something that religious people feel. We talk about it to this day.

When it comes to faith, religion, and spirituality, things are different for our generation than they were for previous generations. We do not speak the same language, go to the same places, name our experiences in the same way, have the same needs, or look to only one or any particular religion to answer our spiritual questions. For those of us raised Catholic, many of us do not have a coherent sense of what being Catholic means, fully understand how much Catholic life changed after the Second Vatican Council in 1962–1965, see why participating in parish life and weekly Mass is crucial to faith and spirituality, and/or feel comfortable naming key experiences in our lives in God-talk, as God moments.

But at the same time, as theologian Harvey Cox has said, ours is a generation

that stays away from most churches in droves but loves songs about God and Jesus, a generation that would score very low on any standard piety scale but at times seems almost obsessed with saints, visions, and icons in all shapes and sizes. These are the young people who, styrofoam cups of cappuccino in hand, crowd around the shelves of New Age spirituality titles in the local book market and post thousands of religious and quasi-religious notes on the bulletin boards in cyberspace. And remember, it was this puzzling and allegedly secular generation that turned out a million of its representatives to welcome Pope John Paul II to that most secular of cities, Paris, France, in the waning summer of 1997.[1]

Sound familiar? As puzzling and unorthodox as we can be, our generation is by no means without interest in or passion for the sacred. As my friend Matt tried to explain how he felt at the Pumpkins concert, for example, he immediately made the connection between feeling free and having a religious experience, even as he made it clear that he was not religious. Like Matt, many in our generation are engaging in all kinds of God-talk. It's just that our God-talk gets communicated less overtly and oftentimes in irreverent, noninstitutional language.

If we listen closely to each other, if we delve beneath the surface of our words, jobs, fashion, and pop culture, what we are all expressing are four profound hungers: We hunger for *healthy personal identity*. We hunger for *intimacy in relationships*. We hunger for *meaningful work*. And we hunger for a *life-giving spirituality*. In many respects, our generation's hungers are human hungers shared by all generations. But as Gen Xers, our hungers have been shaped in a culture of familial and institutional divorce that has led us to satisfy our hungers over a much longer time period than previous generations while relying less and less on institutions to help us along the way.[2]

Before discussing if and how God feeds our hungers, I want to reflect on these four principal hungers of our generation.

Healthy personal identity. Forming a healthy personal identity is a life-long task. While it is true that genetics and the circumstances into which we were born determine a lot about our personal identity, it is also true that each of us has the ability to take control of our lives and shape who we are and who we want to be. In our early years of life we struggle to form our personalities and differentiate ourselves from our families and friends. As we grow up, learn, form friendships, travel, experience people of different backgrounds and values, get familiar with our feelings, gain responsibilities, leave home, find work, and begin our own families (traditional and nontraditional), we are constantly faced with the questions "Who am I?" and "Who am I in relation to others?" At each stage of our life's journey having a healthy personal identity means knowing the nonnegotiable aspects of who we are while being open to loving and learning from others. The quest to form a healthy personal identity is particularly challenging to us as young adults in the diverse culture of shifting values in which we live.

Intimacy in relationships. By the same token, as we seek to know who we are, we struggle to find and feel comfortable with the kind of intimacy that allows us to share ourselves and learn from others. As we grow into adulthood we are challenged to come to terms with our families—some of us lament that our family ties are not stronger while others learn to loosen them. We are challenged to come to terms with our friendships—some of us feel very alone in the world while others try to negotiate changes in their friendships as they fade, deepen, or even become romantic. We are challenged to name the values that are worth keeping and link ourselves with trustworthy teachers and mentors. And, particularly for our generation, we are challenged to make commitments and risk the pain of rejection or loss if they do not last. But in spite of these many challenges, we know that part of a healthy personal identity is healthy relationships.

Meaningful work. One of the most common questions we ask each other is "What do you do for a living?" Our jobs can say a lot about who we are and can dictate how we spend our time and money as well as who we meet, where we go, and what we value. While work is necessary for us to meet our material needs, it is also an extension of how we see our calling, identify and use our gifts, and fulfill our dreams. Many in our generation are not satisfied with just any old work and will jump from job to job in search of meaningful work that allows them to use their gifts and make a positive difference in the world. Beyond having paying jobs, many in our generation also volunteer their time, talent, and energy to service programs that help them meet like-minded people and give back to the community. The quest for meaningful work is part of the quest for meaningful living, and many of us make a solid commitment to our jobs once we find the right ones.

Life-giving spirituality. Many of us claim that we are "spiritual but not religious." The fact is that all people have a spirituality, a way of shaping the spirit or life-energy in each of us, whether we are religious or not. There are different kinds of spirituality, ranging from a spirituality of anger to one of joy. One friend put it best when she said, "Some people wake up and say, 'Good morning, God.' Others wake up and say, 'Good God, it's morning.' There's a big difference between the two spiritualities!" As we seek to know who we are, form intimate relationships, and find meaning-ful work, we cannot help but ask spiritual questions of meaning—Why are we here? What are we supposed to do with our lives? It's pretty safe to say that most of us are seeking a spirituality that gives us hope, conveys meaning, and gives us life. If we seek a relationship with God, our spiritu-ality is aimed at the Spirit itself. The claim of religion is that it provides the foundation and framework for a life-giving spirituality. And, as many of us are discovering, participating in the life of the Church helps us shape our identities, form intimate relationships, perform meaningful work, and nurture a life-giving spirituality. But again, we are much more likely to call ourselves "spiritual" than we are to call ourselves "religious."

In addition to these four key hungers, there are also four key qualities that shape the way our generation goes about its quest for meaning. As Tom Beaudoin points out, we (1) harbor a deep suspicion of religious institutions, often expressed by challenging religious institutions, at-tacking the Catholic Church, and pitting Jesus against the Church; (2) emphasize the sacred nature of experience, whereby we come to our own conclusions instead of being told what to think or feel; (3) recog-nize the religious dimension of suffering in which our pain leads us into new dimensions of awareness; and (4) are comfortable with ambiguity that makes religiousness vague, perhaps, but not any less present.[3]

To help flesh these points out a little more, let me share some real-life stories.

1. We harbor deep suspicions about institutions. My friend Rob is a talented engineer who has shot through the ranks like a meteor. Today he helps run a start-up company that is among the leaders in developing the technology of global tracking devices. If it sounds confusing, it is. Put it this way: Rob's very smart and he's on the cutting edge of a new technology that, among many applications, will allow emergency re-sponse teams to locate people in trouble if they have called 911 from their cell phones.

While Rob has been in the field of satellite networking and communications for several years, he only recently got a personal cell phone, which his co-workers demanded he get. I work with words on a page all day and I've had a cell phone for two years. It's more likely that people need to reach Rob in a hurry than they do me (though I will gladly respond quickly to editing emergencies), but he has opted not to have a cell phone for one reason: he does not want it to rule his life. He says he has better things to do with his time than be tracked down by a noise machine on his belt.

Now, Rob is a former Catholic who in his youth was an altar server—the whole nine yards. But today he describes himself as an agnostic. He knows a lot about the Church, has read much of the Bible, and thinks a lot about spiritual matters. But he says he cannot subscribe to any one religion because they all seem to be more concerned with their own survival than with the God they claim to point to, and they are often riddled with hypocrisy. I usually go to Rob when I'm hungry for a rigorous examination of my faith life. He's more than a worthy adversary and often leaves me wondering why I subscribe to any religion at all, let alone the Catholic religion.

Recently I asked him something I had never thought to ask before. "Rob," I said, "do you think what I do for a living is ultimately meaningless? I mean, in your eyes am I or anyone else interested in religion and spirituality just talking about things that nobody can ever really know for sure?"

"Well," he responded, "no. First of all, I think any job that you enjoy doing and that makes you think is worthwhile. Second of all, I think religion and faith issues are fascinating. They deal with the deepest kinds of questions. I just draw the line when I think people say more than they should about God and God's 'mind.' We all want to know why we are here, if there is anything sacred about life, how we should treat others, and if there is anything after this life. For me, it is just better to believe in a supreme power and leave it at that." Then he said something that has stuck with me, "You know, sometimes I envy you and others who believe in a God they can know. There are times when I go to bed feeling all alone in the world. I imagine people of faith lying there feeling close to God."

Over the years I have met many people who, like Rob, take their spiritual questions seriously but move with great caution when it comes to institutionalizing the way they go about getting to know God. In many cases people are more apathetic about religion than hostile toward it. At the same time, I have met plenty of peers who are quite comfortable with religion and feel that the institution is the backbone of their faith life.

So, whether or not we go about our spiritual quests in the context of a particular religion, the point is that many of us are going about our spiritual quests. While we are wary of institutionalizing our faith, many of us are looking for ways to feed our faith and bring us out of our individual worlds and into community with others. Recent surveys also indicate that among those of us baptized and raised Catholic, our spiritual seeking does not stray very far, if at all, from the Catholic tradition. The question, it seems, is how actively we seek within the Catholic tradition.

2. We place a lot of emphasis on our personal experience. A few years ago I gave a workshop to a large group of my peers on identifying our deepest hungers. During one of the breakout sessions, a young woman raised her hand and said that what she wants most out of her faith life is to *feel* God working inside her. The audience looked as puzzled as I did. Recognizing that she had not made her point clearly, the young woman continued, "I want to experience God, to feel God's presence. And I want God to be in my experience!" Then we got it.

For this young woman, prayer fell flat when nothing happened. God went gray when her mind could not picture his loving presence. Her spirituality dried up when she could not feel its nourishing waters flowing through her daily life.

We are all like that. One of our deepest hungers is to make meaning from our experience and experience meaning in the ebb and flow of our lives. Spiritually speaking, we seek to find the purpose of our lives and to draw as close to the Source of that experience as we can. We want to go through life with our eyes wide open so that we can savor what is good and true and beautiful.

3. We feel we have suffered. At a seminar on issues facing our generation, a fifty-something woman yelled from across the table, "Whenever I hear members of your generation say they have suffered, I just don't get it. What have you suffered? You have not faced any major wars or economic depression like we did. In fact, you have been given more than we ever had."

Of course, she was right. And wrong. The wars our generation has faced have been fought in our own backyards and in our psyches as divorce and drug use and violence and suicide and poverty have skyrocketed. Without whining here, it is a very serious matter that so many members of our generation are dejected, disconnected, and distant. Crises come in all forms, and our generation has faced a crisis of spirit, a kind of existential malaise that followed on the heels of the vivacious sixties and rammed into the uncertain times of the two decades that followed.

One of our deepest hungers is to make sense of suffering: to put it into the context of human experience and face it with spiritual fortitude; to lay our suffering before God and others in our community and ask for the help we need to go on; and even to help others in their suffering.

4. We are at home in ambiguity. In various conversations, I have heard peers talk about things like the death penalty, abortion, euthanasia, divorce, downsizing, homosexuality, women clergy, and a wide range of similar "hot-button" topics as if their attitude today is no indication of their attitude tomorrow. When religion comes to bear on any or all of these issues, many young people will say, "I'm not going to shape my opinion a certain way because someone or some group told me to." Others say they are more about tolerance than judgment. And some just say "whatever."

At the same time, I have encountered many young people who have strong opinions on these and related issues and are either more than willing to act on them or reluctant to do so for fear of being rejected. When it comes to religion, they fear being labeled as sheep who move mindlessly with the flock rather than as independent thinkers. In many of these cases, there is a certain comfort level with ambiguity, a comfort level that other generations claim not to have.

Another of our deepest hungers is to define what we believe based on a wide range of data and stick with it. At least until we see otherwise! The problem is often that we have so many options, models, and data these days that we do not know where to begin or end. Part of spirituality is developing a discipline of discernment that enables us to know better and better what we believe and how to act on it.

As we hunger for healthy personal identity, intimacy in relationships, meaningful work, and life-giving spirituality, where and how we seek makes all the difference as to whether or not we find answers and nourishment. And because we are wary of institutions, emphasize the sacred nature of experience, take our suffering seriously, and are comfortable with ambiguity, we are closed to a Church that has all the answers but open to a Church that is both teacher and student.

For me, and for many young adults, the beauty of the Catholic Church is not that it offers rigid answers but that it embraces and provokes profound questions. Not that it assesses sin, blame, and punishment but that it calls for integration, reconciliation, and accountability. Not that it excludes and divides but that it includes and unites. Not that it fights for a fragile future as an institution but that it fights to be the body of Christ on earth made up of seekers who long to see through the eyes of joy and to serve with passionate love.

Part Two

SEEKING: A WAY OF LIFE

"Ask, and it will be given you; search, and you will find; knock, and the door will be opened for you. For everyone who asks receives, and everyone who searches finds, and for everyone who knocks, the door will be opened."

—Matthew 7:7-8

Introduction

The Age of the Seeker

Several years ago, as I began to think more and more about our generation's spiritual hungers, I sent out an e-mail to about thirty of my friends asking "What do you seek the most in life?" Within a day my mailbox was jammed with responses. As I opened each of the e-mails, I was taken aback by how seriously my friends had taken the question. Even those who began with flip answers—"A supermodel who loves to cook and clean" or "A man who will tend to my every need"—ended up being honest and thoughtful.

As I read through what people said they were seeking—"happiness," "meaning," "fulfillment," "community," "acceptance," "success," "health," "peace," "true love"—I came to one e-mail that stopped me cold.

"I do not know exactly what I am seeking right now," the message said, "but I know that I must continue to seek. Seeking is what keeps us alive."

Instantly these words hit me as being not only a motto for our generation but also universally true for all generations.

All my life I have watched with intense fascination what people say and do, what they believe and how they behave. If you have ever spent time "people watching," you know what I am talking about. Two of my buddies—Rob and Rik—and I grew up hanging out at sporting events, the beach, the 4-H Fair, and places like the arcade and Orange Julius (are they still around?) in the shopping mall watching people and commenting (sometimes defying the rule: "If you can't say something nice about a person, don't say it at all") on what we were learning about human nature. Just about everybody we watched taught us something about human beings and how we did or did not want to be.

As I continue to people watch, it seems to me that we are living at a time of great seeking. Generalizations fly about *who* the seekers are—everyone from Matures to Baby Boomers to Gen Xers to Gen Yers/ Millennials; *what* they are seeking—everything from prosperity to peace; *why* they are seeking—every reason from self-satisfaction to a hunger for God and desire to improve the world; and *how* they go about their searches—in every way from Internet stock trading to prayer and meditation. But if the popularity of "religious" and "spiritual" (I use the terms loosely) books, music, television shows and movies, newspaper and magazine articles, self-help seminars, New Age philosophies, and gurus of alternative medicine is any indication, then it is safe to say that Americans of all ages are seeking a connection to the sacred with great fervor.

A quick survey of the *New York Times* bestseller list over the past several years, for example, reveals many "religious" hardcover and paperback nonfiction titles in the top spots: *Conversations with God: Book 1, Conversations with God: Book 2, The Bible Code, A Simple Path, Simple Abundance, Kitchen Table Wisdom,* the *Chicken Soup for the Soul* series, and *The Art of Happiness.* Past lists have featured *A History of God, Care of the Soul, Crossing the Threshold of Hope, The Celestine Prophecy, The Catechism of the Catholic Church,* and *God: A Biography* as dominant national bestsellers. I myself had the extraordinary privilege of acquiring and editing Joseph Cardinal Bernardin's *The Gift of Peace,* which remained on the *Times* bestseller list for over four months in 1997 and which I will talk about later in this book.

Publishers Weekly, a key resource for anyone in the book industry, has called religion the "publishing success story" of the past decade. But it does not take a publisher to see that people are hungry for the sacred, religion, and spirituality. Just look at the covers of the news magazines in the checkout line at the supermarket. For example, cover stories from the small collection of *Time* magazines I have saved over the past two years include (in order of appearance) "Is the Bible Fact or Fiction?" "Faith and Healing," "Can We Still Believe in Miracles?" "The Right Hand of God," "The Search for Jesus," "And God Said... The Debate Over the Meaning of Genesis," "Jesus Online," and "Does Heaven Exist." *Newsweek* magazine has also run its fair share of religious cover stories, including more recently "The Mystery of Prayer" and "The Meaning of Mary." It is interesting, however, to note that these magazines still march to their own drummers: on November 25,

1996, the week after Cardinal Bernardin died from cancer, *Newsweek* ran a cover story on him called "Teaching Us How to Die," while that same week *Time* ran a story called "Forever Young," detailing ways in which science is keeping us looking and feeling young. In this age of seeking, readers want to explore issues of life, death, afterlife, and transcendence in the here and now.

It's not only periodicals that are feeding their readers' needs for spiritual reading. Television has jumped onto the sacred bandwagon with both feet. In the September 22, 1997, issue of *Time* magazine, reporter Joel Stein says, "This season the networks are paving a multilane highway to heaven with an unprecedented eight shows with religious and spiritual themes." Four of these shows returned after successful debuts: *Touched by an Angel*, *7th Heaven*, *Soul Man*, and *Promised Land*. Joining them were *Good News*, *Teen Angel*, *The Visitor*, and the much-hyped *Nothing Sacred*.

Movies like *Field of Dreams*, *Contact*, *Phenomenon*, *City of Angels*, *The Mission*, *Michael*, *Shadowlands*, *What Dreams May Come*, *The Green Mile* —as well as the soundtracks that go with them and similar spiritually based pop hits—have also topped recent charts as food for the soul.

The beautiful thing about all this seeking is that it is not really new. Since the beginning of rational thought, every single human being has been a seeker. The particularities of our searches—the who, what, where, when, why, and how—may be as unique as each of us and the time in which we live, but the fact remains that by our very nature we human beings are seekers. As my friend said in the e-mail, even when we do not know what we are seeking, we must continue to seek. Seeking is what binds us together, makes us so interesting, and keeps us alive.

5

The Art of Seeking

Seeking is its own art. It is the art of wanting and waiting, toiling and resting, advancing and retreating, grabbing onto and letting go, pursuing and being pursued, struggling and just being. Seeking is the art of trying to *know* and to *create* with our whole selves—mind, body, and soul. It is the art of embracing and being embraced by external and internal knowledge, beauty, truth, and love. It is the art that drives us to do things great and small. It is the art of being human. And it is the art that binds us all together. For while what we find may divide us, it is our never-ending seeking that unites us.

The world that we now know—from time itself to the land and seas, heavenly bodies and our own bodies, the plants and animals, history and human societies past and present—had to be opened, studied, defined, and shaped by countless seekers before us. Explorers like Vespucci, Columbus, and Magellan helped prove the world was not flat and that we could sail around it. Artists like Michelangelo, da Vinci, and Picasso captured the human and material form in marble and paint. Musicians like Bach, Beethoven, and Mozart translated the depths of life into notes and rhythms. Poets like Virgil, Dante, and Chaucer told the human drama in verse. Philosophers like Socrates, Plato, and Descartes explored the meaning of truth and how we know what we know. Scientists like Archimedes, Darwin, and Edison explored why the world is the way it is and invented new technologies meant to make life better. Biologists like Paracelsus, Vesalius, and Harvey went beneath the skin and tracked everything from muscle structure to blood flow. Writers like Shakespeare, Dostoyevsky, and Thoreau probed in plays and essays the meaning of our lives. And theologians like Augustine, Aquinas, and More taught us that if we look deeply into the world we see God's hand at work.

Seeking is nothing new. And it is never easy. Throughout history seekers often have had to ask their questions and chart their paths alone and, worse yet, in the face of opposition from the established order.

For these reasons, one of my favorite seekers of all time is Galileo Galilei (1564–1642). I love Galileo because he was a seeker who would not give up and because his love for God and for science has helped us better understand that we can seek to know God *and* the world around us without contradiction. Faith and reason can go hand in hand.

Like many of us, I learned in high school history class that Galileo is both the father of modern science and the father of the rift between science and religion. We were taught that Galileo, a devout Catholic and a brilliant physicist and astronomer who invented the telescope, followed the lead of Nicholas Copernicus (1473–1543) and boldly went against scriptural interpretation, church teaching, and the science of the time by saying that the earth revolves around the sun. We were told that, for contradicting the centuries-old teaching that the earth (and therefore the human race) is at the center of the universe and that the sun revolves around it, Galileo was condemned by the Church, was made to recant his teachings, and lived out the rest of his life in prison. The saddest part of the story was that Galileo turned out to be right!

I remember being angry at the Church when I learned Galileo's story. Living during a time of great discovery when explorers were charting new courses around the globe, education was being made more accessible to common people, and Gutenberg's printing press was making not only the Bible but the thought of the day available to all who could read, Galileo was condemned for turning his telescope toward the sky and helping humanity better understand the heavens. It still makes me mad.

But, in the Church's defense, the part of the story we did not learn in high school is that the Church had initially warned Galileo not to teach the Copernican model of the universe as *fact* until he could show more conclusively that the earth revolves around the sun. Though he lacked conclusive proof, Galileo went ahead and wrote about and taught his hypothesis as fact on the grounds that scripture was not designed to teach science. And the Church went ahead and condemned him for it on the grounds that he not only lacked sufficient proof for his theory but also directly disobeyed its orders. Contrary to legend, however, Galileo was never imprisoned or tortured by the Inquisition. But in 1633 he was forced to read a statement denouncing his theories as false and upholding all that Holy Mother Church had taught. For the final nine years of his life, Galileo continued to work on his ideas and teach pupils who sought him out. Then, blind and tired, Galileo died on January 8, 1642. Amazingly, perhaps even providentially, Isaac Newton was born that same day and went on to carry the torch of modern science that Galileo had lit.[1]

Since the time of Galileo and Newton, science has steadily marched forward. And over the years the Church has made great strides in understanding and promoting scientific seekers who ask "how" things work. It has also helped address the question of "why" and has looked for meaning in human discovery. Though it was not until 1979, and then again in 1989, that the Vatican, at the urging of Pope John Paul II, acknowledged that Galileo had been poorly treated by the theologians of his time, the Church has made it clear that science and religion are not opposed to each other and are, in fact, essential to one another's missions. As a form of seeking, affirmed Pope John Paul II, "science can purify religion from error and superstition." At the same time, as an equally valid form of seeking, "religion can purify science from idolatry and false absolutism." And each can draw the other into a wider world, a world in which both can flourish.[2]

We live in an age of science. Every day we discover new things about our bodies, the earth, the solar system, the universe. But so often we are led to believe that science has all the answers, that it is based in fact alone, and that it is objective, empirical, and provable. Though science places a great deal of faith in its sharpest minds, methods, and conclusions, faith talk is limited to religious faith. And religious faith, especially in the light of science, can seem more like wishful thinking and contrived explanation than an intelligent path toward meaning and understanding.

The Galileo case is often mistakenly cited as a prime example of how the Church tries to control believers so that they do not seek on their own. Faith is reduced to a "leap" across the valley of reason, as if believing in God and following a particular religion is a matter of the heart and not the head, a kind of seeking that is not rigorous or respectable. But, as Pope John Paul II reveals in his healing statements about the relationship of science and religion, neither discipline has all the answers, both require a certain degree of faith, and each serves the other in important ways.

That does not stop me from wishing that God would just rip open the sky and proclaim, "I exist. Don't you ever doubt it again." But God hasn't worked that way in a long time. So we go with what we know, what seems the surest bet. We go on with our science.

Still, we all have moments in which we know deep down that science cannot answer all of our questions, that it is not the only form of seeking. Once during a long walk along Lake Michigan I knew it in my gut. It was a bright, beautiful, warm summer day and I was heading south into downtown to explore the city. As I slowly made my way, I was suddenly struck by the energy swirling around me. To my left Lake Michigan was filled with people swimming, sailing with the wind, and water skiing behind speedboats. Above me planes circled the city waiting for clearance to land at nearby O'Hare Airport. To my right bicyclists labored their way along the lakefront paths as cars whizzed past on nearby Lake Shore Drive. In a flash I realized that we humans have learned how to dominate the earth, the water, and the sky. By imitating the animals of creation, we have learned how to use our machines to cut across the land on four wheels instead of hooves, soar through the sky with wings of steel instead of feathers, and cross the ocean on fins of fiberglass instead of flesh. Science rules our lives. Our energy comes from fuel and engines.

But what about the energy inside us? As I walked along the lake I was bursting with energy. Certainly the excitement of the city and the rush of people, boats, cars, and planes was energizing me. But there was more. I was amazed at the warmth of the sun, the beating of my heart, the blowing of the wind, the swaying of the trees, and the movement of the day. I wondered who or what was responsible for these energies, for my feeling of being so alive. Was it God?

I left Lake Michigan that day more open than ever to new ways of seeking. Without giving up any interest in science, I looked more enthusiastically to the poets, philosophers, artists, and theologians for insights into what and where to seek. I also sought experiences that would teach me more about the art of seeking and lead me further along the path of discovery.

A few years later I jumped at the chance to go on a Jesuit-sponsored two-week pilgrimage that was to follow the footsteps of Saint Ignatius of Loyola through Northern Spain to Rome. At the time I knew very little about Saint Ignatius except the basics: he was born in 1491 near Azepeitia, Spain, to a noble family and grew up in a royal court; he became a soldier and in 1521 was injured in a battle in Pamplona, Spain,

where a cannon ball hit and shattered his right leg; and in two strokes
of providence he was carried by his French foes home to Loyola Castle
where, instead of dying, he miraculously recovered and went on to
found the Society of Jesus. Though I admired the Jesuits, I had always
felt that Ignatius's story was a little too ideal; it lacked a real-life fleshi-
ness. I couldn't wait to see if there was more to the saint than the books
conveyed, if his life and energy could teach me about the energy flowing through my life.

As our group of pilgrims met at the airport, it quickly became clear
that we were an unlikely bunch—twenty-two women and men ranging
in age from twenty-something to seventy-something. What we shared
in common was that we all worked in one way or another at Jesuit institutions and wanted to know more about the saint who had influ-
enced our lives. The seven Jesuits leading the trip shared with us their
hope that after visiting Madrid, Toledo, Loyola, Burgos, Javier, Bar-
celona, Montserrat, Manresa, and Rome, we would not only know
Ignatius better but also would know God, each other, and ourselves
more intimately.

At the beginning of the trip we were asked to reflect on what it
means to be a pilgrim. We agreed in our conversation that being a pilgrim means leaving what we know and exploring the unknown in the
hopes of coming closer to discerning our true selves and true vocation.
By tradition, pilgrims have been holy seekers, seeking a deeper connection to the energy of life and the source of that energy. As we set out to
follow in Ignatius's footsteps (ironically using modern technology by
riding on an air-conditioned bus that gave us no real appreciation for
how much ground Ignatius covered on foot and animals' backs), we
were asked to put ourselves in his sandals, to experience what he experienced, and to be open to the power of God in our own lives along the
way. The theme at the start of the pilgrimage was simple: "Whoever
labors to penetrate the secrets of reality with a humble and steady mind
is, even if unaware, being led by the hand of God, who holds all things
in existence and gives them their identity."

Long before the trip started I was excited at the thought of traveling with a Jesuit I had known through publishing, Fr. Ed Schmidt. Ed,
who was twice my age, and I had become good friends through conversations about writing and traveling, and I knew I could rely on his
knowledge of history and Europe to help me get the most out of the experience. As the trip got under way, I was also grateful to make friends

with Les, one of the few people on the trip who was my age. Les was a teacher at a Jesuit high school and, though he had been to Spain before, had never hit the Ignatian spots. As it turned out, the more Ed, Les, and I learned about Ignatius and his companions, the more we became companions, which included everything from praying to staying out too late drinking and talking.

After a brief stay in Madrid we took a bus to Loyola, where Ignatius was born and later had his conversion experience. Seeing his family's castle immediately made us wonder why the future saint would willingly go from such privilege to poverty, from a courtly life to a life of service. The Jesuit tour guides explained that Ignatius has been called the "pilgrim saint" because his journey was anything but linear and clear-cut. For example, when he was brought home after being wounded in battle, Ignatius assumed he would recover and resume his life as a soldier. While restlessly waiting for his injuries to heal, he read the only books in the house—the lives of Jesus and the saints. Suddenly he found himself experiencing a peace he had never felt before and decided to dedicate his life to Christ. Though he had no idea what dedicating himself to Christ would mean, he prayed for healing so that he could get on with his new pilgrimage to God and from God to the world.

When he was well enough, Ignatius traveled to the famous shrine of Montserrat in northern Spain where he laid down his sword in front of the Black Madonna and promised to serve her son as a loving pilgrim. Having exchanged his regal clothes for those of a beggar, Ignatius then began a journey to the Holy Land, which first took him to Manresa, Spain, where he spent a year living in a cave praying, begging, and recording his reflections about his new faith life. He eventually arrived in Jerusalem in 1523 and walked in the footsteps of Jesus. Though his trip was cut short because of civil unrest, Ignatius vowed to continue walking in the footsteps of Jesus for the rest of his life. As part of this vow, the pilgrim saint discerned that he needed more academic training, so at the age of thirty-three he entered a grade school and studied Latin alongside twelve-year-olds. His academic journey eventually led him to the University of Paris, where he met several of the companions who would come to be known as the first Jesuits.

In 1539 Ignatius and his companions sought papal approval for a new order they had named the Society of Jesus. This approval was granted in 1540 by Pope Paul III. Ignatius was elected the first superior general of the order and spent his next sixteen years perfecting the now-famous *Spiritual Exercises* (a handbook for retreats) he had begun in Manresa, writing the *Constitutions of the Society of Jesus*, and drafting letters to Jesuits all over the world. Ignatius died on July 31, 1556, and was beatified in 1609 and canonized a saint in 1622. His international legacy is carried on in the grade schools, junior and high schools, colleges, universities, hospitals, charitable institutions, publishing houses, and retreat centers that bear his name.

While the entire journey through Spain to Rome was deeply moving and gave us all deeper insight into the life of Saint Ignatius, the most powerful part of the trip for me was not being in the rooms where he was born, had his conversion experience, traded his sword for the Bible, wrote his Constitutions and letters, or died. No, the most powerful moment for me was praying in the cave in Manresa where, at the same age as I was at the time, Ignatius struggled to discern what God was calling him to do with his life. From the moment I first laid eyes on the cave I could suddenly imagine Ignatius, a small man about five feet tall, panhandling in his beggar's clothing, praying, preaching the Gospel, working among the poor, and writing what would eventually become the *Spiritual Exercises* that have invited so many people into a deeper relationship with God.

As our group gathered for Mass in the cave where Ignatius spent many lonely and many full hours, I felt a very real connection to him. The cave has been preserved alongside the adjoining Santa Cova Church. Throughout the church and inside the cave there are all kinds of signs pointing out significant things about Saint Ignatius and his journey. Amazingly, on the wall next to the spot where I was seated for Mass, I noticed a plexiglass cover protecting some markings and scribbles. A sign under the glass explained that these scribbles were from the hand of Ignatius. I wondered if they were divine revelations known only to the future saint, or perhaps marks of frustration or anger. Whatever they were, they were tangible signs that connected me to him. In that sacred place I heard distant echoes of Ignatius crying out to God, "I believe in you. I want to serve you. Now what will you have me do?" And in that sacred space I heard my own cries echo inside me as Les turned to me and whispered, "I've got the chills. This is so amazing to be here."

The sheer power of Ignatius's seeking reverberated in us all. As the pilgrim saint, Ignatius—like Jesus and all the saints—teaches us that the art of seeking means embracing life's questions, seeking in as many ways as we can, and being open to conversion. Ignatius understood that faith and conversion are an ongoing process and he encouraged us to find God in all things, to see God by our side. As we left the cave at Manresa that evening, I loved being a seeker and I prayed that my seeking would lead me deeper into the heart of life, mystery, and faith.

6

The Great Question of Christianity

One of the best things about Christianity is that it loves seekers. Jesus himself remains one of the most passionate seekers of all time. And in seeking peace and justice, love and mercy, healing and reconciliation, Jesus laid the foundation for the New Testament and the Christian tradition.

When I forget that Jesus and Christianity embrace seekers, I turn to the Bible to remind myself that I am not alone in asking questions and that, no matter what, I am loved. For these reasons, one of my favorite Bible stories is John 1:35-38. There we find John the Baptist standing with two of his disciples. Up until this point John has been the big man on campus, the wild prophet who, with his followers, goes around radically ordering people to repent and make way for the kingdom of God. Yet, upon seeing Jesus walk by, John exclaims, "Look, here is the Lamb of God!" (1:36). With great shock and deep fascination John's followers leave their leader's side and begin to follow Jesus. They want to see for themselves why John so reveres this Jesus.

As Jesus continues on his way, he is keenly aware that he is being followed. In one of the most powerful exchanges in the Bible, Jesus turns to the curious disciples and asks, *"What do you seek?"*

In those few words Jesus asks the great question of Christianity. Instead of being frustrated by the curious disciples and saying, "Please do not follow me, I am busy and there is much to be done," Jesus takes time out of his travels to ask the curious men, who represent us all, what they are looking for, what they are seeking. Nearly two thousand years later, Jesus continues to ask us, "What do you seek?" He invites all of us to bring our questioning, doubting selves to him. He tells us time and again: "Ask, and it will be given you; search, and you will find; knock, and the door will be opened for you. For everyone who asks receives, and everyone who searches finds, and for everyone who knocks, the door will be opened" (Mt 7:7-9).

Recently one of my best friends turned thirty. For most of his life, birthdays had come and gone without much thought; youth seemed almost endless. But this birthday hit him hard. For reasons beyond our understanding, there are times in our lives when our souls tell us to take inventory of who and what we have become and to chart a course for the future. It just kind of happens, and there is no getting around these moments.

When he called me out of the blue to go grab a beer, I was thrilled. I had just been thinking that it had been too long since we last talked. As we had our first pint of Guinness, we got caught up on current events, talked sports, and shared some details on things that had happened since we had last spoken. By the second beer we were telling stories and laughing like no time had passed since our last conversation. We finished the night by jogging each other's memories about our college days—What was her name? Remember that one crazy guy who used to party all week and still manage to ace his exams? Can you believe so and so is married and has kids?

As I drove my friend home at the end of the night, we got into a deep conversation. He shared that he had recently broken up with his girlfriend of a few months. He was also dealing with a job change, and now, faced with his thirtieth birthday, he said he was both feeling nostalgic and wondering about his future. He was as excited as ever about his life, but he was feeling different from the way he had just a few years before. He was experiencing a rite of passage into a new time in his life and his mind was focused on getting a grip on things. As he reflected on his journey, he counted his blessings—a wonderful family, a happy childhood, an excellent education, close friends, a good career, an active dating life. But he also raised the eternal questions: Am I doing what I was meant to do with my life? Does my job make a positive difference in the world? Am I supposed to have a wife and kids? How can I meet the kind of quality people I long to have as friends and to date? Is my life meaningful?

We parked the car outside his condominium and put the flashers on. Then we continued to sit in the car and talk for nearly an hour about what we want out of life. I asked him what he is seeking most in life right now, to which he responded, "You know, I guess like most people I am seeking intimacy—to know and be known." Aware that my friend was raised Catholic and has always taken his faith seriously, I asked him where God fits into his seeking. "I pray sometimes that my life will mean something, that I will be able to share it with someone. I feel that I have lived a good life so far and that there is so much more to look forward to," he explained, "but I need to pray more, to articulate my deepest desires, and to actively engage my faith as a path to finding what I want."

The great question of Christianity asks us what we seek. It also prompts deeper questions. As Aristotle said over twenty-three hundred years ago, "by nature all humans desire to know." We are a questioning animal interested in knowing as much as we can about ourselves, others, and the world we live in. We cannot help but ask questions big and small: Why are we here? Where did we come from? What is the meaning of life? What does it mean to be human? How close is our experience to reality? Why do we suffer? What is death and what is its significance to us as individuals? How can we find happiness? Where are my car keys?

While many of us might not consider ourselves philosophers, we cannot help but *philosophize*. Philosophy is a love of wisdom. It's about lying on our backs, staring up at the sky, and asking "Why?" It's about studying the intricacies of our bodies and asking "How?" It's about taking the long view of human existence and trying to see the threads that sew the varied patterns of life into a meaningful design. The more we contemplate life, the more questions we ask. And the more questions we ask, the more we encounter deeper truths and gain richer understandings of the miracle of life.

Asking good questions and exploring possible answers takes time, patience, study, and guidance. When Jesus asked John's disciples, "What do you seek?" he was also asking them to say something about themselves, about their goals, and about their paths. As my friend suggested in wondering about his life, there are three basic questions we all ask throughout our lives: Who am I? Where am I going? How do I get there? Through time, our lives change, and so do our answers to these questions. But we never stop asking them.

Who Am I?

When I met Kathy she had just moved to the city. At thirty-one, she found herself struggling to get acclimated to her new surroundings, learn the ropes at her new job, and make new friends. She suddenly felt lost. To use her words, she forgot who she was. She even began to question if she had ever known her true self.

We have all been in Kathy's position. But the question *Who am I?* is constantly with us, even in our best moments. If you were to compose a verbal self-portrait, what would you see? How would you describe yourself? How do you think others see you? What are you really good at? What do you do just because you enjoy it? What aspects of your life are you most proud of? What are you least proud of? What parts of yourself would you never trade for anything in the world? What parts of yourself would you like to change? How rich and life-giving are your relationships with family, friends, and co-workers? Where does God fit into your sense of self and your place in the world?

We have heard it said thousands of times that we cannot love others unless we first love ourselves. Loving ourselves, however, does not mean being narcissistic and finding ways to look and feel better than everyone else. Loving ourselves means knowing who we really are, taking an inventory of the things we hold dear, assessing our core values. Loving ourselves means saying yes to who we are and working to grow as best we can with the minds, bodies, and spirits we have been given. Loving ourselves means having the confidence to seek intimacy with others, to reveal and share ourselves, and to help others know and love themselves.

In our culture we take for granted that we are imbued with dignity just for being humans, that we have the freedom to ask questions about our true selves. The Declaration of Independence tells us: "We hold these truths to be self-evident, that all [people] are created equal, that they are endowed by their Creator with certain inalienable rights, that among these are life, liberty, and the pursuit of happiness." But in many ways it is a luxury to ponder who we are and what we want our lives to be about. Tragically, for many people in our culture, these inalienable rights are denied by negative forces like racism, prejudice, discrimination, bigotry, and hate. In far too many places around the world the question "Who am I?" is buried beneath more pressing concerns about food, shelter, clothing, medicine. When basic survival is at stake, it is nearly impossible to ask "Who am I?"

In the Christian tradition, asking "Who am I?" entails asking "Who are we?" People are not judged by social status, race, body type, skin color, looks, or ability. We are judged by how we treat one another, by how we live our lives as part of a bigger whole. If others are denied the right, the freedom, to ask "Who am I?" then there is something wrong with us, all of us. For scripture teaches us that "God created humankind in his image, in the image of God he created them, male and female he created them" (Gen 1:27). If we take this teaching seriously, who we are is caught up in who God is. And God is community—the Creator, Redeemer, and Sanctifier, three persons in one being—who gives birth to community and loves us when we love each other. We also know from scripture that among many names, God is *Yahweh* (I am who am) and *Emmanuel* (God with us); in other words, God is the ground of all being, the one who is always with us from the moment of our birth, through our death, and into eternity. When God is with us, we are not alone. When God is with us, we are with each other.

However, it is easy to forget who we are, as Kathy did. It is also easy to buy into who the culture or others tell us we are. In recent years I have come to love Christianity because, in its light, I am coming to see for myself who I am, who God calls me to be, and who I am as part of humankind. Teilhard de Chardin once said, "We are not human beings on a spiritual journey; we are spiritual beings on a human journey." What a wonderful thought! I pray with the Beatitudes that I may re-member each day that we are all blessed in our physical and spiritual poverty, sorrow, meekness, and hunger. And I pray that we may share our blessedness through our mercy, love, justice, and peacemaking, so that all may know who they are.

Where Am I Going?

As we seek to find the freedom to be who we really are, we are also challenged to answer the question *Where am I going?* While John Lennon was right when he sang, "Life is what happens when you're busy making other plans," it is still true that who we are is tied to con-sciously making decisions about where we want to go in life. We struc-ture ourselves around our goals and dreams, while at the same time we structure our goals and dreams around who we are.

One of the comments I often hear from members of our generation is "I don't know what I want to do with my life." On the positive side, our generation does not want to settle for just any old job or life. We have options and we keep our options open, looking perhaps idealistically for just the right thing. On the negative side, we so fervently avoid routine and have so many options that we barely know where to begin. On the train during rush hour I once heard a young woman say, "I don't really know where I am going with my life, but I have plenty of time to make up my mind."

While we may have time on our side and will live longer than previous generations, it is never too early to think about where we want to go with our lives. If you were to describe where you are in life right now, what would you say? Do you truly know yourself? Do you love yourself? Do you find happiness and fulfillment in your work, relationships, family, and daily activities? Do you spend time doing things that make you feel good? Do you feel free to give and receive love? Do you like your life?

Like most people, I constantly struggle with whether I really know myself, whether I have the right career, whether I am free, and whether I give life to the world. I go through several mini and not-so-mini crises of faith each year and wonder if anything really matters, if God exists, and if God cares. I also carry with me the faces of people in my life who are very close to being their truest selves as well as those who are very far from it. From them I learn what it is to be free from or tied down by fear and insecurity.

What usually happens when we determine that life is going well is that we claim credit for our success and move on. But when we ascertain that life is not going as well as we would like, we look to place blame. We scour our pasts for excuses and explanations. We wonder where God is. We wonder why we feel so alone.

Two of our toughest challenges are to get past claiming sole credit for our successes and to drop the baggage of our burdened pasts. In these moments of clarity and honesty, we are better able to deal with what is good and bad about our lives and look to the future. We can open ourselves to the grace of growth and insight. We can recognize and be drawn toward God's love.

In these moments it is helpful if we ask ourselves what we seek most in life, what kind of person we feel called to be, what gives us the most joy, what gives us the most pain, how we define success, and how we want to be remembered. Answering these questions tells us something very fundamental about who we really are, where we are now, and where we want to go. If we like where we are headed, the question becomes, how can we grow and develop even more? This forces us to wonder what happens if we fall off track and hit rough spots of self-doubt or face unexpected change? If we do not like where we are headed, the question becomes, how can we reassess our goals and point ourselves in a more life-giving direction?

In the Christian tradition, Jesus invites us to join him on the journey of life. If we accept his invitation, we let go of full control over our life's journey and begin to redefine where and how we will travel. Though it sounds like a cliché to say, "God's time is not our time" or "God doesn't do things according to our plans," there is a lot of truth in these statements. When left to ourselves, it is easy to set our sights on selfish things: Am I making enough money? Do I have everything I want? Do people love me enough? Sadly, our paths can easily lead back to ourselves and we can interpret challenges as obstacles rather than as growth opportunities. But when we accept Jesus' invitation to pray, ponder, read scripture, worship, and share our dreams with him and with a community, we are called outside ourselves. "Where am *I* going?" becomes "Where are *we* going, where does God want me and us to go?"

Recently I learned of the powerful example of a man named Thomas who, upon asking himself where he was headed, utterly changed the direction of his life. Thomas grew up in a poor and tough part of Texas in the late fifties and early sixties. Like many of his friends, he became a drug dealer. He made lots of money but lived a fast-paced, high-risk life.

Then one day Thomas woke up to the reality of what his life was all about. He questioned how he could sell drugs to the very same kids whose impoverished, aimless lives secretly broke his heart. He wondered how he could ever be free when he ran from the law and rival dealers on a daily basis. And he trembled to think what would become of his life in the end.

Several years ago, Thomas had a conversion experience and realized the power of faith. He gave his life over to God and eventually became a Protestant minister. He also married a woman who had two teenage children from a previous relationship and made a family. Now, as director of a program to help youth get off the streets, Thomas lives on a small income in a little Midwestern town and has never been happier. In fact, recently he discerned that though the money is tight he and his family would take in three young girls whose mother died of cancer two years ago and whose father recently was arrested for drug dealing and sentenced to several years in prison. Thomas is on the road to adopting the girls because he believes God has given him a second chance at life and he wants to give these girls the best chance of avoiding his mistakes and leading healthy lives.

When asked where he had been going, Thomas says unequivocally, "to an early grave." When asked where he is going today, he says with a smile, "toward the light."

How Do I Get There?

If we seek things such as intimacy, connection, meaning, freedom, and happiness, then the next question becomes, "How do I get there?"

Like many guys, I am notorious for my stubborn refusal to ask for directions, even when I am lost. It's a pride thing. It's also ignorance— to remain lost when all I need to do is admit I'm lost, ask directions, and get back on my way.

If part of the battle in our spiritual lives is identifying who we are and where we want to go, then the other part is figuring out how to get where we are going. Whether we are men or women, air traffic controllers or tourists, saints or sinners, we must stop and ask directions from time to time. It helps, too, if we ask some key questions: Where do you turn for guidance and inspiration? Do you prefer to journey alone or with others? What books, music, television shows, movies, speakers inspire you and help you think about your future? What obstacles block you from getting where you are going? Where, if at all, does God fit into your life and your goals? Do you read the Bible and rely on your faith for direction?

In scripture we learn time and again that for all of our stubborn refusal to ask for directions, we cannot get where we are going unless we open ourselves to Christ. Jesus tells us, "I am the way, and the truth, and the life" (Jn 14:6). The Christian life is a path that leads to life itself. Christianity makes the bold claim that our lives have a direction and a goal and that while we have not reached the final destination, we are on our way. Christianity hails faith in God as "the assurance of things hoped for, the conviction of things not seen" (Heb 11:1). It preaches that the kingdom of justice, mercy, and love is in our midst, but we have to help uncover and activate it.

According to Christianity, the simple truth of the matter is that we need God to help us discern and get to where we are going. In Douglas

Coupland's novel *Life After God*, one of his characters eloquently explains how our faith can help us get where we are going: "Now—here is my secret: I tell it to you with an openness of heart that I doubt I shall ever achieve again, so I pray you are in a quiet room as you hear these words. My secret is that I need God—that I am sick and can no longer make it alone. I need God to help me give, because I no longer seem capable of giving; to help me be kind, as I no longer seem capable of kindness; to help me love, as I seem beyond being able to love."

The great question of Christianity is "What do you seek?" Within that question are the separate questions, "Who are you?" "Where are you going?" "How will you get there?" These questions are not simply for religious people, they are for all people.

The great promise of Christianity is that in asking we receive, in knocking we gain entrance, and in seeking we find. The religious rub here is that in holding Christianity to its promise we are held to asking questions, thinking about why we are here, celebrating the solidarity of all creation, loving and forgiving others, working for peace and justice. Again, these are not actions only for religious people. They are for anyone seeking to live more deeply. They are for us, our parents, our grandparents, our children, and our children's children.

7

"Spiritual but Not Religious"
Why Go to Church?

One of the great buzz phrases of our time is "spiritual but not religious." Seekers of all types are quite comfortable describing themselves as "spiritual" but cringe at the thought of calling themselves (or worse yet, being labeled) "religious." We ask the questions Who am I? Where am I going? and How do I get there? on our own terms and refer mainly to our personal understandings of God or spirituality in formulating our answers. Anything else would be too religious.

At first glance, it would seem that there is an obvious distinction between the terms *religion* and *spirituality*. On one side of the fence, *religion* has a rigid feel to it—bringing to mind an institutionalized system of attitudes, beliefs, teachings, laws, and practices that tell people how to serve and worship God. On the other side of the fence, *spirituality* has an earthier feel to it—calling to mind a free and individualistic way of being that acknowledges and responds to the existence of the transcendent in a personal way.

But if we look deeper, the distinction between religion and spirituality is more an invention of the modern world than an inherent aspect of the nature of the two terms. From the time of Christ through the Middle Ages, religion, theology, and spirituality were intimately interwoven as components of the life of faith that sought to know and respond to God. It was not until the beginning of the fourteenth century, just after the death of the theologian Saint Thomas Aquinas (1225–1275), that theology (words about God) became an increasingly formal academic discipline while spirituality (reflection on the experience of God in one's life) became a more or less underground concern of monks and mystics. As theology became more and more objective and sought to provide ready-made answers to life's biggest questions, it dealt less and less with people's feelings, personal commitment, and conversion.[1] And as spirituality dealt more with otherworldliness, it became disconnected from ordinary human life.[2]

But, again, this was not always the case. Up until the last several hundred years, people did not choose between religion *or* spirituality, they chose *both* religion *and* spirituality. There was no such thing as one without the other. And if we dig deep into the core of the Christian tradition, we find that the real distinction we are called to make is between healthy and unhealthy religion and spirituality.

The root from which the word *spirituality* springs is the Latin noun *spiritus*, which means "spirit." Thus, spirituality deals with what many traditions call the "spirit," or inner dimension of the person where he or she experiences ultimate reality. While the definition of spirituality may be generic, there is no such thing as a generic spirituality.[3]

Moreover, as Ronald Rolheiser brilliantly explains in his book *The Holy Longing*, none of us has an option as to whether or not we have a spirituality. We all have a spirit, a fire, a restlessness, a longing, a disquiet, a hunger, a loneliness, a wildness, an ache, a dis-ease. The question is how we will shape these forces that stir inside us: "Spirituality is not something on the fringes, an option for those with a particular bent. None of us has a choice. Everyone has to have a spirituality and everyone does have one, either a life-giving one or a destructive one....We do not wake up in this world calm and serene, having the luxury of choosing to act or not to act. We wake up crying, on fire with desire, with madness. What we do with that madness is our spirituality."[4] He goes on to explain, "Hence, spirituality is not about serenely picking or rationally choosing certain spiritual activities like going to church, praying or meditating, reading spiritual books, or setting off on some explicit spiritual quest. It is far more basic than that. Long before we do anything explicitly religious at all, we have to do something about the fire that burns within us. What we do with that fire, how we channel it, is our spirituality....Spirituality is more about whether or not we can go to sleep at night than about whether or not we go to church. It is about being integrated or falling apart, about being within community or being lonely, about being in harmony with Mother Earth or being alienated from her."[5]

If spirituality is what we do with our deepest desires, then what, specifically, is *Christian* spirituality?

Spirituality refers to our religious experience, but that experience is always rooted in a particularity: Jewish, Islamic, Christian, or something else. When we speak of Christian spirituality, we are talking about the lived encounter with Jesus Christ in the Spirit. In this sense, Christian spirituality is concerned not so much with the doctrines of Christianity as with the ways those teachings shape us as individuals who are part of the Christian community and who live in the larger world.[6] As we have said, past societies were much more overtly religious than we are—"They simply had less trouble believing in God and in connecting basic human desire to the quest for God and to the obedience that God demands."[7] Today we struggle to see the need for Christian spirituality. Naïvely we believe that we can build our own spiritualities, that we can manage our powerful energies on our own, that in the midst of our busyness we can find all the quality time we need to attend to our spirits, that we do not need institutions to guide us on our way.

Yet when we put ourselves at the center of our spirituality, we are left feeling restless and empty.

Which is why Christian spirituality places Christ at the center of our lives. Through the Incarnation, the central mystery of our faith, Christ became what we are so that we might become what he is. But the Incarnation did not end on the cross. Instead it was released into all of eternity and is just as real today as when Jesus walked the earth. As Rolheiser puts it: "God takes on flesh so that every home becomes a church, every child becomes the Christ-child, and all food and drink become a sacrament. God's many faces are now everywhere, in flesh, tempered and turned down, so that our human eyes can see him. God, in his many-faced face, has become as accessible, and visible, as the nearest water tap."[8] The body of Christ at the heart of Christian spirituality refers at once to the historical Jesus, the Eucharist as God's physical presence among us, and the body of believers who are Christ's earthly body.

Because we are followers of Christ, then, our spirituality takes on a distinctive shape. As Rolheiser points out, when Jesus specifies that following him means praying, fasting, and almsgiving, he points to a spirituality that rests on four essential pillars: private prayer and private morality, social justice, mellowness of heart and spirit, and community as a constitutive element of true worship.[9]

Private prayer and personal moral integrity involve having an intimate relationship with Jesus that prompts us to keep the commandments and love as Jesus loved. Social justice boils down to the fact that we cannot have a relationship with Jesus if the poor are neglected and injustice abounds; in other words, how we treat the poor is how we treat God. Mellowness of heart and spirit are another way of saying that our spirituality is at its best when we are energized with gratitude, warm with love, and rich with meaning. And cherishing community as essential to worship means that we must go to church so that we can engage the tradition of believers before us and interact with the believers in our midst.

This last aspect of Christian discipleship brings us right back to our starting point. "Church" means "religion," and if we are "spiritual but not religious," then why, we wonder, do we need to go to church?

One of the main reasons that a healthy spirituality requires regular church attendance and participation is that, quite simply, we cannot fully grow and develop on our own. We need to root our spirituality in the richest possible soil so that it will bear fruit. Lutheran theologian Martin Marty puts it this way:

> So much talk about "spirituality" today is unrooted, unmoored
> ...there is a marvelous expression of freedom in this kind of
> "pick and choose" spiritual effort; but unrooted spirituality
> tends to come as it goes. There is a momentary satisfaction, but
> without anchor it leaves one adrift.... People brag about how
> spiritual they are—as opposed to "religious"—but unless they
> have some sense of inheriting a tradition, belonging to a com-
> munity, bonding and making a commitment to the generations
> to come, one surmises that their efforts and achievements will
> simply disappear like vapors, so gaseous is such piety.[10]

One of the surest ways we can inherit tradition, belong to community, and make a commitment to the seekers who will come after us is to plug ourselves into parish life and the larger life of the universal Church. It is important to note here that when we speak of "church" we are not referring to some institution that exists solely outside ourselves. *We* are the Church, people of faith seeking communion with God. The issue, then, is not whether we choose spirituality *or* religion, it is whether we make the commitment to root our spirituality *in* religion and vice versa so that the two will last and give life to each other.

One of the questions our generation constantly asks is "Why would we go to church?" While I have asked this question countless times in my own life, more and more I find myself asking, Why would we *not* go to church? Increasingly, I wonder where we can find the moral message of the gospels, the inspiration of the preacher, the concern for the poor, the love of the community, the opportunity for reconciliation, and the blessing to go forth and live good lives all in one place, let alone in one hour on Sunday for the mere cost of a donation to help someone in need.

While no list of arguments will make any of us go to church, Ronald Rolheiser's nine responses to the question Why go to church? provide a terrific starting point.[11] I want to reflect on each one before talking specifically about Catholicism as a religion for seekers.

Why should we go to church?

1. Because it is not good to be alone. While we all need time alone, it is not good to go through life lonely. By nature we human beings are social. We need each other to process our experiences, struggle in our pain, and share our joys. Christianity itself is rooted in a Trinitarian God whose internal relationship flows outward into our individual lives and into our relationships. In our fast-paced, fragmented, and mobile society, it is easy to worry about "number one," to rely only on ourselves. But scriptural wisdom calls us back to the simple truth that we need each other: "Two are better than one, because they have a good reward for their toil. For if they fall, one will lift up the other; but woe to one who is alone and falls and does not have another to help" (Eccl 4:9-10). Scripture also teaches that when we are together God is with us: "For where two or three are gathered in my name, I am there among them" (Mt 18:20). Therefore, attempting to live in isolation or to make our spirituality a private affair rejects a part of our nature and goes against the very manner of living that God intends for us. Going to church, then, connects us with God, each other, and the world.

2. Because we need to be part of the human family. A friend once told me that I have the perfect postmodern family—a biological dad, mom, and brother, as well as a stepmother and two adopted, biracial siblings. I don't know much about postmodernity, but I do know that my family has taught me that *family* is not determined by blood alone. Friends who work in homeless shelters, departments of child and family services, adoption agencies, and foster homes have taught me through their stories that we all need to be loved, to belong. The Christian tradition tells us to love one another, to love as Jesus loves us. While we spend most of our lives trying to distinguish ourselves from others, we eventually come to a point where we feel in our guts the need to be part of the human family. Church offers us a way to humble ourselves, to come together as community, to break bread together, to wish each other peace, and to make a pact that together we will go out into the world as forces of the love we experience together in Christ.

3. Because God calls us there. Since we are created in the image and likeness of God, it helps to know something about God if we are to know something about ourselves. And if the two great commandments are to love God and to love our neighbor, then our spirituality leads us to worship divinity and link ourselves to humanity. While Jesus did not create the Catholic Church, per se, he did create the community whose experience and reflection on encounters with him grew into church. And by going to church in the modern world, we connect ourselves not only to the God who created and brought people together in the first place but also to all those past, present, and future who seek to know God and live in faith every day.

4. Because we need regular reality checks. Since I began going to church more regularly, I have enjoyed inviting various friends or acquaintances to come with me. Some are Catholic, others are seeking a tradition to tap into, and still others are from other traditions. Once I took to church a friend who at the time described herself as a lapsed Catholic. Throughout the whole Mass she paid earnest attention to the readings, homily, prayers, and final blessing. As we walked down the street to brunch after Mass, she got all excited and said, "I really needed that. I heard some things today I really needed to hear and I feel challenged not to be so isolated in my thinking." What my friend, who says she is going to Mass more regularly these days, was articulating is that when left to ourselves we can live unconfronted, even narrow-minded lives. As scripture says, "Give the members of your community a fair hearing, and judge rightly between one person and another, whether citizen or resident alien. You must not be partial in judging: hear out the small and the great alike; you shall not be intimidated by anyone, for the judgment is God's" (Deut 1:16-17). Living in community means opening ourselves to the care and critique of others who call us back to reality and set us on the right course.

5. Because thousands of saints have shown us the way. I used to think saints were for the birds; even the ones like Saint Francis who loved birds. They just seemed too ideal, too perfect. But in journeying in the footsteps of Saint Ignatius, I came to understand saints as ordinary people who lived extraordinary lives of faith. Ignatius, for example, founded a Catholic order that has built countless churches and schools and service programs across the world. And in praying in places where he prayed, particularly in his small chapel in Rome, I realized how crucial church is to nourishing faith and spirituality. Many of the brightest examples of goodness have credited church life as the foundation for their values and actions, and they beckon us all to follow their example.

6. Because we need to help each other deal with our problems. When I visited my brother at his new apartment in San Francisco, we had the chance to attend a Mass in nearby Sacramento celebrating the recent graduates of a certificate program in lay ministry. Among those being honored were my Uncle Walter and Aunt Barb, who had invited us to spend the afternoon with them. Josh had not been to church in a while and after Mass said, "You know, I might start going to church more often." When I asked him why, he said, "Because one thing I really like about church is that all people are welcome." Like him, I had noticed during the Mass that people from all walks of life were there. Some looked broken, others balanced. But we were all there together. When we go to church, we help each other heal what is unhealthy inside us and nurture what is life-giving.

7. Because when we dream with others, dreams come true. A few years ago, the pastor of Old St. Pat's, Fr. Jack Wall, asked some of us to form a group of young leaders. His hope was that we would represent a new wave of leadership in the parish and reach out to our peers. What began as a dream in Fr. Wall's mind grew into a small board and is now a vibrant ministry with a large board, a huge mailing list, and a healthy structure that includes retreats, boat cruises, outreach programs, and fundraising. On a grander scale, the universal Church, flawed as it is, dreams of a better world, brings people together around love and service, and works to build the kingdom on earth. Two are better than one!

8. Because we need to practice for heaven. The concept of heaven is a lot like that of the Trinity—a real show stopper. Scripture and tradition speak of heaven as both a place and a state of being. Catholics hold that upon his resurrection, Jesus established heaven as the fulfillment of union with God and we pray that, if God's grace allows, when we die we will be united body and soul with him and all the angels and saints. While nobody knows what heaven looks like, we have an idea of what it feels like. When things are really good, we say things such as, "I feel like I'm in heaven." If we believe that heaven is the communal embrace of billions of people from all walks of life, then church stretches our hearts into the universal heart we need to live there.

9. Because it gives us joy. There are times—like during Easter and Christmas, but really on any ordinary Sunday—when going to church is simply a joyful experience. The liturgy, message, music, people, babies crying, saints staring, and challenge to do good all combine to make life feel rich and right. Going to church means seeing it all and thinking about what it all means. The Psalmist prays, "Restore to me the joy of your salvation, and sustain in me a willing spirit" (Ps 51:12). Celebrating the countless depths of life together at church reminds us of the risen Christ, loosens our spirits, keeps us human, bonds us together, and brings us joy.

I remember clearly when I finally decided that I believe in God. It was during my senior year of college when I was sitting in one of my philosophy classes listening to a detailed explanation of Immanuel Kant's *Grounding for the Metaphysics of Morals*. In this work, Kant claims he has found by way of logic the supreme principle to ground all of morality, politics, and ethics. He calls this principle the "categorical imperative" and states it as a simple rule: "Always act in such a way that you can also will that the maxim of your action should become a universal law." (In other words, the Golden Rule in more academic language!)

In the midst of taking notes, I suddenly wrote "I cannot not believe in God." That is to say, "I believe in God."

The whole idea of subscribing to a "supreme principle" of morality based solely in logic made no sense to me. It seemed clear that morality and ethics must be rooted in a supreme being, not a supreme principle. As shocking as it was, I had finally resolved my quest to decide if I believed in God or not—right in the middle of a philosophy class.

Throughout college I adored philosophy because it presupposes no other given than a *philo*, a thirst for wisdom. Theology, on the other hand, always frustrated me because it necessarily presupposes a *theo*, God, and I was never able to confidently profess a belief in God. On an intellectual level, belief made no sense. There are no proofs for the existence of God. And leaps of faith seemed to require too much nerve.

Yet in my heart I knew I believed in God; my heart simply had to tell my mind.

While I know that belief is ultimately not a matter of the mind, I remember feeling grateful when the words "I cannot not believe in God" finally came. A whole new world broke open to me.

Around the time that I discovered my faith in God, I also discovered the religious writings of my childhood hero, C. S. Lewis (1898–1963). Though his *Chronicles of Narnia* series is really a Christian allegory, as a child I was too young to understand it at that level. Then one day, while browsing through the library bookshelves for another author's books, I stumbled across a collection of Lewis's religious writings. After standing there and reading just a few selections, I was amazed by how passionately he wrote about his conversion from atheism, the joys of the life of faith, and the importance of rooting spiritual questions in religious tradition. I have since read his *Surprised by Joy, The Screwtape Letters, The Great Divorce, A Grief Observed*, and many other books and have found in Lewis a spiritual mentor whose own conversion from atheism to Christianity has helped me live more deeply into my own questions and to begin thinking about the interplay between faith in God and religious practice of that faith.

In his *Mere Christianity*, Lewis offers a helpful distinction between faith and religion by using the following metaphor:

> The name *Christians* was first given at Antioch (Acts xi. 26) to "the disciples," to those who accepted the teaching of the apostles.... "Mere" Christianity is...like a hall out of which doors open into several rooms. If I can bring anyone into the hall I shall have done what I attempted. But it is in the rooms, not in the hall, that there are fires and chairs and meals. The hall is a place to wait in, a place from which to try the various doors, not a place to live in.... It is true that some people may find they have to wait in the hall for a considerable time, while others feel certain almost at once which door they must knock at.... When you have reached your own room, be kind to those who have chosen different doors and to those who are still in the hall.[12]

In scripture, Jesus tells his apostles at the Last Supper, "Do not let your hearts be troubled. Believe in God, believe also in me. In my Father's house are many dwelling places" (Jn 14:1-2). The house of faith encompasses all religions, and within that house are hallways that are Christian leading to rooms of specific Christian denominations. While it is good to be in God's house and even better to be in the hallway of one of the world religions, it is best to find one of the rooms of religious tradition. For, to use Lewis's language, it is in these rooms where fires, chairs, and meals offer people a place to live.

Having been raised Catholic, I was familiar with the room of Catholicism from an early age. But it was not until I left the room, walked down the hall of Christianity, out the front door of the house of faith, and into the world of agnostic questioning that I began to understand where I had been. Over the years my God moments have brought me back to the house of faith, into the hallways of Christianity, and most recently into the room of Catholicism. It is in this room where I encounter saints, sinners, seekers, spiritual masters, and the wealth of tradition that helps me better know God, myself, and others. While there are many times when I feel like leaving the room or wonder what people in the hall or in other rooms think of us Catholics, I am coming to realize that, for me, this room is a wonderful place to live. And going to church has been a big part of that realization.

8

Catholicism

A Tradition of Seekers, Sacraments, and Imagination

When I found my way back to church, one of the first homilies I heard emphasized that the wisdom of Catholicism is its emphasis on Mass and the sacraments. "We need to go to Mass regularly," said the priest, "because we need to be reminded that we are loved and to love others. We need to be challenged, to break bread together, to offer each other the sign of peace. We need to see with faith eyes." He went on to explain that we need to partake of the sacraments because, as outward signs instituted by Christ, they bring us closer to God.

I really loved what the priest was saying. The more I thought about my journey away from and back into the Church, the more I began thinking of Mass as an opportunity rather than an obligation. Instead of thinking of the Eucharist as an unknowable mystery, I started thinking of it as the physical and spiritual food I need to sustain my body and soul. And rather than limiting my spiritual journey to what my mind alone could grasp, I became more open to the wisdom of others and the power of the sacraments.

For most of my life I had understood religion in a very constricted way. As a kid, I saw the Catholic Church as a scary authoritarian institution rooted not only in 2000 years of history I did not know but also in a mystery far too big for me to ever comprehend. I saw the Church as a body of ancient rules that took the fun out of life. I always wondered if the threat of hell was legitimate or just something the Church used to force people to obey orders, but I certainly was not going to test it too far. I was sure that most questions about God or the Church were generally not allowed and that the allowable questions were already answered in the pages of the catechism. I sat in ornate churches feeling self-conscious as saints frozen in plastered perfection peered down at me in moral condemnation. And I reluctantly took part in liturgies that were often much more boring and confusing than liberating or instructive.

As public school kids, Josh and I received our catechetical and religious education in CCD (Confraternity of Christian Doctrine) classes and at Mass, but neither of us had much of a relationship to Catholicism. When I was twelve and Josh was ten, we moved in the middle of the school year from our mother's house in Minnesota to our father's house in South Bend. My father was remarried by that time, and yet again life took some getting used to. I was in seventh grade and finished that year and eighth grade at Saint Matthew Cathedral School. Josh was in fifth grade and finished that year at a public school before he was enrolled in St. Matt's for sixth through eighth grades. We both had good experiences at St. Matt's, where we experienced daily prayer, took religion classes, attended weekly Mass, regularly went to confession, and were confirmed. But, through no fault of our parents, neither of us really became engaged Catholics. In fact, even though I ended up in Catholic publishing, it was Josh, now a successful businessman in the "dot com" world, who became an altar boy for a couple of years. He claims that he signed up because at the end of the year St. Matt's sponsored a trip for altar servers to the Indiana Dunes along Lake Michigan. I still bet there is more to the story than that.

After junior high, Josh and I both attended a large public high school and had little to do with the Catholic Church except for the "big" events like Easter and Christmas. During high school I discovered my love for reading and writing. To that point I had not put together many of the pieces of my life, so writing became for me a kind of needle and thread as well as a form of therapy. Occasionally, I would write about my relationship to God, but I was so filled with questions that I doubted I was of much interest to him. I believed that Christianity was not a religion for seekers—I thought for sure God was much more on the side of the firm of faith than the weak of heart.

But when I entered college all that changed. In struggling to become my own person, I grew more and more interested in my faith life. As in junior high at St. Matt's, once again I found myself among kids reared on Catholicism from the womb. But this time my friends and I talked about our questions and took a more mature approach to the big faith questions.

Around the time that Kant's categorical imperative sent me into the arms of God and C. S. Lewis's writings held me there, I was introduced to the writings of Saint Augustine of Hippo (A.D. 354–430). The great seeker-turned-Catholic-turned-bishop-turned-saint spoke directly to me, and suddenly I felt freed from an unnatural burden to either accept or reject faith wholesale. In studying Augustine's *Confessions*, I learned that asking questions is not only all right, it is essential to living a healthy faith. Suddenly the quest to know and love God was no longer confined to rules and pre-set ways. Suddenly even the Church looked different to me. Following Augustine's lead, I wondered if the Church could be a home for me, a passionate seeker.

Saint Augustine's life certainly resonates with many young adults: he was highly educated but did not have all the answers; respectful of authority but in tune with his own inner voice and experience; interested in faith, but unsure of which religion—if any—could provide a path to the More of life.

The future saint was born in North Africa to Monica, a Christian, and Patricius, a pagan who converted to Christianity just before he died. At the age of eighteen Augustine took a concubine, to whom he was faithful for fifteen years and with whom he had a son named Adeodatus. While his mother, who served the poor and eventually was named a saint by the Church, prayed constantly for her son's conversion to Christianity, Augustine seemed to move further and further from Christian life. At nineteen he fell in love with philosophy and logic. He regarded scripture, especially the Old Testament, to be stylistically embarrassing and anything but philosophical. Eventually he joined the Manichean religion, which stressed reason over authority, taught that there is a radical duality between Good and Evil, and claimed that matter is created by dark forces and is therefore corrupt and in need of salvation by good forces. He also taught rhetoric and through his connections with prominent Manichees eventually took his concubine to Rome and then Milan, where he got a job as a professor of rhetoric.

Overwhelmed with worry over her son, Monica sailed to Rome to convince him to clean up his act by letting go of his concubine and marrying a woman she had chosen for him. Augustine agreed to follow his mother's wishes, but found that he could not wait to marry the woman his mother had chosen and took another concubine.

While his mother was deeply disappointed in her son, she was given signs of hope when Augustine left Manicheism for Christian

Neoplatonism, which had as one of its chief proponents Bishop Ambrose. Ambrose was an eloquent preacher who helped convince Augustine that the Old Testament was not as crude as he had once thought.
After reading Plotinus and studying scripture, Augustine had a conversion to Christ and, to his mother's great delight, was baptized in 387.
He eventually returned to Africa and established a quasi-monastic community of educated laymen. While on a visit to nearby Hippo in 391 he
was forced by the people of the city to agree to ordination. By 395 he
was consecrated a bishop. As he had throughout his life, Augustine
wrote prolifically. Only after his conversion did he turn his attention to
writing about the goodness of the Creator and creation, the nature of
grace and the sacraments, the wisdom of scripture, and the joy of being
Catholic.

Augustine's *Confessions* is a passionate and moving account of a
young man in search of meaning. Throughout the book he tells of the
crooked path he walked until he found God. Because the *Confessions*
often seem to go overboard with apologies for having lived such a godless life prior to his conversion to Christianity and argue so fervently
for faith, people joke that Augustine had the best of both worlds and
then ruined it for the rest of us. He lived a fast-paced life until the age
of thirty-three, then converted to Christianity and became a bishop,
one of the greatest theologians of the Church, and a saint. Through his
writings, so the argument goes, we learn what not to do on the spiritual
journey to holiness and salvation.

But when I first read Augustine, I did not feel that his legacy is that
he saves us all precious time and energy by teaching us how to avoid the
pitfalls he encountered in his youthful struggle to find his way to God.
Nor did I think his legacy is that seekers should put away their questions and skip steps on the path to faith because he has shown us all the
answers.

Quite the contrary. Reading Augustine opened my eyes to the importance of being a passionate seeker, of using reason to think through
our faith, of being humble enough to accept that we do not have all the
answers. Augustine's legacy is that, like him, we must seek vigorously,
be active participants in our lives, value personal experience, study,
claim hold of our faith, and plug into the treasures of religious tradition. Only by doing these things can we come to understand how the
same saint who said, "Give me chastity, Lord! But not yet!" could later
in life offer the now-famous statement: "You made us for yourself and

our hearts find no peace until they rest in you."[1] Our restless hearts are what make us human and keep us engaged in life. They are what lead us to read, write, enjoy music, make movies, travel, invent, discover, imagine, and live fully.

During the time I have been a parishioner at St. Pat's, the church has gone through a major restoration and renovation. With the support of the parish community, the church has restored to its original glory the beautiful Celtic stained glass and stenciling created between 1912 and 1922 by the renowned Irish artist Thomas Augustin O'Shaughnessy (1870–1956). Today the church, which was built in 1846 and is the oldest public building in the city, is one of the best examples of Celtic art in the country.[2]

During the restoration I noticed that one of the niches along the north wall was empty. After a quick survey, it seemed the other niches provided nice homes for such saints as Mother Cabrini, Martin de Porres, and Kateri Tekakwitha. So I just figured that as part of the restoration one of the saints was getting a dusting and makeover.

Then one Sunday I heard a visitor ask one of the parishioners why the niche was empty. "Oh, it's not empty," she said, "you just have to imagine your favorite saint there." As it turns out, the niche has never held a statue so that people can imagine their favorite saints there.

Sociologist and novelist Fr. Andrew Greeley says that Catholics use our religious imaginations and "live in an enchanted world, a world of statues and holy water, stained glass and votive candles, saints and religious medals, rosary beads and holy pictures." But, he argues, "these Catholic paraphernalia are mere hints of a deeper and more pervasive religious sensibility which inclines Catholics to see the Holy lurking in creation. As Catholics, we find our houses and our world haunted by a sense that the objects, events, and persons of daily life are revelations of grace."[3]

The Catholic imagination Fr. Greeley speaks of is sacramental; that is, it sees created reality as a sacrament, a visible sign of the invisible presence and activity of God. By becoming human, Jesus became the first sacrament, showing us that God is both present and absent, near and far, immanent and transcendent. The Catholic tradition teaches that the seven sacraments—Baptism, Confirmation, Eucharist, Reconciliation, Anointing of the Sick, Marriage, and Holy Orders—were instituted by Christ and that God unfailingly acts in them. But it also teaches that beyond the seven sacraments there are *sacramentals*, which are instituted by the Church, that also bear God. Things like holy water, ashes, palms, candles, rosaries, sacred images, stained glass, and medals remind people of God's presence in their lives and call us to prayer. More than mere trinkets, they serve as symbols that point to what is really real. They center our collective attention and help us respond as a community united in its diversity.

As people of imagination, story, and sacrament, Catholics not only see God in daily life, we celebrate it. The Jesuit poet Gerard Manley Hopkins was able to say "the world is charged with the grandeur of God" because he could *see* with the eyes of faith and marveled at even the simplest leaf blowing on a branch outside his window. It has been said, "once a Catholic, always a Catholic." Even if we do not follow every rule or if we protest certain aspects of the Church or leave the Church altogether, we have a terrible time shaking our love for the enchanted Catholic imagination. According to Fr. Greeley, even lapsed and nonpracticing Catholics have a Catholic sensibility that shapes their lives and the way they see the world. Which is why people as diverse as Galileo, Michelangelo, Bernini, Mozart, Eugene O'Neill, Flannery O'Connor, Graham Greene, Martin Sheen, Madonna, Sammy Sosa, Martin Scorcese, and Mike Ditka can share in common a Catholic way of being.

Of the many expressions of the Catholic sacramental sensibility in music, architecture, art, literature, and even science, one of my favorites is a book of essays called *Meditations from a Movable Chair* by the late Catholic writer Andre Dubus. Each essay is a poignant testimonial to the power of faith by a man who lived passionately, loved his first and second families dearly, suffered mightily after losing the use of his legs when he was hit by a car after pulling to the side of the road to help a young stranded couple, struggled to keep his young family together after he and his second wife divorced a year after the accident, and died much too young in 1999.

In the essay "Sacraments," written several years ago in the present tense, Dubus explains that because he is divorced he cherishes all the more his visits with his young daughters, who live with their mother. On Tuesdays he drives his specially rigged van with high-tech hand controls to the girls' school to pick them up and take them home. Because they do not like the school lunches and are not allowed to bring their own, they are often hungry after school. So, being a loving dad, Dubus brings them sandwiches, potato chips, Cokes, and Reese's peanut butter cups. As he describes the arduous process of negotiating his wheelchair in his small kitchen to make sandwiches for his daughters, Dubus meditates on the sacramental quality of what he is doing. For him, the physical and emotional pain of being crippled and of not being able to move around as easily as he used to is transformed into the very essence of what makes his time with his daughters and his making them lunch so sacred. "On Tuesdays, when I make lunch for my girls," he says,

> I focus on this: the sandwiches are sacraments. Not the miracle of transubstantiation, but certainly parallel with it, moving in the same direction. If I could give my children my body to eat, again and again without losing it, my body like the loaves and fishes going endlessly into mouths and stomachs, I would do it. And each motion is a sacrament, this holding of plastic bags, of knives, of bread, of cutting board, this pushing of the chair, this spreading of mustard on bread, this trimming of liverwurst, of ham. All sacraments, as putting the lunches into a zippered bag is, and going down my six ramps to my car is. I drive on the highway, to the girls' town, to their school, and this is not simply a transition; it is my love moving by car from a place where my girls are not to a place where they are; even if I do not feel or acknowledge it, this is a sacrament.[4]

Dubus goes on to say that if he were "much wiser, and much more patient, and had much greater concentration," he could sit in silence in his chair, look out his windows at a green tree and the blue sky, and know that "breathing is a gift; that a breath is sufficient for the moment; and that breathing air is breathing God."[5]

This is what it means to be Catholic, to see God in the sacraments of daily life.

9

Seeking the God Who Seeks Us

As Catholics, we seek God in all things and we see the world itself as a sacrament that tells us of God and God's love. But the quest for God is nothing new. It has always been and will always be.

What change are the times, the people asking the questions, the questions themselves, the results of the quest, and the way seekers record and "package" their results for others. In writing about the meaning of life and happiness, for example, Augustine brings to bear experiences, education, language, and insights that are quite different from those of Mitch Albom in his *Tuesdays with Morrie* or those of Paul Johnson in his recent memoir *The Quest for God*.

But the quest for meaning—for something More, for the sacred, for God—remains and perdures through every era. The real question is, who controls the quest for God?

While we live in a time and culture of tremendous (re)awakening to the sacred, we have fallen prey to the notion that *we* control the quest. We can send people to moon, to the depths of the ocean, and speeding across the land, so why wouldn't we be able to build a machine (or perhaps a Tower [Gen 11:1-9]) to take us to Heaven? We can split the very atom of our existence, harness the energy of the sun, and send sound and pictures soaring through the air, so why wouldn't we be able to create an instrument to detect the sacred? We have explored the beginnings of our earth and are hot on the trail of the origin of the universe, theorized how humans evolved from primordial sludge, and tracked our history by unearthing ancient cities and texts, so why wouldn't we be able to pinpoint God's exact location in the universe? We have cloned genes, replaced hearts, and mapped the inner regions of the brain, so why wouldn't we be able to know the mind and heart of God?

Part of the reason we have such a hard time finding God is because we see ourselves as gods. There is no doubt, as we noted earlier in talking about the creators, discoverers, and seekers who helped usher in the modern world, that we humans are truly remarkable beings. There is no doubt that with every waking moment we learn something new about everything. But in light of our amazing abilities, we sometimes put ourselves in control of the game of hide-and-go-seek with God: we chart the playing field, set the rules, and determine the winner.

So what is the problem? In his essay "God in the Dock," C. S. Lewis sets it up this way: "The ancient man approached God (or even the gods) as the accused person approaches his judge. For the modern man the roles are reversed. He is the judge: God is in the dock [where the accused sits or stands in court]. He is quite a kindly judge: if God should have a reasonable defence for being the god who permits war, poverty and disease, he is ready to listen to it. The trial may even end in God's acquittal. But the important thing is that Man is on the Bench and God is in the Dock."[1]

There is nothing wrong with asking, as we did at the beginning of this book, the question: Where in the world is God? In fact, we cannot help but ask it! Likewise, we cannot avoid asking another quintessentially human question: How can I find God?

But to explore this latter question more fully, it helps to suspend our trial and take God out of the dock and out of the courtroom all together. It helps to come down off our pedestals and humbly ask where God is and what, if anything, God has to do with us. The Bible teaches us that "fear of the LORD is the beginning of wisdom" (Ps 111:10). The point is that fear—or profound reverence or even plain old respect—is a good starting point in approaching God or, for that matter, knowledge, love, and relationships. If we approach life as if we know everything, we are closed to new experiences and learning. But if we approach life with humility, we are open to new experiences and learning. As for the quest for God, it might just be that for all of our knowledge and instrumentation, God eludes our radar screens only to appear like a log in our eye. It may also turn out that we are not entirely in control of the hide-and-go-seek game with God.

In his book, *How Can I Find God?*, a young Jesuit friend of mine, James Martin, asked people from all walks of life—famous and not-so-famous, rich and poor, young and old, of various ethnic backgrounds, and of different faith backgrounds and from none at all—to talk about where they encounter God. While we may wonder how any of us can honestly search for God if we do not begin already having faith, I join Jim in believing that God is at work in everyone's lives *no matter what.* The more we seek, the more we become able to see. Or, to use the words of the prophet Jeremiah, "When you search for me, you will find me; if you seek me with all your heart, I will let you find me, says the LORD" (29:13-14).

While there are many thought-provoking answers in Jim's book to the question "How can I find God?" I want to highlight four answers (two similar pairs) that are particularly striking.

The first response comes from Chris Erickson, a thirty-three-year-old Nebraska farmer who was raised Lutheran, earned a degree in agricultural economics, and now works the land that has been in his family for over one hundred years. With an ease that leaps off the page, Chris says,

> If someone were to ask how to find God, I would smile and tell them that I see God every day. Being a farmer requires one to work with the earth and nature, and I cannot think of one occupation outside the clergy that would expose a person to God and His Creation more than farming. From the planting of the seeds through the harvesting of the grain, I see God's plan at work all the time.... When we look at God's creation, we see the wonderful work of the Almighty Hand. I find God in the soil I till, the crops I grow, and the water I use—all working together to provide food for many around the world and myself with a living. I see God in other people through their acts of kindness and caring. And I believe you can find God in the way our universe functions, in the intricate and magnificent way it operates and the consistent order with which it functions—all of which point to God as its Creator.[2]

The second response comes from Stacy Laveson, a thirty-three-year-old rabbi who studied sociology at Brandeis University, went on to study at Hebrew University in Jerusalem and Hebrew Union College-Jewish Institute of Religion, and was ordained in 1993. Stacy relays an interesting story:

> I recently had lunch with a friend of mine. After we finished ...my friend looked at me oddly and commented, "You really

have tremendous faith in God." "I do," I responded, "when I remember to."...There are times...when I "forget" to believe in
God. After moments, days, and occasionally even weeks when
God's presence pervades me and the world around me, I suddenly realize that it is gone, that my awareness of God has left
me without my notice....Yet while "forgetting" is not a conscious act, "remembering" is. Only when I look for evidence of
God's presence, only when I recognize that God is part of every
relationship I have, every bite of food I eat, and every drop of
rain that falls from the sky, will my intellectual knowledge of
God be replaced by an intimate awareness of God.[3]

What Chris the farmer and Stacy the rabbi share in common, besides being young adults, is that their quests for God hinge on their
ability to be skilled observers and to name their experiences of life as
gifts from God.

The next two answers from Jim's book look at the question "How
can I find God?" from a completely different angle.

Martin Marty, whom we quoted earlier and who has written nu-
merous books on religion, responds to the question "How can I find
God?" by saying,

Turn it around: How does God find me? If God is, but is ineffable, beyond beyondness, self-contained, forget it. Then God
is unfindable....If God is, and is ineffable, beyond the gods
but still relational, remember it. Then God is findable. "How
do I find God?" Certainly by beginning with a sense of wonder and being ready for awe. God may cause you to be "surprised by joy." But it may take billions of particulars, including
affirmations, recognitions of Christ in the homeless, readings
of Scripture, experiences of friendships, transcendings of despair, for this surprise to work its way, to elicit awe from you.
..."How do I find God?" By listening closely and, with suspicion momentarily suppressed, by responding. Awe-full, isn't
it?[4]

Along these same lines, Catherine Mowry LaCugna, a highly respected feminist theologian and professor of theology at the University
of Notre Dame who died much too young at the age of forty-four in
1997, offers:

One "finds" God because one is already found by God. Anything we would find on our own would not be GOD. If we
think that by our own efforts, our own ideas, we have found
GOD, we may have "found" just a product of our own imaginations, or needs, or wishful thinking.... We are made to know
and love God through love of others, love of self, love of all
creatures. We discover the ever-present God in our own goodness, creativity and capacity for self-transcendence. God desires
nothing more than to be known and loved by us, to be in eternal communion with us—which is why we are indeed already
found by the true, living God.[5]

What Marty and LaCugna share in common is the profound belief
that God is as near to us as we are to ourselves. Both caution us to be
careful, however, to seek the one, true God. As we said at the beginning
of this chapter, all too often, especially in our culture, it is easy to create
and control the God we seek and to put God on trial for not being the
God we had expected. But, as we also said before, if we root our quests
for God in wonder and remain open to awe, our seeking becomes more
capable of leading to seeing.

In my own life, the revelation that I am seeking the God who seeks me
has made all the difference.

As a kid I read the poem "Footprints" but never quite got it. A person is walking along the beach of life with God and both are making
footprints in the sand as they go. At the end of his life, the person looks
back and notices that, when times got rough, there was only one set of
footprints. He assumes that God abandoned him when life got difficult.
But God tells the person that he never left, that the one set of footprints were his as he carried the man in troubled times.

It's a nice thought and all, but, as many have said, it's a little removed from reality. Rather than there being a nice set of God's footprints in the sand as he carries us in tough times, it's more likely that
God's messy footprints would be followed by drag marks as we go kick-
ing and screaming down the beach of our salvation. If a forensics detec-
tive were to stumble upon the scene she'd likely determine, "there's
been a struggle of some sort here."

It was not until I read Francis Thompson's poem "The Hound of
Heaven" (composed in 1890) that I began to understand how intensely

God pursues us with his unbounded love. "The Hound of Heaven" is one of the greatest lyrical poems in the English language for its sublimity of thought, power of expression, beauty of imagery, and verse melody.[6] But its power comes from its portrayal of God as a heavenly Hound that pursues our fugitive souls down the nights and down the days, over hills, through valleys, and across forever. The image of God as the Good Shepherd who seeks out his lost sheep is beautiful. But the image of God as an insistent, unrelenting Hound that hunts the soul that flees from his love and service is simply awesome. The first stanza says it all:

> I fled Him, down the nights and down the days;
> I fled Him, down the arches of the years;
> I fled Him, down the labyrinthine ways
> Of my own mind; and in the midst of tears
> I hid from Him, and under running laughter.
> Up vistaed hopes I sped;
> And shot, precipitated,
> Adown Titanic glooms of chasmed fears,
> From those strong Feet that followed, followed after.
> But with unhurrying chase,
> And unperturbèd pace,
> Deliberate speed, majestic instancy,
> They beat—and a Voice beat
> More instant than the Feet—
> "All things betray thee, who betrayest Me."

The more we seek God, the more God seeks us. And sometimes, when we give up the hunt, it is good to know that we are always being hunted by Love itself *no matter what.*

10

Six Rules for the Road

Seeking is not an art that can be mastered. At least not in this life-time. By its very nature, seeking is fluid, ever-changing. The objects and circumstances of our seeking—the who, what, where, when, why, and how—at this moment in life are very different from what they were in our younger days and from what they will be in our older days.

But, as my friend said in the e-mail, seeking is what keeps us alive; it is what binds us together. So, the quality of our lives and of our faith depends in many ways on the quality of our seeking. In my own experi-ence, the following six practices have helped me become a better seeker, and hopefully they will help you, too. Because my faith is an integral part of my worldview, I have fleshed out each of these general practices with God-moment stories that illustrate how the sacred is present in everything from high school classrooms to baseball games if we learn to look for it.

1. Embrace the Journey

After countless hours of research, outlining, writing, listening, working with patients, lecturing, and discussing, the world-renowned psychia-trist M. Scott Peck boiled the essence of his mega bestselling book *The Road Less Traveled* into the opening line: "Life is difficult."

Our consumer-driven pop culture has produced its own spin on such wisdom. Bumper stickers, for example, give us a range from the fa-talistic—"Life's a bitch, then you die"—to the humorous—"Life's a beach, then you die"—to the commercial—"Life is short. Play hard," or "Just do it." One of the famous lines from the blockbuster movie

Shawshank Redemption tells us that once we realize life is hard, we can "Get busy living, or get busy dying." Translated into consumer language, we can "Get busy buying" and "shop till we drop."

But Dr. Peck's point in telling us that life is difficult is not to prompt us to give up or divert our attention or buy our way into oblivion. Quite the contrary.

Peck's point is to teach us that once we acknowledge that life is tough we are free to *embrace* life to the fullest extent. We let go of misconceptions about what life *owes us* and grab onto the truth that life gives us what *we put into it*. We move from a naïve preoccupation with trying to reach the "top" to a mature acceptance of life as a journey filled with ups and downs and various destinations that change over time. We cease trying to control every aspect of our lives and begin opening ourselves to new possibilities and ways of seeing things.

In faith language, believing in God means believing that our lives both have a purpose and are part of the much bigger picture of all of creation. Faith focuses our attention on the things that matter and helps us put our lives into proper perspective. Through faith we embrace our lives not as the be-all and end-all but as an important part of life itself. We reach beyond ourselves to others and help them embrace life. Instead of seeing each and every fall in our lives as our final step, we walk with Jesus who fell and got up many times on the way of the cross. And if we embrace the cross—the times of physical and mental pain and suffering—we also embrace the joy of the resurrection. Embracing the journey of life, as Blaise Pascal (1623–1662) teaches, means embracing God who helps us stretch our arms wide enough to embrace nothingness and infinity, mystery and meaning, despair and joy.[1]

In high school I scribbled on the cover of a notebook, "Life is a journey to figure out what life is." At the time, the thought was revolutionary for me because I was, like many of my friends, seeking to find some magic key to life that would forever unlock all the doors that lead to fulfillment and happiness. The journey part of life scared me, so, rather than embrace it, I sought to take the mystery out of it by conquering it.

As a public school student, I had a healthy diet of subjects that included the usual fare of science, math, literature, history, health, and so on. My electives included Latin, debate, and journalism. And I played on the baseball and tennis teams. Overall, I was blessed with a well-rounded education that fed my mind, body, and to some degree, spirit.

But I was naïve because I believed that if I sifted through my education I would find the key to life that I was looking for. I did some thinking about God and occasionally went to church with my family, but faith was not part of my curriculum and was more of an afterthought than a motivator or instructor.

When I wrote the words above on my notebook, I was a senior in the advanced placement English class with Mrs. Smith. She was explaining that the beauty of literature is that it is always new, always alive. "Even though we tend to think of literature, especially the 'classics,' as being locked in some irrelevant, dead past," she would say, "the words, stories, and insights are always being read and received in different ways by different readers in different times—they are always fresh."

I enjoyed thinking of literature as being "alive" because it freed me to read and interpret it in my own way. My reverence for writers and the critics and professors who explain their work did not wane in that moment. It just became nuanced so that, instead of being intimidated or even bored by them, I decided to join them and add my own flair as a reader.

As I listened to Mrs. Smith, I made a connection between what she was saying about literature and how it applied to life. After all, I thought, literature is about life, even when it is fictional. The beauty of life is that it is by definition "alive" and therefore open to change and new interpretations and meaning. So my early hope to evade the journey of life by "figuring it out" was transformed into *embracing* the journey of life by enjoying the ride.

A few years later, when I was in college, Alasdair MacIntyre, a famous philosopher and by far the toughest professor I have ever had, told our ethics class, "You have not read a book once until you have read it twice. The first time through you become familiar with the author's language, structure, logic, and overall thesis. The second time through you see more clearly what the author is conveying, and you not only grasp the author's meaning but also generate your own insights and meaning."

Suddenly I was reminded of Mrs. Smith's class, but this time something else clicked for me: my faith. I asked myself, How deeply have I been reading the book of life? And what do I know about the Author of life?

My experience at Notre Dame led me to think about my faith a lot. But even then I was "reading the book of life" only once, and probably too quickly at that. I have always wanted answers as fast as possible. So the instruction to read and re-read texts made sense to me. It also opened my eyes to the reality that when it comes to faith especially, the journey to know and understand God is ongoing. Either embrace it or spend a lifetime being frustrated!

2. Be Awake, Aware, and Alive

The art of seeking requires us to be awake, alert, and alive. It also requires us to be open, daring, and bold enough to think "outside the box." Rather than seeking through other people's eyes and accepting at face value what *they* seek and ultimately discover, we must train *ourselves* to be skilled observers who seek and find for ourselves. Of course, we have much to learn from others and we must always embrace our journeys in light of community, but it is crucial to believe that *seeking is not only all right, it is essential* to our lives. Socrates had it right: the unexamined life is not worth living!

My friend John Cusick is fond of saying, "You do not see the world for *what it is*, you see the world for *who you are*." In other words, while many disciplines such as psychology claim objectivity, there is no such thing as pure human objectivity. Each of us is shaped by a particular set of circumstances defined by everything from our genes to our upbringing to our education. Skilled observers are not objective robots who coldly take in and assess data but individuals who pay careful attention to what is going on inside and outside themselves.

In the past seven years we have witnessed a dramatic increase in the number of people who change careers to make more time for other parts of their lives, take paid and unpaid sabbaticals from work, escape on extended vacations, or search their souls at retreat centers. Many of these people explain that they just had to "get off the merry-go-round," "relax," "step back and gain a perspective on life," and simply, "reenergize." In these moments outside the day-to-day grind, we examine our lives from a calmer, clearer vantage point. We observe our lives from something like a third-party perspective, replaying tapes of our experience and watching and assessing ourselves at work, at home, at play, and in general.

But being a skilled observer involves much more than occasionally retreating from and assessing life. Being a skilled observer means *moving attentively inside each moment of each day.* If we truly embrace the journey of life, then we awaken to life as it is happening. We engage in the direction and activity of each day. We observe what we are feeling and learning. And we dive into even the most frustrating and perplexing mysteries.

A wonderful insight into the importance of being skilled observers comes from the British composer Harrison Birtwhistle. In 1997 Birtwhistle debuted an orchestral work entitled "Exody 23:59:59." The title, he told the *New York Times*, is twofold: Exody is a reference to Exodus and captures a sense of leaving, of journeying; 23:59:59 is military time for the second before midnight and captures a moment in time before a new calendar day begins. Writing toward the end of the last millennium, Birtwhistle composed his piece to capture the significance of leaving one era and entering another.

When asked to describe his musical creation, Birtwhistle responded, "The piece is like a journey" and then explained:

> I'm interested in the whole notion of what a journey is. Whenever you're traveling, there's the prescribed place you're attempting to get to, but there's also the moment where you are within the journey—the scenery, if you like. Even more interesting for me is the question of right and left, the fact that when you're looking at something, along the journey, you're all the time cutting out other things. You can't see everything all the time. And so the question of continuity and discontinuity also interests me—how you make discontinuities that in another way add up to a continuity.[2]

The quote may not immediately sound exciting (I've seen audiences glaze over when I've read it aloud!). But if we break it down, we can see that Birtwhistle is teaching us that *being skilled observers is one of the most crucial aspects of being human.* If we are seeking such things as meaning, fulfillment, and happiness as we go along in life, then we are called to (1) keep our "eyes" open, (2) carefully choose what we "focus" on, and (3) recognize that even when we focus on all the right things, we are still limited and challenged to make everything add up, to find continuity in discontinuity.

To the first point, if we go through life zoned out and passive, then we cannot be active and tuned in to the everyday happenings. Worse yet, if we go through life with our eyes half shut, then we only catch a small portion of the experience of living. If we are anemic in our thinking, closed to new ideas, prejudiced against the "other," then all we will ever know of life is what our limited perspectives allow us.

To the second point, if we keep our eyes open but focus only on less-than-life-giving things, then we are going to miss the really important stuff. There are those who are skilled observers when it comes to pointing out all the things that are wrong with the world and all the reasons life is miserable. But there are also those who see everything through rose-colored glasses and miss the lessons to be learned in such things as suffering and sorrow. The point in being skilled observers is to be realistic and balanced.

To the third point, even if we choose to focus on all the right things, we cannot take it all in. We are limited even when we are fully aware, which means we must rely on God and others to help us make a healthy worldview out of the fragments we take in. Interestingly, the word *religion* comes from two Latin roots *re* (again) and *ligare* (to tie together), which means "to tie together again." The goal of religion, then, is to tie the events of life together so that they make sense and lead to fullness. At its best, religion's foundation in scripture, ritual, and tradition gives us a lens through which we can combine all the fragments of life into a whole picture.

I grew up in a family of Cubs fan. My dad has written several books on the Cubs and is a lifelong fan of the team. Some of my fondest memories of childhood include going to parks with my dad and brother and pretending to be Cubs players as we "had a catch" and called the play-by-play. The few times we made the 110-mile drive into Chicago from South Bend and watched the real Cubs play are burned in my memory. My favorite of these was my "golden" birthday (I turned 12 on August 12, 1982), when my family got ten of my best friends and me seats behind home plate, arranged for the scoreboard to read "Happy Birthday Jeremy Langford," and the bat boy gave me a foul ball from Jay Johnstone's bat.

Today I live down the street from Wrigley, which as far as I can tell is one of the truly authentic slices of heaven on earth. A few seasons ago I was at the park in June watching the Cubs play the Arizona Diamondbacks. As one of the team's promotions to draw people, it was billed as "'70s Night," which meant the Village People were in town

blaring their ever-famous song "YMCA" and fans were dressed up in
their best J. J. Walker and Mary Tyler Moore outfits. All around us people were wearing wigs, tight bell-bottom pants, big-collared shirts, and
funky jewelry. And on this night Wrigley Field was transformed into a
time machine lost somewhere in the seventies.

There were 39,000 people jammed into the park, which holds
only 35,000, to watch our beloved Cubs play ball. True to their history (and for those of you who do not know, the Cubs have not won a
World Series since 1908 or a pennant since 1945 or a division cham-
pionship since 1989), the Cubbies played as poorly as they did in the
seventies. They lost 5-4, and all four of their runs were from single-
shot homers. Every time a Cub hit a home run, the fans went crazy.
Not so much because it meant we might win but because we were less
likely to lose. Truth is, the fans that night did not much care who won
or lost, or even how the game was played. They were just enjoying
themselves.

Trying to be a skilled observer, I looked around the park for signs
of deeper things than just a bunch of people watching baseball. I overheard a guy behind me telling his friends what a great night it was, so I
pretended to be looking for a hot dog vendor and I turned around to
see what this reveler looked like. Forgetting briefly that it was "'70s
Night," I was surprised to lay eyes on a young man with his shirt wide
open revealing fake chest hair and a big gold medallion. But I got a
good look at his face and saw his joyous expression.

With a hot dog in one hand and a beer in the other, he looked at
his friends, a large group of young women and men, and quoted a line
from a popular beer commercial, "It doesn't get any better than this."
Now, I know he wasn't talking about baseball because it gets a lot better
than that! And I'm sure he'd had better beer than Old Style, though it is
the nectar of the gods at Wrigley Field. So, somehow, watching this
game and being with his friends put him in the mood to say, "This is
great!" And when the Cubs hit a homer in the next inning, the guy behind me high-fived his friends and huddled them in a circle for a group
hug.

I loved the fact that in the midst of watching baseball, a secular
sport where multimillion-dollar players whine about not making
enough money, this guy celebrated his friendships. And for a brief moment I made a connection between how I felt at the game that night
and how I often feel at Mass. When Mass is done right, we all join to-

gether as fans of the Jesus event and the gospel message. Instead of high-fives, we join hands in the Our Father and offer each other the sign of peace. Instead of passing pretzels and beer down the row, we pass the collection basket. And instead of pouring back onto the streets with a game on our minds, we feel charged to go and "love and serve the Lord."

3. Log the Experience

No matter how good we become at embracing our journeys and sharpening our skills as observers, all is lost unless we savor the richness of life. The art of seeking requires us to take note of where we have been, where we are now, and where we are going. I call this "logging the experience."

The value of personal experience in our journeys of life and faith can never be overstated. We hear all the time that young adults place great emphasis on experience, which does not mean that we reject everything at face value or consider rules and eternal lessons irrelevant. We simply like to "see for ourselves." I wish more people placed so much emphasis on the importance of experience.

Logging our experiences can be done in many ways. Some people compose music or paint or write poetry or call a friend or take photographs or dance or sing. There is no right or wrong way to log experience. The point is simply to do it. Taking time out of each day to reflect on life as it is happening is crucial for making continuity out of discontinuity and for seeing the larger tapestry of our lives.

Keeping a journal has always helped me log my own experiences. Ever since I can remember I have written down my thoughts. Sometimes I have written daily, other times only when I felt the urge. The effect has been that, from my earliest childhood scribbles to my adult entries typed on the computer, I have kept track of the threads that hold my life together.

By logging the experience, we claim it, mine it for its riches, come to understand it better, and record it for those days when life seems empty and devoid of meaning. In his poem, "The Dry Salvages," T. S. Eliot says it best: "We had the experience but missed the meaning / And approach to the meaning restores the experience / In a different form, beyond any meaning / We can assign to happiness." As we get

into the habit of logging the experience, we become better at string-
ing our experiences together and seeing the meaning in them. Henry
David Thoreau called the practice of meditating on and writing about
experience "sucking the marrow out of life."

As a kid I was always fascinated by my parents' den. A sunny room off
to the side of our house, the den was a sacred place where my mom
and dad would spend much of their time, especially in the evenings,
reading and writing. My brother and I also spent a lot of time in the
den because on the side opposite my parents' desks was the family
television.

Ironically, I learned to read later in life than most kids. Our house
was filled with books but I struggled in school to learn to read and spell
and often gave up hope. But thanks to Sr. Dolorosa (whose name means
"sorrowful one" even though she was always happy), who spent many
hours tutoring me after the other kids from Saint Joseph's Grade School
had gone home, I eventually learned the joy of reading. The floodgates
opened and I was forever checking out books and filling notebooks with
words I had learned at school.

But it was not enough to write in my notebooks on the floor of my
parents' den or at the kitchen table. I wanted my own den, a room of
my very own to log my experiences.

Having learned of my dream, my mother helped me convert my
bedroom closet into my very own office. Then she made some soft sug-
gestions about the need for office equipment, helped me set up a table
and chair, and gave me some shelves that she had made. But she respected the fact that this closet office was mine and let me do things my
way.

Pretty quickly into "operation office," my brother Josh came
snooping around. Forever my shadow and companion, Josh saw something going on here that said, "stay out."

"Whatcha doin?" he asked.

"None of your business," I snarled back.

Never one to take no for an answer, Josh found ways to break into
my closet office and join me. I think most of my time in there was spent
trying to hold the door closed so Josh couldn't interrupt my "important
endeavors." When I wasn't around to guard my office, Josh would sneak
in and do what I did in my parents' office: root through things looking
for clues. Time after time I would find evidence that an intruder had

been in my office, and time after time Josh would deny it with a guilty smile streaked across his face.

Bringing to life the phrase, "if you can't beat em, join em," Josh eventually decided to convert the closet in his room into his own damn office. Josh was a bit on the messy side, so clearing his closet of everything from dirty laundry to mason jars of dead bugs took some work. But he got the job done. Within a day or so, Josh had an "office," desk and all. The only problem was, now that he had an office, he didn't know what to do in it. I smile now imagining him sitting in there for what must have seemed endless minutes wondering what one does in an office and, more specifically, what I was doing down the hall in my closet office. It was not long before Josh's office was once again a messy closet, only this time it had a desk and chair!

Years later, Josh asked me, "What *were* you doing in your closet office when we were kids?" I admitted, "Probably wondering what *you* were doing." We laughed our heads off.

I remember pretending that I was busy, like the boss was breathing down my neck or I had some major deadline. But most of the time I was in there I was just being me. I spent time organizing my desk, sharpening pencils, putting books I never read on my shelf, filing papers that contained nothing more than scribbles. But I also spent time imagining great adventures, dreaming up stories, thinking about my experiences, and trying to live up to having the huge responsibility of maintaining a closet office.

Twenty years later my mother came to Chicago to see the apartment I had just moved into. Much larger than my first two studio apartments right after college, this one allowed me to set up a home office, where I work as an editor during the day and write in the early morning and late night. I love the office because it's where I think, dive into books, listen to my stereo, stare out the window, and log my experience.

In a true God moment, the first time my mother looked around the room and saw the desk, computer, bookcases, and reading chair, she smiled one of those motherly smiles and said, "Oh, your little closet office!" I felt instantly grateful for all the times my mom had read stories to Josh and me, taken us on adventures, and helped me make the most of my closet office so that I could log my experiences. Virginia Woolf was right: we all need a room of our own to do our best thinking.

4. Seek Out Kindred Seekers and Mentors

Though I did not fully understand it at the time, one of the best pieces of advice I ever got was from my cousin Tom: "Value the friendships you make in high school and college, because you can't be friends with everyone, and real friendships are rare. The bonds you form during those years are unlike those you'll form at any other time in your life."

Because he was in college and I was in high school at the time, I only half listened to what he was saying. At that age, we think we know it all. Though I had always valued my friendships, I was out to win popularity contests and be friends with everyone. It seemed very odd, even cynical, to say that of all the people we know, only a select few ever really become true friends.

But for some reason, Tom's advice stuck in my mind. As I developed my personality, sense of self, values, dreams, and ideals, I began to recognize that some of my friendships gave me more life than others.

By the time my grade school and high school friends and I entered college, it became more and more clear whom I would stay in touch with on a regular basis and whom I would be satisfied to see back in the old neighborhood on breaks and down the road at reunions. We were scattered all over the country in different schools pursuing different courses of study. We were off making new friends and having experiences apart from each other. And it took some serious effort for my best friends and me to stay in touch and grow and develop together.

Throughout college, Tom's advice rang more and more true. From the guys in my dorm to the women and men in my classes, I could pretty quickly tell whom I wanted to be friends with. Growing into young adulthood means coming to terms with where we have been in life so far and where we want to go. For me, seeking out kindred seekers became crucial to who I was and who I was becoming. I also began to understand how important mentors are in the whole process of growth, and so I sought out mentor friendships with some of the professors and "seasoned people" I knew would ignite a fire in me.

As I better understood that I could not be true friends with everyone and that mentor friendships are different from peer friendships, I concentrated my energies on the people who were most life-giving and who helped me be my true self. I also came to realize, however, that peer and mentor friendships need not be based on having the same views, beliefs, or interests. Quite the opposite. Some of my closest friends and mentors have views that are almost completely different from mine, in some cases especially when it comes to faith issues. Yet, we benefit one another through talking about and experiencing life together. We are kindred spirits in our quests to suck the marrow out of life.

While there are several people in my life who have mentored me, my friend Richard has been one of the most significant. Early in my job as an editor, Richard, a co-worker at the time, asked me for a ride home one day after work. More than thirty years my senior, Richard fascinated me—he was clearly well educated and always had great tales to tell of travels all over the world, but I did not really know him. From the first car ride home we became fast friends and I came to learn that after nearly earning a Ph.D. in literature he had shifted his goals from teaching to a career in advertising. Eventually he became an executive, but his work was really a means to feed his love for travel, art, books, opera, symphony. Later in life he became a freelance editor and now works for many interesting publishing houses.

After a few car rides home, Richard asked me if I would be interested in taking on some freelance work to supplement my entry-level income. I was grateful, and together we edited projects on the weekends and in the evenings. Richard helped me become a better editor. But, more important, I found a mentor and a friend who has taught me about literature, music, art, travel, and life. Though we no longer work together, Richard and I are like family and regularly get together. I always learn new things and am forever grateful that he has taken the time to teach and coach me over the years. Thanks to his example, I mentor others when I have the chance, especially those younger than I.

C. S. Lewis so valued friendships that in a letter to his friend Arthur Greeves in 1939 he said, "My advice to any young [person] is live close to your friends above all else." I read these words as I was contemplating a job change that would take me away from Chicago. Because many of my friends live here, I was very torn. After the interview, I flew home and thought long and hard about my goals and quality of life. I eventually made up my mind that, no matter what, I would not take an offer. As it turned out, I did not get the offer. But I still believe that if it had come, especially at that stage in my life, I would have opted for remaining near my friends rather than for a little more money and a better title.

To this day my closest friends and mentors from high school and college remain so. And I've been blessed with rich peer and mentor friendships with a few others along the way.

The first day of college was as scary as it was exhilarating. At Notre Dame, men and women are separated into their own single-sex dorms. As incoming freshmen, we were informed of our dorm, room number, and roommate assignments just before the fall term. Back then, we were permitted to rank our top three dorm preferences, but we could not select our rooms or roommates. I was fortunate to get my top choice of Sorin Hall, the oldest dorm on campus, and was eager to meet my roommate and the other guys in the dorm.

As we all descended on the campus and gathered with the rector and resident assistants for "freshman orientation," we had the chance to size each other up. Then, as we moved our stuff into our rooms and began getting acclimated to dorm life, we got the chance to talk and get to know each other.

One of the first people I met was Andy Pauline from Potomac, Maryland. We became instant friends, sharing similar stories of high school; love of books, music, and sports; and an overall enthusiasm for the next four years. Within the first week of school, other guys in the dorm thought Andy and I had known each other all our lives.

While we had just met, two of Andy's high school pals—Tom Gerth and Jay Kelly—were also assigned to Sorin. All three were graduates of Georgetown Preparatory School in Maryland. Tom was from Rockville, Maryland, while Jay had been a boarding student from Flint, Michigan. It did not take long for me to build friendships with Tom and Jay, which made people wonder even more how long we'd all known one another.

Throughout freshman year the four of us were pretty much inseparable. As a local yokel from South Bend, I loved being pals with these East Coasters. I was so interested in where they came from, and they were so willing to show me, that for spring break that year we all drove out to a frozen Maryland in Tom's Volkswagen Rabbit. While I loved my first tour of Washington, D.C., I loved even more seeing Georgetown Prep, especially the sports facilities that had made Andy, Tom, and Jay heroes in their own minds! It was also a joy to meet Andy's and Tom's families, where Jay had been so welcome when he was a boarder at Georgetown.

Late freshman year Jay developed a severe pain in his right leg. It got so bad that he limped with each step and eventually had to go to the doctor. He was told that it was either a pulled muscle or a pinched nerve. The pain did not subside by the end of the semester, so we all prayed that Jay would get better over the summer. At first he was told that special exercises would help rid him of the pain and get him going again, but there was no diagnosis. By the middle of summer the worst came true: Jay was diagnosed with Ewing's sarcoma, a rare form of cancer. The pain in his leg was caused by a tumor along his side and back. I will never forget the round of phone calls between the four of us and another of our close friends, Terrence Murphy. Jay was in real trouble and we were all trying to digest the news and be there for him.

Jay was well into chemotherapy when school started up again. He was unable to make it back to Notre Dame for the first semester because he was going through testing and treatment in Boston and recovering in Flint. All of us wanted to be there for Jay as often as possible, but it was Andy who took the lead. He organized road trips to Flint and made sure that Jay's friends all over campus stayed in touch. During fall break of that year, 1989, Jay was in Boston for radical surgery to remove the tumor. Andy, Tom, and I drove to Maryland and then took the train to Boston for a day visit with Jay. It was very tough to see him in such bad shape, but his faith, humor, and strength gave us all courage enough to process the situation and hang out with him, just like the old times.

Later on, Jay made a few visits to campus, but he was not able to enroll in classes. Instead, he went to a local college in his home town and worked at rehab with a determination I had never seen before.

Throughout that summer, Jay held onto the hope that he would be able to come back to campus for junior year and continue his education. But he was able to enroll in classes only for a brief while before having to go back to Flint for more tests and treatment. We continued to visit him and occasionally he was able to make it down to South Bend with his family. It was all very confusing and sad. We all knew that young people are not supposed to die.

Once, during the time Jay was on campus taking classes and Andy and I were studying with him, I could no longer hold back asking, "Jay, are you mad at God?" With a look of calm understanding, he said, "Jer, there have been times throughout this whole thing when I've gotten mad, even at God. But I always come back to God. What upsets me most is that I have so much I want to give. But things happen for a reason, and in the end God is all we've really got."

When Jay died on July 15, 1991, I tried to remember his words. But my anger and sadness overcame me and I think I genuinely hated

God. It was only with the help of Andy, Tom, and Terrence that I, and they, were able to make any sense of Jay's death and understand what he had said about not being mad at God. It was not God I was angry with. It was loss itself.

The beauty of the friendship between Jay, Andy, Tom, Terrence, and me was that we delighted in being together individually and in a group. Somehow we knew that no one of us alone could bring out the entire best in the other, so we enjoyed watching the interaction that took place as our personalities, humor, opinions, and dreams intermingled.

Jay's death represented a terrible beauty that is the very heart of loss itself. For loss is not loss unless something was gained to begin with. As C. S. Lewis says in his essay "Friendship,"

> If, of three friends (A, B, and C), A should die, then B loses not only A but A's part in C. In each of my friends there is something that only some other friend can fully bring out. By myself I am not large enough to call the whole man into activity; I want other lights than my own to show all his facets....Of course the scarcity of kindred souls...sets limits to the enlargement of the circle; but within those limits we possess each friend not less but more as the number of those with whom we share him increases.[3]

When Jay died, Andy, Tom, Terrence, and many others lost parts of each other that only Jay could bring out. But, at the same time, in being blessed to know Jay and to have him as part of our close circle of friends, we gained the grace of catching glimpses of one other that otherwise never would have seen the light.

5. Live into Your Questions

When faced with the "big" questions of life—Where do we come from? Why are we here? Is there a God? Why do we suffer?—we have many options as to how we will respond. We can avoid such questions or, worse yet, be paralyzed by them. Or, we can dive head first into them.

The first two reactions are the easiest, and therefore are perhaps the most natural. In today's culture of quick bits of information and instant gratification, there seems to be no room for tough questions that

require our time, that frustrate us, that seem to have no empirical answer. We want to dominate information, put it at our disposal, use it for
power. Anything else is for the philosophers and theologians to ponder.

But in our quest to quiet questions, we really only bury them in
shallow graves that still allow them air. And as they lie just beneath the
surface, they infect us with a dis-ease that keeps us restless until we dig
them up and face them head-on.

It takes a certain combination of courage, patience, and humility to
face the big and tough questions of life. Often, the answers are slow to
come, if they ever do. And we are left with more questions than we
began with.

The other side of that coin, however, is the fact that our questions
can empower us. Free from fear, we can, as the German poet Rainer
Maria Rilke so wisely states, "live into our questions" as a way of embracing their energy. If we embrace our journey of life, if we are skilled
observers, if we log our experiences along the way, and if we seek out
kindred seekers and mentors, then we are much more open to living
into our questions. As Rilke suggests, living into our questions means
facing them and working through them. And, as my friend wrote in his
e-mail, even if we do not know what we are seeking, we know that we
must continue to seek. For, in the words of the poet Lord Alfred
Tennyson in *Ulysses*, our purpose is to "sail beyond the sunset, and the
baths / Of all the western stars... / To strive, to seek, to find, and not to
yield."

Every year in the dead cold of winter eighty young adults make their
way from the city and suburbs to a special place in Warrenville, Illinois,
called the Cenacle Retreat House. Having signed up months in ad-
vance, these twenty- and thirty-somethings eagerly await the weekend
of the annual retreat sponsored by the Young Adult Ministry Office of
Chicago. Many of them have never been on a retreat before. Others
have some retreat experience and feel it is again time to prayerfully
pause for a weekend. Still others are all but professional retreatants who
would not miss this or most any other large-scale retreat for anything in
the world.

This past year the weather conspired to test the will of the young
adults who had signed up for the annual retreat. The Thursday night
before the retreat weekend it snowed with a vengeance. At times big
fluffy flakes floated from the sky; other times icy pellets encased the

earth in a dangerous glaze. By Friday afternoon, nearly two feet of snow challenged everyone in the Chicago region to try going about their lives as if they could defy nature. It was a near-record day for absences from work. Nature had won, forcing even the busiest people to stay home.

I was scheduled to help lead the retreat that weekend and wondered if I would be able to get from my apartment to Warrenville. All the reports said no and told us to "stay home." But, due to good snow plowing and cautious driving, I made the fifty-mile drive west. Miraculously, almost every one of the eighty retreatants also made it.

After we all kicked the snow off our boots, got situated in our rooms, and warmed up, we met in the common area and hunkered down for the weekend. Kate DeVries, John Cusick, and I welcomed everyone and joined them in letting our worries melt away like the snow and enjoying this chance to be with God and each other. As an icebreaker (literally!), we asked the retreatants to introduce themselves, offer one reason they were on the retreat, and share something they hoped to get out of the weekend.

After about forty people had spoken, the next in line was a tall, fresh-faced young man. Before saying anything, he leaned way back in his chair and looked off into the distance in a most ponderous way. He sighed deeply, introduced himself, and in a frustrated tone told us he was an architect. Then, after a pause, his face lit up and he explained, "I am here because God keeps popping up in my life and I'm starting to like it." He concluded by telling us that he hoped to get a lot out of this weekend because he was plagued with questions and was discerning what his faith meant and if God was calling him to do something different with his life.

Later that night I spoke on some of what I've written in this book— the art and importance of seeking, asking questions, being awake. During a break, the young architect approached me and explained that he was mired in questions and felt trapped. He said that he enjoyed being an architect and that his parents had supported and encouraged him to go into that profession. But he also said that as he sat at work designing "windows and bathrooms," he felt there was something else he wanted to do with his life. He told me that during his work breaks and over lunch he logged onto the Internet and researched Catholic web sites for what books he should be reading, what prayers he should be saying, and what the path of Catholicism looked like. He was feeling overwhelmed by his duties at work, his parents' hopes, and the zillions of questions and new information his research of Catholicism was yielding.

I immediately loved this young guy for his questions and passion. But I also perceived a very real lostness that caused him frustration, anxiety, confusion, and heartache. He wanted Truth, he wanted answers, he wanted clarity, and he wanted them NOW. I knew some of what was going on inside him—we all do—because I had been there at his age and am often still there six years down the road. So, after talking with him about his questions, what he was reading, and what he was learning about the Catholic path, I invited him to get excited by his questioning.

"What do you mean," he asked.

I explained that asking questions is what makes us human. And the more we ask, the more we find; likewise, the more we find, the more we ask. And on and on *ad infinitum*. Asking questions keeps us alive, engaged, interested.

He liked the idea of being excited by his questions, and even offered a smile. But he wanted to ponder this notion a little more. All I could think to say was Rilke's line: "Live into your questions." Face them, grapple with them, share them with others, write them down, put them away for another day. Whatever you do, do not let them sap *your* energy. Rather, harness *their* energy and know that you are alive because you question. The answers will come. They will even change. But the asking always remains.

As group members got situated in their chairs for another segment of the retreat, the young architect-philosopher and I finished our conversation with a thought from C. S. Lewis that has always helped me when my questions, especially those about faith and Christianity, cause me anguish and seem to lead nowhere:

> There are certain things in Christianity that can be understood from the outside, before you have become a Christian. But there are a great many things that cannot be understood until after you have gone a certain distance along the Christian road. …Whenever you find any statement in Christian writings which you can make nothing of, do not worry. Leave it alone. There will come a day, perhaps years later, when you suddenly see what it meant. If one could understand it now, it would only do one harm."[4]

Talking with the young architect helped me live into my own questions. I do not know if it was a God moment for him, but it was for me.

6. Have Fun!

Religion and spirituality often get a bad rap as being heavy stuff for serious, somber people. Pondering ultimate meaning, struggling to find God or to help God find us, nurturing hope in the face of suffering, denying ourselves boundless pleasures, going to church, reading the Bible, and living according to values and codes sound like all work and no play. And no matter how hard we work, it seems there is always more than enough cause for us to feel guilty and fear being condemned to hell.

So why bother building a faith life, let alone one rooted in scripture and religion?

Quite simply, because faith is fun. In fact, in religious language, it is joyful.

The Bible is filled with stories of people whose faith not only saved them from utter despair but led them to sheer joy. Think of the joy of Abraham and Sarah when they learned that in their nineties they would bear a son named Isaac, whose name means "may God laugh," and become the ancestors of all nations. Think of the joy of the Israelites when, after forty years in the wilderness with Moses, they were able to reclaim their homeland. Recall the joy of those who were healed by Jesus and ran to share the good news. Imagine the joy of those, especially the marginalized, who ate, drank, and laughed with Jesus.

The Catholic tradition is all about joy. The Church teaches that the seven gifts of faith—by way of the Holy Spirit—are wisdom, understanding, counsel, fortitude, knowledge, piety, and fear of the Lord. With each of these gifts, we become more open to understanding who God is and who we are as created by God. We become more open to receiving the gift of life and using our own gifts. And as a result, we receive the twelve fruits of faith: charity, joy, peace, patience, kindness, goodness, generosity, gentleness, faithfulness, modesty, self-control, and chastity.[5]

Saint Thérèse of Lisieux (1873–1897)—the famous French Carmelite nun sometimes known as the Little Flower—accepted her life and her faith as gifts from God. She entered the convent at the age of

fifteen and took the name of Thérèse of the Child Jesus and the Holy
Face. From the very beginning she formed a playful relationship with
the child Jesus, which she describes in her internationally beloved auto-
biography *Story of a Soul*: "I wanted to amuse Jesus; I wanted to give
myself up to his childish whims."[6] Her favorite image of Jesus was a
statue of him as a child that stood in the courtyard of her monastery. As
the artist of her order, Thérèse was responsible for painting the statue
and loved to spend time coloring it and imagining herself playing with
Jesus. She believed that Jesus is with us all at all times, and her "little
way" of spiritual childhood teaches us to have an attitude of unlimited
hope in God's merciful love and remains a witness to us all that even the
most ordinary human experience bears the extraordinary power of
God's love.

As a young woman, Thérèse wrote, "Joy is found in the inner recesses of the soul. One can possess joy in a prison cell as well as in a
palace."[7] In many ways, Thérèse's cloistered life in the convent was akin
to life in a prison. But in the silence and solitude, she soared as an artist,
writer, and master of the soul. In her early twenties she was diagnosed
with tuberculosis and suffered severely until her death at the age of
twenty-four. As in her best moments, Thérèse found joy in her darkest
moments, rooting her entire being in faith: "Since the time I took my
place in the arms of Jesus...nothing escapes my eyes; I am frequently
astonished at seeing so clearly."[8]

What Thérèse and people like her see so clearly is that faith is not
only joyful but fun. As we seek to understand why we are here, to find
community, to love and be loved, and to spread justice, faith begs us to
enjoy our lives, to be joyful people, to have fun in our solitary moments
and with each other.

He danced in the aisles. He couldn't help it. The joyful music, the tone
of the homily, the expressions on the faces of those in the pews around
him, and the love he felt sent lightning through his legs and he just had
to dance.

I'd been watching him the whole Mass, this little "special needs"
boy bobbing from side to side in the row in front of me. I'd also been
watching the reactions of his parents and siblings as they tried to keep
him quiet and still so as not to disrupt those of us trying to pray. His
sister laughed at him, lovingly but with a tinge of embarrassment. His
brother ignored him. His mother tenderly ran her fingers through his

hair and stroked his face to calm him down. And his dad steeled his facial expression, trying not to show how much he wished that his son could just be "normal."

But in spite of their efforts, the little boy whispered loudly to his family, "dance," and tugged on their shirts to join him until he finally bolted into the aisle and got his groove on. As the first-rate music—electric guitar, synthesizers, horns, and a full choir—filled the church, the little boy laughed and danced and waved at the band and singers. They waved back and played right to him, pointing their instruments and faces in his direction.

Just before the mother went to retrieve her son, the boy's father put his arm around her as if to say, "Let him go, he's having a blast." His hard face had melted into pure love. When the boy finally made his way back into the pew, his dad hugged him and looked proud, for in that moment, his son had taught him the power of faith and of joy.

PART THREE

SEEING: BEING TRANSFORMED AND PERCEIVING IN A NEW WAY

"One thing I do know, that though I was blind, now I see."
—John 9:25

Introduction

Navigating the River of Life

In his wonderful book *Life on the Mississippi*, Mark Twain tells of his love for the river and his journey to becoming an expert steamboat pilot. Twain's description of how he came to see and know the river provides a perfect analogy for how we come to see and know the sacred that flows through everyday life.

From his earliest days, Twain had one permanent ambition: to be a steamboat pilot. Other ambitions of all sorts came and went throughout his childhood, but he never lost his focus on the river and his dream of someday navigating a ship on it. Steamboat captains were the modern-day equivalent of "cool"—they had a way with people, they were adventurers, and they were paid handsomely for their skills. As enticing as these things were then or are today, however, Twain's passion for piloting ran deeper. Quite simply, he loved the river and wanted to be part of it.

Twain eventually ran away from home, vowing that he would not return until he was a pilot. After leaving Hannibal, Missouri, he made his way to Cincinnati and soon thereafter boarded a vessel named the *Paul Jones* bound for New Orleans. While on the ship, Twain made a deal with the ship's captain, Mr. Bixby: if the seasoned pilot would teach him to navigate the river, then the young, aspiring pilot would pay his mentor five hundred dollars out of his first wages upon graduating.

As Twain says sarcastically, "I entered upon the small enterprise of 'learning' twelve hundred or thirteen hundred miles of the great Mississippi with the easy confidence of my time of life. If I had really known what I was about to require of my faculties, I should not have had the courage to begin."[1]

After many trips up and down the river, Twain realized just how hard it was to skillfully navigate it. He filled his notebook with the names of towns, "points," bars, islands, bends, reaches, and so on, but sadly none of it remained in his head. Each time he thought he knew enough to at least navigate the ship in the daylight, Mr. Bixby would test him and show him that there was still much to learn. If Twain proudly pointed out where a "snag" (an underwater tree stump or branch) lay hidden in the distance, Bixby would counter by asking him to describe the shape of a distant sandbar from memory or to rattle off the depth of the water at various points along the river.

Frustration eventually set in and Twain threw up his hands saying, "When I get so I can do that, I'll be able to raise the dead, and then I won't have to pilot a steamboat to make a living. I want to retire from this business. I want a slush-bucket and a brush; I'm only fit for a roustabout. I haven't got brains enough to be a pilot; and if I had I wouldn't have the strength to carry them around, unless I went on crutches."[2]

But the stubborn Mr. Bixby, who had come to respect and love the young Twain, would not let the cub pilot give in and assured him that one day he would be able to "read the river" and be a damn good pilot.

Twain hung in there and, as is the reward for perseverance and diligence, eventually "got it":

> It turned out to be true. The face of the water, in time, became a wonderful book—a book that was a dead language to the uneducated passenger, but which told its mind to me without reserve, delivering its most cherished secrets as clearly as if it uttered them with a voice. And it was not a book to be read once and thrown aside, for it had a new story to tell every day. Throughout the long twelve hundred miles there was never a page that was void of interest, never one that you could leave unread without loss, never one that you would want to skip, thinking you could find higher enjoyment in some other thing. There was never so wonderful a book written by man; never one whose interest was so absorbing, so unflagging, so sparkingly renewed with every re-perusal.[3]

Twain's experience of coming to "see" the river is filled with all the passion and joy that comes from any true moment of seeing. As young spiritual seekers, we are like Twain was at the same age, only we are hungry to "see" the river of life and to navigate it to the best of our ability, snags and all. We want to see God's loving presence in our lives and the world around us. But, like Twain, we know that such seeing requires us to embrace the journey; log the experience and fill our notebooks with teachings, principles, experiences, inspirations, and interpretations; be skilled observers; seek fellow seekers and mentors; live deeply into our questions; and have fun.

Sometimes the journey to catch a glimpse of the sacred, to see God in the moment, can be frustrating and overwhelming. Seeking sight within the context of Christianity does not make things any easier. In meditating on this very issue of seeking yielding to seeing, C. S. Lewis tells us in *Mere Christianity*, "If you are thinking of becoming a Christian, I warn you that you are embarking on something which is going to take the whole of you, brains and all. But, fortunately, it works the other way round. Anyone who is honestly trying to become a Christian will soon find his [or her] intelligence being sharpened: one of the reasons why it needs no special education to be a Christian is that Christianity is an education in itself."[4]

When we finally get it, as Twain got the river, the sacred lays itself open to us in ways that are "dead to the uneducated passenger." We suddenly realize that "seeking" is only one step, literally only one letter, away from "seeing."

11

The Great Invitation of Christianity

Earlier we recounted the gospel story in which John the Baptist was standing with two of his disciples when he saw Jesus walking along in the distance and exclaimed, "Look, here is the Lamb of God!" (Jn 1:36). Deeply fascinated by the person who has provoked such high praise from their leader, the disciples leave John and follow Jesus to see for themselves what he is all about. Jesus quickly becomes aware that he is being followed, turns toward the two men, and asks what we have said is *the great question of Christianity*, "What do you seek?"

At first, the disciples' response sounds a bit stupid: "'Rabbi' (which translated means Teacher), 'where are you staying?'" (1:38). But upon deeper reflection we recognize that they are really asking Jesus to show them where he comes from, where he dwells, what it is that dwells in him, where he is going, and what his mission is all about. By their interest in him, the disciples are also asking Jesus tell them something about themselves, about life itself.

At this crucial moment in the story, Jesus, like Mr. Bixby in Twain's experience, could have played hard to get, could have told his followers he was far too busy with more important things than idle conversation. But instead he extends *the great invitation of Christianity*: "Come and see" (1:39).

That beautiful moment in the story made all the difference for the curious men, for the twelve apostles, and for Jesus' friends and family. It has also made all the difference for those of us who struggle to follow him today. By extending the intimate invitation to "come and see" who he is, what God's kingdom is all about, Jesus asks us to see who we really are, what the world is really supposed to be: sacred, holy, beloved.

The challenge for our ancestors and for us is to accept Jesus' invitation to come and see. In today's fast-paced world, we squint to make sense of the blurs streaming past our faces. Meaning transmorphs and contorts, eluding our grasp. Knowledge is revised and supplanted by yet more knowledge. Truths come and go. Gurus and self-proclaimed prophets have their moments and fade into the distance.

So we feel right down to our guts that if our spiritual quest to know God and to live out our connection to the sacred is to take root and yield fruit, it must be planted in fertile soil. When properly understood, Christianity provides rich soil that nourishes and water that quenches our hungry and thirsty souls. The rituals, the interpretation of scripture, and even the rules are a living spirituality that challenges and informs us and slowly but surely helps us take the blinders off and see. Like a slow trickle that becomes a stream that becomes a river, the habit and practice of faith in the context of Christianity works on us until we are bursting forth with the energy of life itself, until we have eyes to see and ears to hear.

The young priest-theologian Robert Barron says it best in his book *And Now I See...A Theology of Transformation:*

> Christianity is, above all, a way of *seeing.* Everything else in Christian life flows from and circles around the transformation of vision. Christians *see* differently, and that is why their prayer, their worship, their action, their whole way of being in the world have a distinctive accent and flavor. What unites figures as diverse as James Joyce, Caravaggio, John Milton, the architect of Chartres, Dorothy Day, Dietrich Bonhoeffer, and the later Bob Dylan is a peculiar and distinctive *take* on things, a style, a way, which flow finally from Jesus of Nazareth. Origen of Alexandria once remarked that holiness is seeing with the eyes of Christ, Teilhard de Chardin said, with great passion, that his mission as a Christian thinker was to help people *see,* and Thomas Aquinas said that the ultimate goal of the Christian life is a "beatific vision," an act of *seeing.*[1]

This act of seeing is what we are about as human beings. It is what the scriptures are about. It is what the Catholic tradition is about. As part of our faith we believe that if we love God and each other and open ourselves to God's grace through Jesus and the Holy Spirit, we will come to see God face to face in the afterlife. Because the subject matter —God—is always partially beyond our reach, and because we are often blinded by sin (that is, pride, envy, anger, laziness, greed, lust, gluttony), our task requires us to pray, study, serve others, and remain open to grace. Nine hundred years ago, Saint Anselm of Canterbury (1033–1109) taught that faith does not mean believing things because we are told to. He said that we must see through our own lens of "faith seeking understanding"; that is, believing in God means using our minds and hearts to better understand God. For it is only through experience, question, objection, argument, witness, and radical openness that we can "come and see" what the Christian life shows us.

12

What Does It Mean to See?

Seeing has many dimensions. In a physical sense, if our bodies are intact we literally see through our eyes as images and colors hit our retinas and are interpreted by our brains. In a metaphorical sense, we "see" once our minds finally grasp something we have struggled to understand. In a spiritual sense, we "see" when we interpret our lives and the world through the eyes of faith.

In scripture we encounter many stories of blindness and sight, darkness and light. All four gospels teach us that Jesus himself is the light and that if we walk with him we will be able to live in the light and let the light live in us so that we can be light for others. For this reason, Matthew and Luke focus on the importance of having healthy eyes (that is, a healthy way of perceiving spiritually): "Your eye is the lamp of your body. If your eye is healthy, your whole body is full of light; but if it is not healthy, your body is full of darkness. Therefore consider whether the light in you is not darkness. If then your whole body is full of light, with no part of it in darkness, it will be as full of light as when a lamp gives you light with its rays" (Lk 11:34-37; cf. Mt 6:22-23).

All three of the synoptic gospels use the metaphor of a lamp being lit to teach us the importance of sharing the light of Christ with the world: "No one after lighting a lamp puts it under the bushel basket, but on the lampstand, and it gives light to all the house. In the same way, let your light shine before others, so that they may see your good works and give glory to your Father in heaven" (Mt 5:15-16; cf. Mk 4:21, Lk 11:33). John finishes this idea by quoting Jesus as saying, "Whoever believes in me believes not in me but in him who sent me. And whoever sees me sees him who sent me. I have come as light into the world, so that everyone who believes in me should not remain in the darkness" (Jn 12:44-46).

Throughout his ministry, Jesus healed those who lived physically and metaphorically in the darkness. But he did more than help them see in a human way; he shared his light with them so that they could see who he was and who they could become. Time and again Jesus shows us that believing and seeing are paths to each other—seeing leads to believing and believing leads to seeing. He also shows us that seeing with the eyes of faith is often a gradual process and that when we come to see with the eyes of faith, we sometimes have to convince others that what we see is real by standing firm in our faith.

Seeing leads to believing. We have all used the phrase "I'll believe it when I see it." We live in a world of facts, technology, and science, and we demand to see things for ourselves before we believe them. Throughout the gospels Jesus understands that people need to see before they believe, so he performs miracles as a way of helping them better understand all that he is teaching. In Matthew 20:29-34, for example, Jesus and his disciples are leaving Jericho when two blind men sitting on the side of the road hear of their passing by and shout, "Lord, have mercy on us, Son of David." The crowd orders them to be quiet, but the men only yell louder. Jesus stands still and asks them, "What do you want me to do for you?" They ask him to open their eyes. "Moved with compassion," Jesus heals them. In response to the gift of sight, the men follow him. In this story, Jesus does not ask the two blind men anything about their faith. Instead, he is so moved with compassion by their pleas that he heals them on the spot. But once they are healed, they immediately follow him, showing us that seeing leads to believing. And both believing and seeing lead to following.

Believing leads to seeing. It would sound strange to say, "I'll see it when I believe it." But in a real sense this is what faith is all about: believing so that we can see in new ways. While faith is a leap, it is not a leap into the dark. As Jesus often shows, faith is a leap into the light, into seeing. For example, in Matthew 9:27-31, Jesus had just brought back to life the dead daughter of a leader of the synagogue and had healed a hemorrhaging woman when two blind men cried out to him, "Have mercy on us, Son of David!" Jesus said to them, "Do you believe that I am able to do this?" to which they responded, "Yes, Lord." Then he touched their eyes and said, "According to your faith let it be done to you" and their eyes were opened. Then Jesus ordered them not to tell anyone of the event. But the men could not help themselves—their faith led them to see and they ran to share the good news with others, to help people understand that believing leads to seeing.

Coming to see is a process. One of the technologies of our day is Lasik surgery, a quick and relatively painless procedure that uses a laser to correct people's vision. A few of my friends have had Lasik surgery and say the results are immediate: one minute they couldn't see anything without their glasses, and now they will never need glasses again. But, as Jesus teaches throughout the gospels, especially as he works with his disciples to explain his miracles and parables, spiritual seeing is not so automatic; it is a process. For example, in Mark 8:22-26, when Jesus reaches Bethsaida some people bring a blind man to him and beg Jesus to touch him. Jesus takes the man by the hand, leads him out of the village, puts saliva on his eyes, and asks, "Can you see anything?" The man looks up and says, "I can see people, but they look like trees, walking." Then Jesus lays his hands on the man's eyes again and this time the man can see clearly. In our own lives, coming to see God's presence in our lives and sharing that presence with the world is often a process that requires the faith to be patient and trust. The essential point is that Jesus sticks with us the whole way.

Seeing means standing firm in our faith. One of the biggest obstacles to believing in a good and loving God is suffering. Though Jesus was raised from the dead after being crucified on the cross, we have a hard time grasping the resurrection and an even harder time seeing how it applies to our lives today. But the saints teach us that suffering leads to greater compassion. As Edith Stein (1891–1942)—who converted from Judaism to Catholicism, became a Carmelite nun, and was killed in the Holocaust—tells us through her witness and her words: "I spoke with the Savior to tell him that I realized it was his Cross that was now being laid upon the Jewish people, that the few who understood this had the responsibility of carrying it in the name of all, and that I myself was willing to do this, if he would only show me how."[1] Spiritual masters like Henri Nouwen teach us that living a good life means befriending pain, suffering, and the inevitability of death.

In the gospels, Jesus works to transform pain and suffering into wisdom and witness. For example, in John 9:1-41 when they encounter a man born blind, the disciples ask Jesus, "Rabbi, who sinned, this man or his parents, that he was born blind?" Jesus tells them, "Neither this man nor his parents sinned; he was born blind so that God's works might be revealed in him." After a brief exhortation foreshadowing the end of his life and explaining that he is the light of the world, Jesus spits on the ground, makes a mud paste that he rubs onto the man's eyes, and tells the man to wash in the pool of Siloam. When the man returns, he can see.

The crowds are so amazed that they do not believe this is the same man they knew as a beggar born blind. He explains to them that he is one and the same and that all he did was follow Jesus' instructions. The Pharisees accuse the man of being naïve and the one who healed him of being a sinner. The Jews bring in the man's parents who attest to the fact that he was born blind and are unable to provide an explanation as to why he can now see. Then the skeptics call the man back and demand that he admit that Jesus is a sinner. The man responds simply, "I do not know whether he is a sinner. One thing I do know, that though I was blind, now I see." After they ask him how it is that Jesus healed him, the man rebukes the accusers, "Never since the world began has it been heard that anyone opened the eyes of a person born blind. If this man were not from God, he could do nothing." Calling him a sinner, they drove the formerly blind man out.

What we learn from John's story is that encountering Christ helps us see who God is and who we are. Though we may be able to only utter the words "All I know is I was blind, and now I see," we can join Saint Edith Stein in holding firm to our faith even in the face of suffering. And we can join Saint Augustine in seeing the making of the mud paste as a metaphor for the Incarnation. When the divine power of Jesus mixes with the earth, a balm is created that, when rubbed onto our eyes, leads us to see in a new way.[2]

But what is it that we come to see, and how do we come to see it?

The earliest gospel writer, Mark, tells us that after Jesus was baptized and tempted in the desert, he went into Galilee and began to preach. The first words out of his mouth summarize everything about his life and ministry: "The time is fulfilled, and the kingdom of God has come near; repent, and believe in the good news" (1:15). Jesus wants us to see the kingdom of God in our very midst.

As Fr. Barron points out, there are many interpretations of what *kingdom* means. While agreeing that it can refer to a political realignment of Jewish society, a purely spiritual condition beyond the world, and a change of heart in an individual, *kingdom* "has a primary referent *in the person of Jesus himself.* Jesus wants us to open our eyes and see *him*, more to the point, to see what God is doing in and through him. He himself *is* the Kingdom of God coming into the world with transformative power."[3] He is the coming together of the human and the divine who offers healing, forgiveness, and salvation through a renewed friendship with God.

But, again as Barron points out, the Incarnation is not something to be admired from the outside, but rather an energy in which to participate. When we open our eyes and see the light, we are not to admire it but to embrace it and let it pour back out of us. We are to let the same word that was incarnate in Jesus be incarnate in us today.

So, we move to the second of our two questions: how do we come to see the kingdom? Mark makes it clear that we are to "repent and believe in the good news." As Fr. Barron points out, *repent* has taken on a moralizing tone aimed at one's behavior and actions. But *repent* is a poor translation from the Greek, *metanoiete*, which is composed of the roots *meta* (beyond) and *nous* (mind or spirit), and means something like "go beyond the mind that you have." In other words, Jesus is interested in helping us see differently, to see at a deeper level who we are: beings created in the image and likeness of God. Jesus wants us to see with the eyes of trust instead of fear, hope instead of cynicism, joy instead of sorrow, solidarity instead of discrimination, surrender instead of ego, love instead of hatred.

Once we see the kingdom, the coming together of the divine and the human, what are we to do?

Mark tells us we are to "believe in the good news." As with the word *repent*, the word *believe* has been poorly translated and has come to stand for dry assent to religious propositions for which there is little or no evidence. But *believe* is not so much a way of knowing as a way of *being known.* To have faith, then, is "to allow oneself to be overwhelmed by the power of God, to permit the divine energy to reign at all levels of one's being." Belief is surrendering to the God who wants to become incarnate in us. "Fired by the God-consciousness, in touch with the divine source within us, drinking from the well of eternal life, we are inspired simply to pour ourselves out in love."[4]

13

What Happens When We Don't Get It?

Throughout our journey of faith to know and be known by God, it is easy to get discouraged and lose heart. The evening news is enough to make us throw our hands in the air and say "There is no God!" Facing personal suffering and tragedy forces us to ponder the biggest questions about life and can send us into spiritual tailspins. Religious dogma, teachings, and rituals can seem so arcane and esoteric that they are rendered impotent by the modern world. Our minds can seem too small to grasp the concept of God, let alone to know, love, and serve him. And spirituality can seems as light as gossamer in the wind.

But, as we have said before, questioning, doubting, pondering, rebelling, and even quitting are a natural part of faith. What we often forget is that wrestling with faith is nothing new. In scripture and tradition we encounter plenty of people who did not "get" what they were witnessing or being asked to believe or what it means to be created in God's image. In the Old Testament, Job represents the classic human struggle to understand God and God's ways. In the New Testament the disciples and even Jesus' own family often fail to get what the Son of God/Son of Man is doing. In early Christian communities believers often felt their faith falter, especially in regions where they were misunderstood and persecuted for their claims and practices. And throughout the history of the Catholic tradition even the sturdiest leaders have fallen to their knees in desolation and despair.

What is important, then, is *not* that we often fail to "get it," but what we learn from Jesus in our greatest moments of blindness, misunderstanding, and doubt.

If we turn to scripture in search of kindred doubting souls and lessons to help bolster our faith, we see that the synoptic gospels of Matthew, Mark, and Luke include three cycles of three predictions of

Jesus' suffering and resurrection, three misapprehensions by the disciples, and three discourses on discipleship (Mk 8:31-38; 9:31-37; 10:32-
45; Mt 16:21-28; 17:22-23 and 18:1-5; 20:17-28; Lk 9:22-27; 9:43b-48;
18:31-34). While all three gospel writers tell similar stories, Matthew's
are most helpful in illustrating the disciples' misunderstanding and what
lessons Jesus teaches them as a result.

1. In the first cycle, Jesus tells the disciples that he must go to Jerusalem
and undergo great sufferings at the hands of elders, chief priests, and
scribes; be killed; and on the third day be raised. Upon hearing this,
Peter takes Jesus aside and rebukes him, "God forbid it Lord! This
must never happen to you." Jesus responds, "Get behind me, Satan!
You are a stumbling block to me; for you are setting your mind not on
divine things but on human things." Then he explains to the disciples,
"If any want to become my followers, let them deny themselves and
take up their cross and follow me. For those who want to save their life
will lose it, and those who lose their life for my sake will find it. For
what will it profit them if they gain the whole world but forfeit their
life? Or what will they give in return for their life?"

Like Peter, we often find it difficult to believe in a God who became
flesh and allowed himself to be killed on a cross. Like Peter, we lose our
focus on the resurrection and fixate on the cross as the end of the Christ
event. And, like Peter, we inhibit our minds from seeing with the eyes of
faith. But Jesus issues a stern wake-up call: if we worry only about how
Jesus' death on the cross makes us look as believers, then we will not be
able to carry our own crosses and follow him to the resurrection and beyond. If we cling too tightly to the things of this life, we will forfeit living fully here and now and in heaven. And if we see only through our
limited human eyes, we will fail to receive and serve Christ.

2. In the second cycle, the disciples respond to Jesus' foretelling of his
death and resurrection by asking him who the greatest among them is.
Calling a child over and placing him among the disciples, Jesus explains: "Truly I tell you, unless you change and become like children,
you will never enter the kingdom of heaven. Whoever becomes humble
like this child is the greatest in the kingdom of heaven. Whoever welcomes one such child in my name welcomes me."

In our culture it is so easy to ask if we are the best, the most recognized, successful, happy. But Jesus teaches that the more we compete
with others, the less free we really are. By telling the disciples to "be-

come like children," Jesus is trying to help them worry less about their social status and more about both being humble and welcoming those who are without social status and power. Real power and status come from solidarity with the downtrodden, marginalized, and dispossessed.

3. In the third cycle, after Jesus foretells his death and resurrection, the mother of James and John asks him to declare that her sons will sit on his left and right in his kingdom. Jesus explains that the Father will determine who sits at his left and right and that "whoever wishes to be great among you must be your servant, and whoever wishes to be first among you must be your slave; just as the Son of Man came not to be served but to serve, and to give his life as a ransom for many."

As Matthew tells the story, we cannot help but sympathize. What mother would not want her children to have the best place in this life and the next? In the Gospel of Mark, the eager disciples James and John go to Jesus on their own. Again, we can understand. But in addressing the situation, Jesus points to himself as the answer: he is not concerned with his social status or position on earth or in heaven. He is here to serve and to free people from the bondage of limited, small thinking. By emulating him, we become free to be fully alive and we trade social status for the chance to help others become their best selves.

Beyond these examples, the gospels are filled with stories that help us recognize our hunger and thirst to understand, to *feel* our faith as a part of being human. Throughout my own life I have found the two stories of the miraculous feeding of the multitudes very helpful in facing my fears and living into my doubts so that I can better see what it means to believe in God.

As Matthew and Mark tell it, upon learning of the death of John the Baptist, Jesus took a boat to a deserted place by himself. But crowds of people hungry for his message followed him on foot. When he went ashore, he had compassion for them and healed their sick. As evening fell, the disciples came to Jesus and told him to send the crowds away so they could go into the villages and buy food for themselves. Instead, Jesus commanded the disciples to feed the people. They were perplexed at this, and they told Jesus that all they had were five loaves and two fish. Commanding them to bring the food to him, Jesus ordered the crowd to sit on the grass and then blessed and broke the loaves and gave them to the disciples, who gave them to the crowds. When all was said and done, the entire crowd of five thousand had eaten and there were twelve baskets of food left over.

Immediately after feeding everyone, Jesus made the disciples get into the boat by themselves and go to the other side of the Sea of Galilee while he dismissed the crowds. As the disciples made their way, a great storm rose up and tossed them around. Early the next morning they saw Jesus walking toward them on the water. Thinking he was a ghost, Peter issued a test, "Lord, if it is you, command me to come to you on the water." Jesus commanded him to "come," so Peter began walking toward Jesus until he became frightened, began to sink, and cried out "Lord, save me!" Jesus reached out his hand and saved Peter, saying, "You of little faith, why did you doubt?" When they got into the boat, the wind ceased. And those in the boat worshiped him, saying, "Truly you are the Son of God" (Mt 14:13-33; Mk 6:32-52; cf. Lk 9:10-17; Jn 6:1-21).

It is hard to understand how Peter and the other disciples could have had such little faith after witnessing Jesus' many miracles, including the miraculous feeding of the crowd. But, at the same time, we can all relate to Peter's sinking for lack of faith. We all get that sinking feeling, even when we are not trying to walk on water. But if we see with the eyes of faith, we realize that, no matter what, Jesus reaches out his hand and saves us.

Yet, like the disciples, we need more than one helping hand. In the second feeding story the disciples' lack of faith once again blocks them from seeing what is really going on. After having miraculously fed the five thousand, Jesus performs the same miracle by feeding four thousand people in Gentile territory on the east side of the Sea of Galilee. After all have been fed physically and spiritually, Jesus boards the boat with his disciples and returns to Jewish territory. When they reach the other side, the disciples realize that they have forgotten to bring any of the leftover bread and begin discussing it among themselves. Like a "Who's on First?" skit, the disciples pass the blame and squabble about why they are hungry. We can imagine Jesus' frustration as he picks up on the conversation! Imagine his face as he says to them, "You of little faith, why are you talking about having no bread? Do you still not perceive? Do you not remember the five loaves for the five thousand, and how many baskets you gathered? Or the seven loaves for the four thousand, and how many baskets you gathered? How could you fail to perceive that I was not speaking about bread?" (Mt 16:5-12; Mk 8:14-21; cf. Lk 12:1; Jn 6:32-36).

Like the disciples, we fail to "get" Jesus' message again and again. And it is heartening to know that we sit with the disciples wondering where the bread is when we ask: Where will my next paycheck (monetary bread) come from? Where will my next meal (literal bread) come from? Where will my next satisfying relationship and job and faith experience (spiritual bread) come from?

When we worry about the "bread" before our eyes, we are blind to Jesus' deeper message: "I am the bread of life. Whoever comes to me will never be hungry, and whoever believes in me will never be thirsty. But I said to you that you have seen me and yet do not believe. Everything that the Father gives me will come to me, and anyone who comes to me I will never drive away" (Jn 6:35-37).

In response to our failed efforts to see with the eyes of faith, Jesus teaches, explains, feeds, and embraces us. Like the father in the synoptic gospels, if we cry out "I believe; help my unbelief!" Jesus cannot resist the opportunity to help and heal us (Mk 9:14-29; Mt 17:14-20; Lk 9:37-43a). As human beings we are allowed to fear, to doubt, to sink, to miss the point. But if we remember Jesus' question *What do you seek?* and accept his invitation to *"Come and see,"* our darkest moments lead us deeper into the heart of the mystery that gives us light by which to see.

14

Walking the Tightrope over the Abyss

It is one thing to struggle to see with the eyes of faith when things are going well in life. It is quite another to do so when life is not going well or, worse yet, when life is as dark as it gets.

If there is one thing we all fear, it is that life is meaningless, that in the final analysis all our hoping, waiting, seeking, dreaming, planning, and experiencing amount to nothing. That, while we spend our days working toward fulfillment, peace, freedom, and happiness, we are simply tricking ourselves, diverting our attention away from the fact that with every minute, hour, day, week, month, and year we are moving closer and closer to our inevitable deaths. And that, in the end, our lives, no matter how full, will fade into oblivion without so much as a whimper. Shakespeare's Macbeth horrifies us all when, upon learning that his wife has committed suicide, he proclaims:

> Tomorrow, and tomorrow, and tomorrow,
> Creeps in this petty pace from day to day,
> To the last syllable of recorded time;
> And all our yesterdays have lighted fools
> The way to dusty death. Out, out brief candle!
> Life's but a walking shadow, a poor player,
> That struts and frets his hour upon the stage,
> And then is heard no more; it is a tale
> Told by an idiot, full of sound and fury,
> Signifying nothing.[1]

It is part of human nature to fear—to downright dread—meaninglessness. From the beginning of time we have looked into the sky and wondered why we are here and what the purpose of our lives is. In our darkest moments, we see ourselves as mere accidents coming from nothing, living for no real reason, and heading back toward nothing. We race to our scientists, philosophers, psychologists, and theologians for explanations and direction. We construct our own theories and structures to comfort and protect us like safety nets. But we are all swallowed by the shadows at some time or another.

The sixteenth-century mystic Saint John of the Cross called the moment of our greatest dread the "dark night of the soul." It is the moment when we come face-to-face with our deepest fears and stare meaninglessness directly in the face, when everything about ourselves, the universe, and anything beyond is consumed by the abyss of nothingness.

We all know the abyss. And we know people who have been or are now engulfed in it. As I was writing this chapter, for example, I ran out to do some errands. Lost in the mundane tasks of grocery shopping, I felt a complacent contentedness in my young adult life. I had just returned from a relaxing vacation and was reenergized to write, run errands, and enjoy better balance in my life. Just before completing my errands I decided to get a haircut. I found a parking spot, fed the meter, and darted into a Great Clips. The small Vietnamese woman at the counter was on the phone and appeared to be in a serious conversation. I stood for what seemed an eternity before she motioned to her left and told me to take a seat. Being impatient and a little concerned that my meter would run out and I would get a ticket before I got my haircut, I reluctantly took a seat. Within a few minutes the woman hung up the phone and called me over. She led me to her station, sat me down in the swivel chair, wrapped the smock around me, wet down my hair, and asked me what I wanted her to do. I told her a trim was all I needed.

As she began cutting my hair, a Chinese woman came into the shop and my Vietnamese haircutter asked me to wait a moment. She and the Chinese woman spoke intensely, hugged briefly, and then parted ways. The Vietnamese woman returned to her task with tears in her eyes. I did not want to pry, but she started cutting haphazardly and then, in a moment I will never forget, lowered her hands, looked in the mirror at me, and said in broken English, "When you walk in, I was on phone with my Buddhist priest. Then I left you to see my friend, who was teacher at the school where my son went. She came here comfort me because my son was killed two weeks ago."

I sat there dumbfounded, offering befuddled condolences. She told me that her sixteen-year-old son was her only child. He had been shot in the head and left in an alley near his school in a respectable suburb where things like that are not supposed to happen.

Then she reached into her purse and pulled out a printout of a *Chicago Tribune* article that she had downloaded from the Internet detailing the murder of her son and the ensuing investigation. She wanted me to read the article in its entirety. As I read about her son—his achievements, his personality, his bright future—I felt sick. This grieving mother was staring right into the abyss of loss. And moments earlier I had been dancing on clouds. Then she showed me a picture of her son that she kept on her key chain and told me that he had just been beginning to look at colleges when his life had been stolen from him.

"Am I taking enough off? You want shorter?" she asked, trying to complete her duties with what little energy she had left.

"That's fine," I said, as my uneven haircut did not mean a thing to me in light of this woman's pain. While she whisked the loose hair off my neck, I asked her if she had taken some time off to begin processing all that had happened. She said she had but that she needed to work to help pay bills. She mentioned that her husband was back at work already, too. And then she reiterated that her son was her only child. I asked how her husband was doing and she said he was barely making it.

As she escorted me to the counter to check out, she asked, "Did you hear about the woman who was murdered this week? Her killer cut her into pieces. I feel so bad for her family. We live in a terrible world."

I hugged her but her body felt lifeless and her face told me that hugs were of no use right now. As I paid and left the tip I told her that I would pray for her and her family. She thanked me and turned away.

Walking back to my car I felt terrible for this woman, her husband, and their friends and family. Her abyss had crept into my life and the great *why* of it all overwhelmed me as it has so many times in my life.

The chance meeting with this woman hit me even harder because I had been re-reading some of Friedrich Nietzsche's works for this book, especially *Thus Spoke Zarathustra* and *The Gay Science*. Nietzsche's writings about the abyss have haunted me since I first read him. As the notes in my worn copies of his books reveal, I have not read Nietzsche since college. But I have never forgotten him. In many ways, Nietzsche both terrified and enlivened me at that crucial stage in my life.

A German existentialist philosopher who lived from 1844 until 1900, Nietzsche is best known for declaring the "death of God" and ushering in the *übermensch*, or rare "overman" who can elevate himself above the all-too-human masses and achieve a position in the cosmos that the Bible and Christian theology would consider our divine birthright. As an existentialist, Nietzsche held that because there is no God each of us is totally free and therefore utterly responsible for creating our own essence. In other words, unlike Christian theology, Nietzsche's view is that our existence precedes our essence and that all we are is what we make of ourselves. There is no such thing as being created in the image and likeness of God. *We* are our own god, and this life is all we have to work with.

However, contrary to nihilists (who hold that existence is utterly meaningless), Nietzsche held that while the world is a godless and irrational affair of ceaseless striving and suffering, life still has meaning and can be affirmed. His proclamation that "God is dead" was not his own, he said, but a matter of cultural and intellectual fact. God was a failed hypothesis that had begun with the human desire for a source of meaning and value transcending this world and ended when there was no longer anyone who believed in an eternal and infinite God. In the place of God, Nietzsche worked feverishly to create a new set of values and to encourage people to strive to rise above common humanity and become their own brand of *übermensch*. He wanted the *übermensch* model to help people *create* meaning and make the most out of life, since life is all there is and we only live once.

What scared me most about Nietzsche when I was in college was that, as an astute student of culture and one of the greatest writers of the last two centuries, he had said very convincingly what countless others were unwilling to say but felt in their hearts: "God is dead." I first read Nietzsche while also reading other powerful critiques of faith by the likes of Sigmund Freud (who said faith is delusional), Karl Marx (who called religion the "opiate of the people"), and Ludwig Feuerbach (who said that religion is a childish crutch to teach morals and must be thrown away once people realize they are their own gods). My own faith at that time was questionable—actually, barely existent—and I was left adrift by encountering so many arguments against faith and God. Yet, at the same time, Nietzsche's writings, along with those of others, afforded me the chance to strip my own wavering faith down to its bare bones and to rebuild it from the ground up.

I mention all this because it is Nietzsche who first introduced me to (1) the cultural fact that though many *speak* of God, far fewer truly *believe* in him, (2) the notion of the "abyss" that threatens to swallow us at every turn, and (3) the experiment of envisioning the world without God.

In one of the most famous passages of all his writings, Nietzsche tells the story of a madman who "lit a lantern in the bright morning hours, ran to the market place, and cried incessantly: 'I seek God! I seek God!'" Those in the marketplace at the time laughed and jeered at the man, whom they viewed as being mad for not being able to find God. "Is he lost?" they asked tauntingly. "Is he hiding?" "Is he afraid?" "Has he gone on a voyage?" Of course not, they claimed, *God is everywhere.* There is no need to seek him in the daylight with a lantern![2]

But the madman turned the tables and transformed laughter into dread. Jumping into their midst, he pierced them with his eyes and exclaimed:

> Whither is God?...I will tell you. *We have killed him*—you and I. All of us are his murderers. But how did we do this? How could we drink up the sea? Who gave us the sponge to wipe away the entire horizon? What were we doing when we unchained this earth from its sun? Whither is it moving now? Whither are we moving?...Has it not become colder? Is not night continually closing in on us? Do we not need to light lanterns in the morning? Do we hear nothing as yet of the noise of the gravediggers who are burying God? Do we smell nothing as yet of the divine decomposition? Gods, too, decompose. God is dead. God remains dead. And we have killed him....How shall we comfort ourselves, the murderers of all murderers? What was holiest and mightiest of all that the world has yet owned has bled to death under our knives: who will wipe this blood off us? What water is there for us to clean ourselves?[3]

When he finished, his listeners stared at him in amazement. The madman then smashed his lantern against the ground and proclaimed that he had come too early, that the people in the marketplace had not yet realized not only that is God dead but that they had killed him.

If we go to the marketplace today, we hear a great deal of God-talk. It would seem that God is very much alive in the minds and hearts of those in the marketplace. In fact, as we said earlier, God is part of the marketplace as books, music, seminars, retreats, and all things religious/spiritual are selling very well these days. At the same time, the marketplace is its own god and the more God goes up for sale, the more we are left wondering which "God" is being sold and for what purpose. The marketplace is its own abyss, its own nebulous mixture of being god while selling, buying, and bartering God.

Nietzsche recognized the ways of the marketplace and, in declaring the death of God and lifting up his *übermensch*, he hoped to move humanity from mass mediocrity to a richer way of living. In *Thus Spoke Zarathustra*, Nietzsche offers us Zarathustra as an *übermensch* who has gone to the mountains, realized certain truths, and returned to the valleys to elevate all who will listen. As he enters the marketplace to preach about the "overman," the townspeople are gathered to watch a tightrope walker perform. After hearing a lengthy discourse about the overman being the one who dispenses with the "other world" and embraces this world, the people laugh at Zarathustra and clamor for the tightrope walker to begin his act.

As the tightrope walker inches his way onto a rope strung between two towers over the marketplace, Zarathustra begins a new discourse: "Man is a rope, tied between beast and overman—a rope over an abyss. A dangerous across, a dangerous on-the-way, a dangerous looking-back, a dangerous shuddering and stopping. What is great in man is that he is a bridge and not an end: what can be loved in man is that he is an *overture* and a *going under*."[4]

Nietzsche's madman and tightrope walker are ingenious literary devices because they are memorable characters who tell us about the culture we are part of *and* teach us about the culture Nietzsche wants to develop. He begins in the sleepy world we know (God is nominally alive and well); wakes us up to the world that, as he sees it, really is (God is dead); and he creates a new world (in God's place, the *übermensch* leads us out of the delusional dichotomy between the "other" world and this world by grounding us in the earth). It is up to us to accept Nietzsche's critique of the present world and promises of the world he wants to develop.

But as much as Nietzsche wants us to accept that God is *dead* and therefore all things are possible, our faith tells us differently. Our faith tells us that God is *alive* and therefore all things are possible. As we will discuss more fully in the next chapter, because God is, we are. And because God loves us, we are able to walk the tightrope over the abyss; in fact, we are able to *be* the tightrope over the abyss.

I learned what it means to both walk and be the tightrope over the abyss from meeting Terry Anderson at a talk he gave to the First Friday Club of Chicago in 1996. Like so many around the world, I had known Terry Anderson as the American Associated Press reporter who, while on assignment in the Middle East, was taken hostage by radical Shiite Muslims in Beirut, Lebanon, in March 1985 and survived nearly seven long years of captivity until he was released in December 1991. As a college student, I had followed Terry's story and remembered him for his courage, faith, and remarkable ability to articulate what it was like to live in chains for so long. Having the chance to meet him was a profound privilege.

As a crowd of nearly 350 people crammed into the Red Lacquer Room of the famous Palmer House Hotel, I caught a glimpse of Terry off to the side of the stage sipping a glass of water and looking out over people's faces. Over the years I had seen newspaper and television images of Terry in various states, mostly unshaven and disheveled. Seeing him in a suit with a well-trimmed mustache struck me immediately. So did the fact that, though he had been released from his tiny cell four years earlier, it was probably still very strange for him to be in places like the grand ballroom of the Palmer House speaking about faith, hope, love, and freedom.

When I was introduced to Terry I wanted to embrace him, because he had embraced the abyss of pure desperation and emerged not only a survivor but a living testament to the power of faith and hope. But I just shook his hand and told him how much I admired him and looked forward to his reflections.

To this day I still replay Terry's talk in my mind. From the moment he humbly took the stage until he descended from it to a standing ovation, he proved himself to be one of the most genuine human beings any of us could ever meet. He framed his story not in terms of a hero who had triumphed over his enemies but in terms of a lapsed Catholic who had found God in the darkest night of his soul and whose deep faith both saved him and led him down the path of forgiveness.

Terry explained, as he does more thoroughly in his 1993 book, *Den of Lions*, that about two years before he was captured he had begun to do some serious thinking about his life and faith. He said that he had never been introspective, never stopped pushing long enough to think about where he was going, what he was becoming. As a journalist, Terry lived a fast-paced, hard-drinking, womanizing, and "arrogant" life of privilege that allowed him worldwide travel and special access to almost any place and anyone. But, as he says, he was a mess physically and morally. So, he decided to make some radical changes—cut back on drinking; exercise more; and, tough as it was on his eight-year-old daughter Gabrielle, ask his wife Mickey for a divorce for both their sakes. He eventually entered into a relationship with Madeleine, the woman he had planned to marry and who became pregnant before his kidnapping.

Because he was a lapsed Catholic, Terry also began to read the Bible and return to his roots. One day, while on a short vacation in England, Terry decided to stop into a church. In his book he recounts that he "sat down in a pew and just looked at the altar, at the cross with its crucified figure. I didn't pray," he says, "but I felt a perfect sense of being at home, where I belonged."[5]

As Terry struggled to find balance in his life, he did pray—for more time to attend to his faith. He kidded that the old adage "Be careful what you pray for" holds true, because soon thereafter, when he was back in Beirut, he was kidnapped, blindfolded, chained to a wall, and left alone in a dark cell with all the time in the world to ponder his life.

In his book, Terry explains that a month into his imprisonment he searched for God in the shadows: "I almost chuckle sometimes—this punishment, if punishment it is, seems perfectly designed for my sins and weaknesses, as only God could. I drank too much—no alcohol here. I chased women—no women here. I'm arrogant—what better than to put me in the hands of these so-arrogant, uncaring young men. I've been careless of others' feelings—these people give not one tiny thought to mine. I've been an agnostic most of my life—my only comfort here is a Bible, and my prayers."[6]

As it turned out, Terry's greatest comfort came from the Bible and, in an ironic twist of events, the priest whom he credits with welcoming him back into the Catholic Church. Having been given a Bible after weeks of demanding one, Terry read it voraciously. But the guards kept taking it away and later returning it. Terry thought it was a form of psychological torture. But, as it turned out, Servite Father Martin Jenco, one of the first American hostages, was in the cell next door and was asking for the Bible, too. Like a backwards game of "hot potato," the guards would transport the Bible between Martin's and Terry's cells depending on which prisoner requested it. When Terry was eventually informed that his neighbor was a priest, he laughed to realize why the Bible was so often ripped from him. Then he asked the guards to honor his religious tradition and allow him to meet with the priest to confess his sins. Amazingly, the guards not only complied but also granted his request to be alone with Fr. Martin with the door closed.

Before the guards left, the two blindfolded men—a priest and a lapsed Catholic—found each other and shook hands. After the guards shut the door, the two men removed their blindfolds and Terry saw a gentle, white haired, bearded man dressed in shorts and a T-shirt sitting cross-legged on the neighboring cot. He opened with "hi" and from there bared his soul to Fr. Martin as quickly and fully as he could. As he recalls,

> By the end of our session, the bare floor around us is littered with crumpled tissues. Both he and I are crying. Finally, I kneel beside him. "Father, forgive me, for I have sinned, in word and in thought, in what I have done and what I have not done."
>
> He rests his right hand on my head. "In the name of a gentle, loving God, you are forgiven." He pulls my head gently to his shoulder and hugs me. We sit back and look at each other. In a few moments we hear a guard turning the lock on the door, and we pull our blindfolds down over our eyes.[7]

Upon returning home and writing about his experience, Terry crafted a poem that teaches us all that at the moment we stare into the abyss and think we are alone our faith tells us otherwise:

"Faith"

> Where is faith found?
> Not in a book,
> or in a church,
> not often or
> for everyone.
> In childish times
> it's easier;
> a child believes

just what it's told.
But children grow
and soon begin
to see too much
that doesn't match
the simple tales,
and not enough
of what's behind
their parents' words.
There is no God,
the cynics say;
we made Him up
out of our need
and fear of death.
And happily
they offer up
their test-tube proofs.
A mystery,
the priests all say,
and point to saints
who prove their faith
in acts of love
and sacrifice.
But what of us
who are not saints,
only common
human sinners?
And what of those
who in their need
and pain cry out
to God and go
on suffering?
I do not know—
I wish I did.
Sometimes I feel
all the world's pain.
I only say
that once in my
own need I felt

a light and warm
and loving touch
that eased my soul
and banished doubt
and let me go
on to the end.
It is not proof—
there can be none.
Faith's what you find
when you're alone
and find you're not.[8]

15

The Courage to Be... Fully Alive

For many, especially Nietzsche, belief in God is submissive and destroys one's ability to affirm oneself. For such thinkers, it is the individual alone who can affirm his or her own being alive.

In response to Nietzsche and the death-of-God movement, the twentieth-century Protestant theologian Paul Tillich (1886–1965) wrote a masterpiece of spiritual insight called *The Courage to Be*. There he makes the case that Nietzsche is the most impressive and effective representative of what could be called a "philosophy of life." That is, as Tillich sees it, by preaching the *übermensch* Nietzsche puts forth a philosophy that says human beings can affirm life to its fullest, even in the face of that which negates life: death, ambiguity, doubt, fear, anxiety, despair, emptiness, meaninglessness, mediocrity, decadence, apathy, and so on.

But in Tillich's estimation, Nietzsche's claim that God is dead denies one essential fact: "Every courage to be has an open or hidden religious root. For religion is the state of being grasped by the power of being-itself. In some cases the religious root is carefully covered, in others it is passionately denied; in some it is deeply hidden and in others superficially. But it is never completely absent. For everything that is participates in being-itself, and everybody has some awareness of this participation, especially in the moments in which he [or she] experiences the threat of nonbeing."[1]

These moments in which we embrace our being in the face of nonbeing are what I have been calling "God moments." In Tillich's language, a God moment is when we have the courage to affirm our essential nature, our inner aim, *in spite of* everything that works to prevent us from affirming ourselves (everything from a mean boss to inner despair to feelings of worthlessness). The power of this self-affirmation "in spite of" is the power of faith, the state of being grasped by the power of being that transcends everything that exists and in which everything that exists participates.[2] It is also accepting God's acceptance of us.

As we discussed in chapter 7, when we root our spiritual quests in religion, we become better equipped to move forward. In Tillich's language, we become better able to affirm our very being in spite of everything that blocks us from our truest selves: "Religion asks for the ultimate source of the power which heals by accepting the unacceptable, it asks for God. The acceptance by God, his forgiving or justifying act, is the only and ultimate source of a courage to be which is able to take the anxiety of guilt and condemnation into itself. For the ultimate power of self-affirmation can only be the power of being-itself. Everything less than this, one's own or anybody else's finite power of being, cannot overcome the radical, infinite threat of nonbeing which is experienced in the despair of self-condemnation."[3]

In other words, God is far from dead and Nietzsche's übermensch can never contain the infinite power of being that we participate in when we say yes to life in God, especially in the face of the abyss.

We all know the abyss. We all know fear, despair, self-condemnation. But through our faith, we root our courage to be in the God "who appears when God has disappeared in the anxiety of doubt."[4] We accept God's acceptance of us. And we root our relationship to God in a Church that "preaches the Crucified who cried to God who remained his God after the God of confidence had left him in the darkness of doubt and meaninglessness."[5]

As we look back on the past, face the present, and plan the future, how many of us can say that we truly know and love ourselves? How many of us find fulfillment and happiness in our jobs, our relationships, our families, our daily activities? How many of us are free enough to accept and grow in love? And how many of us are so bubbling over with life that we cannot help but love and give life to others?

It goes without saying that we live in a complex world full of obstacles that block us from being our truest, best selves. As if it were not enough to know that life is fragile, daily we hear about or directly encounter war, poverty, crime, injustice, prejudice, environmental crises, political scandal. Daily we are barraged with information that "feeds our minds," new technologies that "enhance our lives," products that we simply "cannot live without." And daily we are pulled between despair and hope, caring for others and getting what we can for ourselves, polishing our public personas and working on our inner selves, meeting our material needs and feeding our spiritual hungers.

Yet, for every external obstacle to deeper fulfillment, there is an internal one. All too often *we* are responsible for not being who we really are. We allow our pasts to weigh us down, we let go of dreams for more "practical" pursuits, we permit our fears get the best of us, and we buy into some strange notion that the world will reject us for being ourselves.

The challenge of faith, then, is as radical as it is simple: Be who you really are. Be who God calls you to be.

More than eighteen hundred years ago Saint Irenaeus (130–200), one of the greatest bishops and theologians of the early church, said the same thing in a different way: "The glory of God is a human being fully alive."

Think about that—the greatest statement of faith, the strongest show of gratitude for life itself, is to live as fully as we can.

We have long learned from scripture and tradition that God created the universe and everything in it out of love, that we human beings are created in God's image and likeness, and that God so loved the world he sent his only son to become what we are so that in the end we might become what he is.

These tenets of our faith are not easy to understand. Indeed, they are imbued with mystery. But they speak to us, challenge us, and call us to see ourselves, the world, and others through the eyes of faith. They beg us to ask, "Am I fully alive?" And "If not, why not?"

If we desire to be fully alive, what is required of us?

Above all, we need *courage*. Not just any courage, but the courage that comes from God and frees us to affirm ourselves in spite of all else, that frees us to grab onto the essentials of life and to let go of the nonessentials, to form our identity and live in accord with it, to curb our passions and quell our fears, to move from mere survival to true joy. Courage releases us to say Yes to our own true being. To find freedom, peace, meaning, fulfillment, happiness. To go beyond ourselves and love others. To dance and sing and sleep and do it all over again. To be who we really are, who God calls us to be.

We also need to accept God's acceptance of us. For even in our direst moments of meaninglessness, emptiness, hopelessness, anxiety, doubt, and fear, God—the source and ground of all being—accepts and loves us. By accepting God's love in return we do not remove the obstacles that prevent us from being our truest selves, we affirm ourselves *in spite of* them. One of the greatest forms of prayer we can offer is to be still and know that we are loved, no matter what.[6]

16

Accepting God's Gift of Peace

The Spiritual Wisdom of Cardinal Joseph Bernardin

When I first moved to Chicago in February of 1993, the only cardinals I knew of were the bird and the St. Louis baseball team with whom the Cubs have a longstanding rivalry. While Cubs baseball is its own religion, the more I heard Chicagoans talk of "the Cardinal," the more I realized that I had moved to a Catholic town that loved its spiritual leader, Cardinal Joseph Bernardin.

From the newspaper and television I came to know something of this man Bernardin. A regular figure in the public eye, he carried himself with dignity, was a leader on the international stage, openly and honestly answered questions from the media, and responded passionately to the concerns of his flock. At that time, he was still responding to protesters and answering questions over the recent decision of the archdiocese to close several parishes and parochial schools as part of a new budget meant to strengthen the economic health of the church in the city. I watched the Cardinal's genuine care and respect for dialogue and I instantly liked him. At a time of great spiritual seeking in my life, he seemed like a leader I could trust.

The more I watched Bernardin, the more I liked him. But in early November, the Cardinal was faced with a devastating blow to his reputation. On Wednesday, November 10, rumors began circulating the country, and indeed the globe, that a United States cardinal was to be accused of sexual misconduct. By the next day it appeared that Bernardin was to be named in the suit. My heart, like those of so many others, sank. There had been a rash of sexual misconduct cases involving priests, and it seemed Bernardin might be one of them.

But during the first days of the accusation something amazing happened. People from all walks of life throughout the city proclaimed that Cardinal Bernardin was innocent, that there was no way he could be guilty of such charges. Their trust in the Cardinal was not blind faith or wishful thinking; it was based on the connection they felt to one who had led an upright life and had somehow reached into their hearts in the midst of the flurry of everyday life. No matter where I went, people were talking about the case and proclaiming the Cardinal's innocence—bus drivers, waiters, bookstore clerks, lawyers, and teachers refused to believe someone they trusted so much could be guilty of such a crime. Like many, I could not help but to turn my despair into hope as I got caught up in the goodwill of those who supported Bernardin.

By Friday the charges were made formal. A man named Steven Cook claimed that he had been sexually abused as a seminarian in the Archdiocese of Cincinnati when Bernardin was archbishop there. Even before the Cardinal received the charges that day, the Cable News Network (CNN) had been airing a trailer for a story to air on Sunday called "Fall from Grace" dealing with sexual misconduct by clergy and promising an interview with Cook implicating Bernardin in a scandal. As the news went around the globe—including to Tonadico di Primero, Italy, the town of the Cardinal's ancestors—something seemed fishy about the whole thing: why would CNN have an exclusive interview with Cook before his charges were made formal if there wasn't a bigger conspiracy at work?

As it turned out, Cook recanted his charges and admitted that he was in fact part of a failed plot to hurt the Cardinal and claim a multi-million dollar reward. But the essence of the story is not that a good man was falsely accused of something he did not do and then was acquitted. The essence of the story is that faith really matters and that Joseph Bernardin taught us all something about what the walk of faith looks like.

Knowing that he was innocent of the charges, Bernardin felt very hurt and, as he later wrote in his memoir *The Gift of Peace*, sat quietly for a moment and asked himself a simple question: "Was this what the Lord had been preparing me for, to face false accusation about something that I knew never took place? Spurious charges, I realized, were what Jesus himself experienced. But this evolving nightmare seemed completely unreal. It did not seem possible that this was happening to me."[1] As friends and relatives from around the world called him to ask about the rumors and charges, he could see media trucks parked outside the window of his office at the chancery and outside his home. While he later said he felt very alone, he truly believed that "the truth will make you free" (Jn 8:32). He first issued a brief statement declaring his innocence and, following the formal accusation, held a press conference that remains one of the greatest testaments to faith in modern times.

Standing before a crowded room of reporters, the Cardinal went against his lawyers' advice and answered any and all questions. That morning he had prayed the rosary and meditated on the first sorrowful mystery, trying to understand the Agony in the Garden and draw from Jesus' strength. That strength allowed him to respond to personal and embarrassing questions that reached their height when a rookie reporter went so far as to ask, "Cardinal Bernardin, are you sexually active?" Even the most hardened reporters gasped at the question. But Bernardin paused, feeling the enormous gulf between the reporter's world and his own, and responded, "I have always led a chaste and celibate life."[2] His response was the lead story in several papers the next day as people remarked on his composure and their own sense of his innocence. One reporter told me that he had gone into the press conference looking for a "good story" and instead found a "good man" whose faith in God and in humanity were transformative.

We can tell a lot about people by the way they handle adversity. Cardinal Bernardin held fourteen press conferences in the week after he was falsely charged. He submitted his case to a review board that was part of a progressive process he had helped to create for handling sexual abuse charges against priests. He visited the young seminarians studying at the University of Saint Mary of the Lake in Mundelein, just outside Chicago, to assure them of his innocence and make sure their own vocations were not in jeopardy. And, most amazingly, he wrote his accuser, Steven Cook, offering to visit him and pray with and for him. The Cardinal knew he was innocent, but he worried about the effect of the charges on believers, the Church, and his accuser. He said publicly that he was praying for his accuser, and he meant it.

It took one hundred days before Cook dropped the false charges on February 28, 1994. As the news spread across the world, including through the very same CNN that had rushed to judgment earlier, people of all faiths and none at all shared their joy. But as elated as he was, Cardinal Bernardin could not help feeling that he should reach out to Steven Cook, who had likely suffered abuse and had left the Church, faced public scorn for accusing the wrong person, and was now dying of AIDS.

Just after Christmas that year, Bernardin contacted Steven through his mother, Mary, and requested a meeting. Steven enthusiastically agreed to meet in Philadelphia. On December 30, the two men, each accompanied by a friend, sat together and talked. Steven apologized for all the pain he had caused, and the Cardinal not only accepted Steven's apology but prayed with him for his physical and spiritual well-being. After the profound moment of forgiveness and reconciliation, Cardinal Bernardin asked Steven if he wanted to take part in celebrating the Eucharist. Steven said he had felt alienated from God and the Church for a long time and in anger had even thrown the Gideon Bible against the walls of various hotel rooms over the years. Cardinal Bernardin hesitated for a moment and offered Steven a Bible he had inscribed. Steven took the Bible and held it to his heart. Then Bernardin explained that an anonymous man had given him a hundred-year-old chalice and asked him to use it someday if he ever had a chance to celebrate Mass with Steven. Steven tearfully said that he would like that very much. Later, Cardinal Bernardin called the meeting the most profound reconciliation in his priesthood. And Steven was so moved that he asked the Cardinal to share the story with the world, which he did. The Cardinal and Steven stayed in touch until Steven died on September 22, 1995. His mother reported that her son died fully reconciled with the Church, which she saw as Cardinal Bernardin's gift to her family.

After facing the false accusation and seeking forgiveness and reconciliation with such grace, Cardinal Bernardin turned the corner only to find out that he had pancreatic cancer. Diagnosed in June of 1995, Bernardin explained that his two worst fears had come true in a short span—being falsely accused and finding out that, like his father who had died of the disease when Joseph was only four years old, he too would die of cancer.

As before, he shared the news openly and honestly. It was incredible to watch the outpouring of love. Even tough city reporters had to hold back their tears as they inquired about the details. One question people frequently asked the Cardinal was which he considered worse, the false accusation or the diagnosis of cancer. Without hesitation he said the false accusation was much worse.

I can remember reading about the Cardinal's health in the papers every day. But what I remember most are the stories of how he transformed his suffering into deeper compassion for others. Having successfully made it through surgery and chemotherapy treatment, the Cardinal was told that the cancer was in remission. But his ministry to those suffering from illness was only beginning as he regularly visited hospitals, wrote letters, and emphasized the need for good health care in this country. Each story about the Cardinal was like a testimony to the power of faith, and, like so many, I felt my own faith growing in his light.

I never imagined that I would have the chance to meet Cardinal Bernardin in person, let alone work with him. But in September 1995, a Pulitzer Prize–winning photographer named John H. White approached Loyola Press, where I was an editor at the time, with a project he had been working on since 1982 called *This Man Bernardin*. We immediately signed a contract with John, and through him and the project, a remarkable collection of black-and-white images of public and private moments in the Cardinal's life, I had the life-changing opportunity to work with and get to know Cardinal Bernardin. What follows are five key themes from the spiritual wisdom he left us as his legacy.

The Power of Prayer

The first time I met Cardinal Bernardin face to face was March 22, 1996. I was in his office to interview him for captions I was writing for John White's photobook *This Man Bernardin*.

During the six months leading up to the meeting I had immersed myself in John's soul-catching photographs detailing everything in the Cardinal's life from quiet moments in his study to celebrating Christmas Mass at Holy Name Cathedral. When I asked John why he, as an African-American from the Methodist Episcopal Zion tradition, had spent fourteen years photographing the Cardinal's life and ministry, he explained, "Because inside this man Bernardin is a light that illuminates the world. I want to share that light with as many people as I can." By listening to John's stories, studying the Cardinal's writings, and reading the chapter openers written by the Cardinal's long-time friend and biographer Eugene Kennedy, I began to recognize the "light" he emitted through his strong sense of himself and deep faith. I had been struggling with my own faith at the time and was overwhelmed by the Cardinal's faith in God and desire to serve as an instrument in his hands.

I had never intended to write the captions for the book, but John insisted, saying simply, "I trust you." Even when my first efforts yielded such lifeless slogans as: "Here Cardinal Bernardin gets out of a car," or "Cardinal Bernardin smiles as he pushes a child on a swing while visiting a local Catholic school," John would smile and say, "Well, you're certainly not wrong, but you might try to write something with a little more life." One day he encouraged me to set up an interview with the Cardinal to discuss the photos and to make the book more personal and interesting. After many reluctant phone calls to the Cardinal's secretary, I finally landed an appointment. John's only caution was that the Cardinal was very disciplined as to how he spent his time, so if the interview was set for one hour, one hour was all I would get.

Though I was accompanied by John's good friend and colleague, Rich Cahan, I arrived at the chancery the day of the meeting feeling nervous. Yet, when Cardinal Bernardin stepped into the hallway to lead us into his office, I was amazed at how familiar he seemed to me and how calm he made me feel. As he shook our hands, I knew I was in the presence of a holy person.

Moving carefully because of an ailing back and the many months of recuperation from cancer surgery and treatment, the Cardinal escorted us to a round marble table in the middle of his office. The three of us took our seats, and the Cardinal spent a quiet moment looking at the images before him. He seemed at once humbled by and grateful for the project. Rich and I looked at each other and silently logged our mutual understanding of what a privilege it was to be sitting with *this* man at *this* time in his life. The media had covered the Cardinal and given people glimpses into his life. But this was different.

Rich and I began with a seemingly simple question: "Cardinal Bernardin, why do you pray?" After a short pause he explained, "Because prayer connects me with the Lord. I begin each day with an hour of prayer. It grounds me. Prayer is very important."

Accepting the answer as a pretty "Cardinal thing" to say, we started to move on to the next question. But before either of us could utter a word, Cardinal Bernardin grabbed my arm and exclaimed, "I really believe that!" I was so taken aback, I nearly fell off my chair. Then, gazing intently at us, he explained that prayer had always been an enormous part of his life. For the Cardinal, the work of prayer, the chore of it, gave way to the immeasurable benefits of it. "It is something," he later told me, "that grows on a person, and the sooner people make a practice of praying, the more connected they will become with God and things that really matter." He was genuinely concerned that we believe him *not* because he was a cardinal archbishop, but because he was a person of faith. His "I really believe that" flowed through everything the Cardinal did.

As Cardinal Bernardin later explained in *The Gift of Peace*, it was not until he was a busy bishop that he learned he had to set aside quality time to pray. Though he preferred to work late and sleep as long as possible, he developed the spiritual discipline of getting up very early and devoting the first hour of his day to God. Far from a perfect pray-er, Bernardin found that each morning drew him closer to God and that the effects lasted throughout the day. As part of his ritual he prayed the Liturgy of the Hours (the public prayer of the Church consisting of readings and prayers throughout the day), said the Rosary, read scripture and spiritual books, and offered his intentions for all those in need. The Cardinal said that when he was ill he often found it hard to pray but because he had developed such a rich prayer life he knew how to connect with God even in the worst of times. When I asked him what advice he would give to young people on prayer, he said simply, "It is never too early to learn how to pray. Developing a healthy prayer life connects us to God and to all."

Accepting the Gift of Peace

On August 28, 1996, Cardinal Bernardin saw his doctor, Sr. Ellen Gaynor, for an examination that would determine whether or not he could have back surgery to alleviate a painful case of spinal stenosis. Until then, all indications were that the cancer was in remission and his health was good. But during the exam Dr. Gaynor discovered that the Cardinal's cancer had returned, this time in the liver. In keeping with their honest relationship, she told him that he had only a year or less to live.

In that moment, Bernardin later wrote, "I immediately identified with Jesus in the Garden of Gethsemane. At that moment—on the eve of the suffering and death that would complete the mission his Father had given to him—Jesus was very lonely, as was I." That moment, however, passed rather quickly. "Quite simply," the Cardinal said, "I am grounded in the Lord and realized that I had been asked to enter more deeply into the mystery of his death and resurrection. I am also grounded in his Church to which I have dedicated my life and ministry for more than four decades and in which, in good times and bad, I have been buoyed by the loving support of its bishops, priests, deacons, religious, and lay faithful."[3]

Two days after receiving the bad news, Cardinal Bernardin held a press conference before a crowded room of reporters. When he shared that his cancer had returned, reporters teared up and his dear friend John White fell to his knees in sadness. But Bernardin lifted people's spirits by saying, "I have been assured that I still have some quality time left. My prayer is that I will use whatever time is left in a positive way, that is, in a way that will be of benefit to the priests and people I have been called to serve, as well as to my own spiritual well-being."[4]

He went on to say that he was working even harder to practice what he had preached for so long: to trust God completely. He said in all sincerity that he was at peace in the face of the cancer and his impending death, that he considered this as God's special gift to him at that moment in his life. Then he shared the wisdom that his friend and spiritual writer Henri Nouwen had taught him, "We can look at death as an enemy or a friend. If we see it as an enemy, death causes anxiety and fear. We tend to go into a state of denial. But if we see it as a friend, our attitude is truly different. As a person of faith, I see death as a friend, as the transition from earthly life to life eternal."[5] He concluded by praying with and for people of all faiths and asked for their prayers in return.

Watching the press conference on television, I was so moved that I wrote the Cardinal a letter and faxed it to his residence. I told him that I was praying for him and thanked him for his strong witness to the power of faith. I said that I was amazed he could view his cancer as a gift from God.

Later when I was working with him on his as-yet-unnamed memoirs, I realized that I had misunderstood what he had said in that press conference. "Cardinal," I apologized, "I made a big mistake in my recent fax. I thought you saw the *cancer* as God's gift, but you were talking about being at *peace* at this time in your life, weren't you?" He smiled and explained that many people had misunderstood what he had said. "It's interesting isn't it," he offered, "we can understand cancer, but peace is less tangible, less comprehensible."

As he worked tirelessly to complete his book and help make peace more tangible, he offered a profound prayer:

What I would like to leave behind is a simple prayer that each of you may find what I have found—God's special gift to us all: the gift of peace. When we are at peace, we find the freedom to be most fully who we are, even in the worst of times. We let go of what is nonessential and embrace what is essential. We empty ourselves so that God may more fully work within us. And we become instruments in the hands of the Lord.[6]

As Cardinal Bernardin taught so well, God offers us all the gift of life and the gift of peace. It is up to us to accept and share these gifts on the path to wholeness and happiness.

"One Can Easily Distinguish Essentials from Peripherals in the Spiritual Life"

Twelve days after announcing the return of his cancer, Cardinal Bernardin flew to Washington, D.C., to receive the Presidential Medal of Freedom—the highest award given to a civilian. During the ceremony, President Bill Clinton praised the Cardinal for being a bridge builder and for teaching people that time is too precious to waste on acrimony and division. Reporters at the White House met with Cardinal Bernardin later that afternoon and asked him what he hoped to do with his remaining time on earth. He told them that he had lived a full life and that, while he had always tried to focus on the essentials and therefore was not racing to make up for lost time, he did want to write a book of personal reflections. I immediately wrote him a personal letter inviting him to publish his book and offering to serve as his editor. He responded with a simple yes to both the invitation and the offer.

Working closely with his special assistant Reverend Al Spilly and me and asking for feedback from his friends Eugene Kennedy and Monsignor Kenneth Velo, the Cardinal recorded his thoughts on living and dying in the light of the Lord's love, on finding the freedom to be his truest self, and on discerning the essentials from the nonessentials in life.

He was sixty-eight and dying of cancer. I was twenty-six and sorting through life's possibilities. Somewhere in this meeting place between age and youth, priest and lay person, author and editor, we found common ground and formed a friendship that continues to shape my life.

The times I met one-on-one with Cardinal Bernardin toward the end of his life, it always took me a moment to get used to being with him. His body was giving way to the cancer, but his mind and his spirit were keenly focused on and energized by his faith and trust in God. No matter how hard I tried to remain strictly professional, I could not help but think of the Cardinal as a friend. Quite simply, I really liked him. And it was difficult to know that our time together was so limited.

I once asked him if it made him uncomfortable when people called him a holy man. Waving his hand in the air as if to bat away the comment, he said, "I'm just trying to live my life the best I can. I'm an ordinary human being and the Lord doesn't expect any more from me than he expects from you. We may be called in different ways, but neither of us is more important than the other."

He went on to explain that, to become closer to God, to close the gap between who we are and who God calls us to be, we must focus on the essentials of Jesus' life and message. "One can easily distinguish essentials from peripherals in the spiritual life," he explained. "Essentials ask us to give true witness and to love others more. Nonessentials close us in on ourselves."

Perhaps nothing has fed my own spiritual life more than this insight. I often stop and ask myself if the ways I am spending my time, money, energies, and talents enact my Christian faith and lead me to love people more or if they selfishly close me off from God, myself, and others. In a world that emphasizes individualism and promotes a "get-while-the-getting-is-good" mentality, it is often difficult to direct our lives toward community and to, in the words of Saint Thomas Aquinas, "will the good of the other" while expecting nothing in return.

Throughout his entire life, Cardinal Bernardin resisted the temptation to close in on himself. As a young priest, bishop, and archbishop, he sought the advice of others to help him develop his spiritual life in the midst of his hectic schedule. In the late seventies he gave away all of his money except what he needed to maintain his checking account. In the eighties he listened to and addressed the concerns of protesters outraged by his decision, for financial reasons, to close some of Chicago's oldest and most beloved parishes and schools. After the false charges of sexual misconduct against him were dropped, the Cardinal not only forgave but also reconciled with his accuser. And throughout his entire battle with cancer, he learned how to more fully empty himself and to walk with the afflicted, especially cancer patients and the severely ill.

The Cardinal showed us all the truth of James's statement: "Faith without works is dead." He often said his greatest sermon would be the way he lived out the rest of his life. It was.

An Instrument in the Hands of the Lord

I met with the Cardinal in the library of his residence two weeks before he died. During our conversation, he told me that the previous evening, in what turned out to be his penultimate public appearance, he had celebrated an emotional Mass and was touched by the actions of a woman who was fighting cancer.

As he handed me a crumpled piece of paper, he said, "Last night during the distribution of Holy Communion I noticed a young lady creeping up, and when she got to the sanctuary, I could see that she was growing even more reluctant to do anything. I didn't want to add to her anxiety, so I didn't look at her directly. But out of the corner of my eye I could see what was happening. Finally she got enough courage to come up the three steps and put something on the floor. Well, I couldn't reach it, and so I said, 'Why don't you just give it to me personally?' She was in tears as she gave me this note. She had written it during the Mass."

Unfolding the note, scrawled in shaky handwriting with a nearly inkless blue pen, I read the words of a woman in her thirties struggling with how to handle her cancer and thanking Cardinal Bernardin for "saying Mass while not feeling so good." She thanked him for being such a tremendous source of hope and inspiration. At the end of the note the woman had written "P.S. Pray for me. I intend to live to 95 years old."

While the Cardinal recalled his story, many things ran through my mind. I felt an instant connection to this hesitant young woman. It was difficult not to be in awe of Cardinal Bernardin. (Someone once told me that he overheard a parishioner approach the Cardinal and become so nervous all he could think to say was, "It's nice to meet you, Your Majesty.")

What struck me the most about the Cardinal's story, though, was the way he drew this young woman to him without making her feel uncomfortable. Like Jesus, who ministered to the people even from the corner of his eye, Cardinal Bernardin knew how to cut through all the nonessentials to what was truly essential: being present to other people as an instrument in the hands of the Lord.

The Cardinal taught me that to share God's love we must first know that we are loved and that we all have special gifts. Then we must use and develop our gifts. Finally, and most important, we must recognize that our gifts are not our own—they belong to God and are ours to share. The last stage is crucial, for in acknowledging where our gifts come from we get out of the way and allow God to truly work through us. We come out of the darkness and "in God's spirit,... we call each other out of our self-made graves" and into the light of life.[7]

"Letting Go Is Never Easy. Indeed, It Is a Lifelong Process"

The last time I saw Cardinal Bernardin in person was October 29. He was exhausted, his back was hurting, and his breathing was labored. But he still wanted to go over the nearly final draft of his book and to share with me a very personal open letter that he had decided to write to his readers.

We took our usual seats, he on the south end of his off-white sofa and I on the adjacent rust-colored guest chair. As we organized our papers that morning, the clock on the shelf behind the couch marked the hour with eleven soft chimes. Ordinarily I loved the sound of that clock, but today it only served as a reminder of how precious the Cardinal's time was.

Under the gentle light given off by the lamp on the end table between us, the Cardinal carefully organized the pages in his hands. I noticed his expression of determination, his deliberate movements, and the sound of his breathing.

Holding up a handwritten draft of his letter, the Cardinal asked, "Can I read this to you?"

"Of course," I said. I emptied my mind and asked God to help me be fully present to this moment.

As Cardinal Bernardin began to read, his loving spirit came through in his heartfelt words and the soft sound of his weary voice. "My dear friends...," he began.

I closed my eyes tightly and just listened. Toward the end of his reading, he came to these words, "On a very personal note, I invite those who read this book to walk with me the final miles of my life's journey." He paused, then finished reading.

Looking up, filled with emotion, Cardinal Bernardin asked me what I thought. "Perfect," was all I could say. He smiled wanly and said,

"I cannot do much better than that. It was written in tears." It was also received in tears.

As we continued to work that morning, the Cardinal would periodically prop his arm on the edge of the couch, rest his chin on his palm, and close his eyes. His fatigue, he told me, was so pervasive that he never felt rested. But he assured me that he was paying close attention, as he always did. I asked the Cardinal, "Would you like to stop and do this later?"

He looked at me and said what I had known but did not want to accept, "There isn't any later."

A week earlier I had suggested to the Cardinal that his book might include samples of letters people had written him, especially cancer patients with whom he had corresponded. At the end of our meeting that day he told me that the letters were across the hall in his office.

I had read in the newspapers that Cardinal Bernardin kept many of these letters in his desk drawer until it overflowed and he had to file them elsewhere. As we rose to go to the office, the Cardinal took hold of my arm and we slowly walked together.

When we reached the office, the Cardinal sat down in his chair, which was rigged with a special cushion to support his aching back, and breathed a sigh of relief. His office was dark, but he did not need much light to find what he was looking for. Reaching down he pulled open a deep drawer, revealing an enormous stack of letters in all shapes and sizes. Some were typed, others handwritten.

"These I have saved for a long time now," he explained. "I have always tried to write people back. They mean a lot to me." Then he reached in, scooped up a handful in his white hands, and gingerly placed the letters in a brown grocery bag for me. The letter that now sat atop the stack in the drawer was written on pink stationery and had a photograph of a young woman attached to it. "This letter," said the Cardinal, "was from a young man whose wife had cancer. He wrote to ask me to pray for her, which I did." Another handful revealed another letter and another memory. And another. And another.

I watched and listened as the Cardinal emptied the drawer, filling the bag and sharing his thoughts as he recognized the letters and recalled the lives they represented. He had talked a great deal about letting go, which he described as the "ability to release from our grasp those things that inhibit us from developing an intimate relationship with God." Time and again he shared how hard—even frustrating and unsettling—it was for him to empty himself of his grandest plans and smallest distractions so that the hand of God's purpose could truly enter his life. "Letting go is never easy," he said. "Indeed, it is a lifelong process." It had taken him a lifetime to learn how to let go, to let God, and his gesture of handing the letters over revealed that he had prepared himself for his impending death.

Taking the bag of letters, I stood at the opposite side of the Cardinal's desk, looked him in the eyes, and said I would pray for him, as I always did. He leaned back in his chair, folded his arms across his chest, and smiled softly. After a moment he said, "I hope you don't mind, but I'm going to just sit here a while and rest." We said good-bye and he closed his eyes. As I walked out of the office, I turned and stared at him for a minute as he rested. It was the last time I would see him alive. He passed away on November 14.

What Have We Had in Our Midst?

On November 20, the day of the Cardinal's funeral, I awoke with a deep sense of loss. I had been invited to attend the ceremony with my friend Fr. John Cusick, and when I got out of the cab to meet him at Holy Name Cathedral I was overwhelmed to see people of every age and background huddled together, shivering, blowing into their hands, and wiping tears from their eyes as they awaited the liturgy to warm their hearts.

The scene was reminiscent of the previous forty-two hours during which a continuous line of more than two hundred thousand people had come to view the Cardinal's body and to say good-bye.

Following the funeral, thousands of us lined State Street as the cortege prepared for its long, slow journey west through the city to Mount Carmel Cemetery where Joseph Bernardin was entombed that evening. Within fifteen minutes the pallbearers placed the Cardinal's casket inside the hearse and closed the door.

The drivers and passengers in the cortege climbed into their vehicles as well, and the sound of doors closing against the backdrop of profound silence marked the Cardinal's final journey to and from the cathedral. I stood there numb, unable to string together the fragments of my thoughts. It was all too immense.

Suddenly a woman beside me asked her friend in a tone of frustrated wonder, "What are we looking at? Help me place this event. What have we had in our midst?"

The friend replied, scanning the crowd, "A very special man."

Tears began to roll down my face. Exactly, I thought.

As the procession slowly pulled away I wondered how those of us gathered could possibly express how we were feeling about our brother Joseph. Chicago's simple reaction was to break out in applause. The clapping and waving hands of people from all backgrounds followed the Cardinal all the way to the cemetery. Even in death, he brought people together and taught us to accept God's gift to us all: the gift of peace.[8]

PART FOUR

ACTING: FAITH WITHOUT WORKS IS DEAD

To each is given the manifestation of the Spirit for the common good. To one is given through the Spirit the utterance of wisdom, and to another the utterance of knowledge according to the same Spirit, to another faith by the same Spirit, to another gifts of healing by the one Spirit, to another the working of miracles, to another prophecy, to another the discernment of spirits, to another various kinds of tongues, to another the interpretation of tongues. All these are activated by one and the same Spirit, who allots to each one individually just as the Spirit chooses. For just as the body is one and has many members, and all the members of the body, though many, are one body, so it is with Christ.

—1 Corinthians 12:7-12

So then, whenever we have an opportunity, let us work for the good of all.

—Galatians 6:10

Introduction

Praxis Makes Better

One of the most positive things about our generation is that we are hungry to serve a world in need. Tired of empty promises, increasingly alarming news about the sad state of the world, and partisan and special interest politics that lead nowhere, we want action. Contrary to what many of the stereotypes lead people to believe, far from being aimless slackers we are working to build better lives for ourselves and others. Our generation may be set apart from others in that we rarely align ourselves with any one party, often have a diverse interest in a range of issues, are grassroots-based in approaching problems, are more tolerant of everything from lifestyles to ethnic backgrounds, are skeptical of marketing and advertising, and are techno-savvy.[1] But we are not only working with existing action-oriented groups and leaders, we are developing new and exciting ways of fostering social awareness and nurturing change. The more we celebrate our diversity, question convention, explore, and invent, the more we are discovering that we have the power to lead our nation—and indeed the world—into a truly global, color-blind, nonideological, and borderless milieu of thought, action, and production.[2]

In some way or another social service has always been a part of my life. My family and extended family members have been deeply involved in the Peace Corps, mentoring programs, prison ministry, advocacy, and work with at-risk children. And I have been blessed to have friends who also believe in service. From grade school through high school I marveled at the zeal with which some of my friends ran canned food drives and fundraisers for charity. While in college, many of my friends spent at least one summer or academic break doing service projects everywhere from Appalachia to inner-city San Francisco. Following college, several of my friends devoted the first year or two after graduation to working with the poor at home and abroad, teaching in urban schools, assisting AIDS patients in hospitals through religious and non-religious institutions such as Holy Cross Associates, the Jesuit Volunteer Corps, Catholic Charities, Teach for America, the Peace Corps, the Inner City Teaching Corps, the YMCA/YWCA, homeless centers, children and family services, and Greenpeace. Years later, many of these same friends have either made a living out of non-profit service-oriented work or have found a way to weave service into the routines of their lives.

My experience is by no means atypical. No matter where I go, I run into young adults who share their stories of service and take pride in the fact that, while our generation may be off the political radar screen, we are in many ways leaders of a new movement of service. Gallup polls regularly reveal that young adults' commitment to hands-on help is at its highest in forty years. A recent article in the *New York Times* reported that today's young adults are choosing teaching as a profession in record numbers despite low pay. Other newspapers such as *USA Today* and business magazines highlight our generation's commitment to balance, which often means finding jobs that do not demand eighty-hour work weeks, that allow us to work from home, and/or that fit our interests even if they do not pay as well. An emerging trend among young people is developing a spirituality of work that allows the whole person to flourish and feel fulfilled.

One of the most successful volunteer organizations today is City Cares of America. With thirteen thousand volunteers and more than seventy-five thousand members, the organization's success comes from its flexible and varied volunteer opportunities for busy young professionals. Started in 1986 in New York by six young friends who struggled to find realistic volunteer opportunities, the organization, which does everything from mentoring to building houses to planting trees, has expanded to twenty-six cities throughout the nation, from Los Angeles Cares to Chicago Cares. Another volunteer organization is Do Something, which was founded in 1993 by a group of young people that included actor Andrew Shue of *Melrose Place* fame. The objective of Do Something is to build safe and happy communities through grants, awards, and recognition for entrepreneurial young adults who develop community service projects from drug rehab to legal services for immigrants. Also started in

1993 was the volunteer organization Jumpstart, which was founded by two Yale students who believed that university and college campuses provide a natural resource to communities in need of additional support for young children. Today Jumpstart exists at eleven universities and has linked itself with Americorps, the government initiative to get young people involved as mentors to at-risk children.[3]

While there are countless examples of our generation's interest in social justice, one of the primary problems we face is not a lack of desire to make a difference but the inability to orchestrate our passions and initiatives into a cohesive political and social force. We dislike or reject the label and attributes of "Generation X," but we have yet to represent ourselves as fully as possible in political and civic arenas. Less than 30 percent of Americans and even fewer young adults say they trust the government or feel that policy makers address their concerns, but less than a third of us eighteen and older have voted in the last three presidential elections. We are involved at the grassroots level of service, but we do not march in the streets or conduct rallies. We are deeply invested in technology and information, but we have yet to pool our collective knowledge or mobilize those of our peers who remain disenfranchised. We believe in helping the poor, but we are either less inclined or less aware of the need to get at the root of social problems by affecting changes at the structural level.

Meredith Bagby, a young adult who reports on our generation's financial interests for CNN's Financial News Network, issues this challenge to all who believe we can make a difference:

> Our role in American history seems clear: If our parents' generation was about dismantling the status quo, our generation will be about building new institutions, moral codes, families, churches, corporations.... Our job is to make order out of the chaos—to resurrect America from the ashes of burning crosses, draft cards, and bras, from the humiliation of public betrayals, from the rubble of riots from Kent State to Rodney King, from the shells of cities rotted by crime and despair, from the wreckage of broken homes. If our parents were the revolutionaries, then let us be the rebuilders.[4]

I take Meredith's challenge seriously, and it is my contention that one of the greatest vehicles for social change is religion. In the context

of this book, we are talking about the Christian call to love others as
Jesus loves us. We are also talking about the powerful tradition of
Catholic social teaching that both grows out of the lived response to
Christ's call and forms a context within which we are inspired and edu-
cated to serve the common good at every level, from that of politics to
that of our homes.

As I mentioned at the beginning of this book, I have spent many
years being an uneasy Catholic, wandering toward and away from, inside and outside the Church. While I cannot explain exactly what it is
about being Catholic that makes me uneasy, I can tell you that a large
part of it is caused by the fear of being *irrelevant*. In other words,
though my mind and spirit are invigorated by my Catholic upbringing
and my exploration of philosophy, theology, and spirituality, I have been
deathly afraid of being *religious*, let alone admitting to anyone else that I
am an active member of a religion. Perhaps you have felt the same way.

Why? Maybe because religion by its very nature banks on the existence of a mysterious-yet-real-and-knowable God. Or because religion
is an institutionalized system of attitudes, dogmas, beliefs, teachings,
rules, and rituals that are often confusing to its members and near impossible to explain to nonmembers. Or because religion can be rigid
and appear to be totalitarian and dictatorial to the point of denying its
members the ability to think independently. Or maybe because religion
is countercultural and gets slammed for being "different" or "geeky" or
downright "stupid."

At the height of a recent crisis in which I thought about calling myself "spiritual but not religious" and letting my faith journey go at that,
I met a non-churchy friend of a friend who had just come back from a
day of volunteering as a tutor in a poor section of town. She was filled
with the kind of joy that comes only from helping people in need. After
she told us of the child she had helped work his way through a spelling
test, she said the most amazing thing: "You know what else? I had
signed up for this volunteer day through a friend, and at the end of the
day, it turned out that the group sponsoring the tutoring was from a
Catholic parish! I'd been thinking about getting into church and developing my faith life, and this experience made me feel like faith really
matters."

Suddenly something clicked for me. The times I've felt faith in
God and participation in religion are irrelevant, I have been living in
the abstract. I have been approaching faith purely on the intellectual

level, looking for test-tube proofs for God's existence and logical arguments to support religious belief. But the times I have felt that faith and
religion are not only relevant but absolutely relevant, I have been *acting*
on my beliefs and *working* for good in the world. Seeing this young
woman so excited about her service experience and her desire to root
that experience in a religious tradition that at its core reaches out to
those in need made me feel good about being Catholic. It also made me
want to get more involved!

The twelfth-century saint and church reformer Peter Damian once
quipped: "If philosophy were necessary for salvation, God would have
sent philosophers to convert the world instead of fishermen." How
true! But at the same time, it is also true that we need philosophers and
theologians to help us reflect on our experience of God and the way we
act in light of our faith. The Greeks called this process of thinking and
acting *praxis*. Praxis is theory and practice wedded together in an ever-
revolving cycle that spirals to deeper truths. Through *praxis*, and not
simply *practice*, we put our thoughts, wonderings, and convictions into
motion—we bring them into reality. At the same time, we let reality
stimulate our thoughts and we reflect on the world around us. Consequently, our desire to understand what it means to be Catholic requires praxis—*thinking and doing; living and reflecting.* One without the
other is impotent, but together they can give birth to an overwhelming
number of opportunities for growth and understanding.

The dance of theory and practice helps us balance our faith lives
and be free to think about and act on our faith without having all the
answers. Serving others, like the young volunteer did, leads us to reflect
on our experience and want to tap into the wisdom of a tradition that
teaches us the value of life and inspires us to serve more fully. Practice
does not make us perfect; it makes us better. The Catholic tradition,
with its strong commitment to social justice, helps us serve and be
served much better than if we go it alone.

17

The Call and Cost of Discipleship

Tapping into Christianity, and more specifically the Catholic tradition, sets us on our way toward a life of discipleship. At its best, discipleship is not about buying into the letter of the law or a bunch of doctrines and moral codes. It is about following Jesus along his path, accompanying him, and making him the companion on our journeys toward deeper love, meaning, and fulfillment. In scripture, *disciple* refers to one of the twelve in the inner circle of Jesus' followers (also called *apostles*, "those sent out"). But, as Jesus makes clear many times, his disciples are far from exclusive; they are called to make "disciples of all nations" (Mt 28:19) so that we all might become one family who serves, prays, loves, lives, suffers, dies, and rises with Jesus. Discipleship, then, is a whole matrix of values, behaviors, and actions that derive from close association with Jesus and are nurtured through our life as Christians. In our modern-day quests to feed and act on our faith, we can look to the New Testament and the Christian tradition for models of discipleship. There we find that discipleship takes many forms and challenges us to use our creativity, gifts, and passions today.

Responding to Jesus' Call

If you have ever tried to organize a group of people to join you in a cause, you know how hard it can be not only to convince others that the cause is worth their time but also to get them to show up for meetings and events. A former co-worker of mine, for example, was into several causes that she believed others would embrace if they only took the time to listen and participate. A local leader in Amnesty International, she spent countless hours organizing protests, printing flyers, making phone calls, and pleading with people to march at death-row prisons and write letters to government officials to put an end to the death penalty. She also educated anyone who would listen about the importance of boycotting companies that use child labor or promote unfair working conditions. Some people in the office used to remark, "That Erin sure is tough to be around. She's into so many causes that she has to alter the way she lives. She can't buy certain products or say things that might sound 'politically incorrect.' Why bother!" But Erin went on trying, sometimes getting people to join her and always offering a strong witness to the power of conscientious living.

The New Testament is loaded with stories of Christ's call and his hearers' responses. At first glance, it seems Jesus had it easy—he did not have to run around posting flyers on trees saying "Meeting tonight at 8 P.M. at the synagogue to discuss the reign of God. Be there or be square." He called and people responded. In Mark's gospel, for example, when Jesus calls the first disciples, they respond without hesitation:

> As Jesus passed along the Sea of Galilee, he saw Simon and his brother Andrew casting a net into the sea—for they were fishermen. And Jesus said to them, "Follow me and I will make you fish for people." And immediately they left their nets and followed him. As he went a little farther, he saw James son of Zebedee and his brother John, who were in their boat mending the nets. Immediately he called them; and they left their father Zebedee in the boat with the hired men, and followed him. (1:16-20)

While Matthew's account of the calling of the first disciples (4:18-22) is similar to Mark's, Luke's and John's are different in that the disciples had previously heard of Jesus and either feel unworthy to follow him or are a bit hesitant. Luke, for example, has Jesus get into a boat with Simon and from the water teach a crowd of people standing on the shore. When he has finished speaking, Jesus tells Simon, who has not caught anything all night, to put his net into the water for a catch. Simon is skeptical but he does as Jesus says. Soon he realizes that his net is full. He motions to James and John in the next boat to help him, but when they divide the fish into their boats, both begin to sink. Falling to his knees out of fear and awe, Simon tells Jesus, "Go away

from me, Lord, for I am a sinful man!" Jesus responds by saying, "Do
not be afraid; from now on you will be catching people." When the
men bring their boats ashore, they leave everything and follow Jesus
(5:1-11).

In John's account of the calling of the first disciples (1:35-51),
which we briefly covered in chapter 11, the first disciples come from
among the disciples of John the Baptist. As the Baptist is standing with
two of his disciples in Bethany, he sees Jesus walk by and proclaims,
"Look, here is the Lamb of God!" The two disciples follow Jesus, who
turns around and asks them "What are you looking for?" When they
respond with their own question, "Where are you staying?" Jesus invites them to "come and see." They follow Jesus and, after spending the
afternoon with him, recognize him as the Messiah.

But did Jesus really have it so easy? Without the modern conve-
niences of television, cell phones, faxes, e-mail, and newspapers, he had
to share his message by walking door to door, riding on donkeys' backs,
rowing a boat. He had to rely on word-of-mouth accounts of his miracles and teachings. He constantly had to help his apostles and those
who heard his message understand what he was revealing to them. And
all the while, he was considered suspect by government officials who
pointed out that Jesus was not only breaking with tradition by seeking
out disciples instead of letting them come to him, but was also preaching that he was the Son of God and healing in God's name. As time
went on, fewer and fewer people responded to Jesus' call out of confusion as to whether he was who he said he was or out of fear for their
lives. Only the true diehards followed Jesus into Jerusalem at the end of
his earthly life. And, in many ways, following Jesus today is no easier.
But he continues to call us.

Whom Does Jesus Call?

Of great significance are the people Jesus called and the radical nature
of his call. Rather than seek out the righteous of his day, Jesus called
those on the margins. For example, he called a tax collector named Levi
(named "Matthew" in Mt 9:9) who immediately left his job in a toll-
booth to follow Jesus. Later, Jesus ate dinner in Levi's home with many
tax collectors and sinners, which scandalized the scribes and the
Pharisees. Upon learning that they had questioned his disciples about

the company he was keeping, Jesus exclaimed, "Those who are well have no need of a physician, but those who are sick; I have come to call not the righteous but sinners" (Mk 2:15-17).

The nature of Jesus' call was radical and immediate. For example, when he ordered some of his disciples to journey with him to the other side of the Sea of Galilee where the Gentiles lived, one of them said, "Lord, first let me go and bury my father." Jesus quickly responded, "Follow me, and let the dead bury their own dead" (Mt 8:18-22). When he was questioned as to why he and his followers did not fast as John the Baptist and his followers did, Jesus answered with three analogies: the wedding guests cannot fast while the bridegroom is with them, no one sews a piece of unshrunk cloth on an old cloak, and no one puts new wine into old wineskins. In other words, Jesus is ushering in the kingdom and in the process is dispensing with the legalistic tradition of his time. When he and his disciples reaped grain fields and healed a man with a withered hand on the sabbath, the Pharisees questioned him. In the first case Jesus responded by saying, "The sabbath was made for humankind, and not humankind for the sabbath; so the Son of Man is lord even of the sabbath." In the second case he responded by asking, "Is it lawful to do good or to do harm on the sabbath, to save life or to kill?" (Mk 2:23–3:6).

In reshaping the laws of his time, Jesus called those willing to see with the eyes of faith, those willing to put human-made power structures in service of a higher power of mercy and love. Today he calls any of us who are willing to look more deeply into the law and order of our time and who refuse to accept injustice and oppression.

What Does Jesus Call Us to Do?

Answering Jesus' call was and is serious business. Before he appointed the twelve apostles from among his many followers, Jesus went out to the mountain and "spent the night in prayer to God." The next day he called his disciples, chose twelve of them to be his apostles (Lk 6:12-16), sent them out to "proclaim the message" (Mk 3:13-19a), and "gave them authority over unclean spirits, to cast them out, and to cure every disease and every sickness" (Mt 10:1-4). Once he had chosen the apostles, Jesus sent them out two by two. He ordered them to take nothing for their journey except a staff—no bread, no bag, no money in their

belts. They were to wear sandals and not to put on two tunics. He said
to them, "Wherever you enter a house, stay there until you leave the
place. If any place will not welcome you and they refuse to hear you, as
you leave, shake off the dust that is on your feet as a testimony against
them" (Mk 6:6b-30; Mt 10:9-14; Lk 9:1-10a).

During Jesus' lifetime, the twelve apostles were privileged beyond
privilege to witness the kingdom of God firsthand. Following Jesus'
death and resurrection, the first Christians were so charged with the
grandeur of God that they could not help but proclaim the good news
as far and wide as possible. The epistles of Paul and the gospels are the
first written accounts of the experience of being grasped by the power
of salvation and, especially in Paul's case, of the transformation that
takes place in developing "eyes to see and ears to hear."

In trying to understand the essence of discipleship, it is worthwhile
to reflect on what we learn from Paul's experience. As the infamous persecutor of Christians traveled along the road to Damascus to destroy
the Christian church there for breaking away from Jewish law and proclaiming newfound freedom in Jesus Christ the Son of God, Saul (as he
was then called) was suddenly knocked to the ground in a flash of light
and heard a voice say to him, "Saul, Saul, why do you persecute me?"
When he responded, "Who are you, Lord?" the reply came, "I am
Jesus, whom you are persecuting. But get up and enter the city, and you
will be told what you are to do." Saul got up from the ground but could
not see. When Saul reached Damascus, the Lord had one of his followers, Ananias, lay hands on the blind man to restore his sight. Filled with
the Holy Spirit, Saul regained his sight, was baptized, and within a day
was preaching Jesus as the Son of God (Acts 9:1-25).

Though he himself does not say much about the events of his conversion experience, Paul (as he was called after his conversion) spent the
rest of his life writing and preaching from the road and in jail because
of the faith instilled in him: "I have been crucified with Christ; and it is
no longer I who live, but it is Christ who lives in me" (Gal 2:19-20).
Paul, writing between A.D. 50 and 58, offers the oldest accounts of the
Christian experience and is the first interpreter of the gospel and
founder of churches. As a result of his efforts, the Christian movement
became a world religion. And because of his Christian zeal for evangelization, Saul the persecutor became Paul the persecuted. While the
New Testament does not mention his death, Acts 21–28 details his ar-
rest and transportation to Rome and reliable tradition depicts him as a

martyr who was beheaded for his Christian discipleship during the persecution of Nero in the mid 60s.

The Cost of Discipleship

The story of Paul's persecution points to what has been called "the cost
of discipleship." In Luke's gospel Jesus makes it very clear that he demands complete and lasting loyalty:

> Whoever comes to me and does not hate ["turn away from"]
> father and mother, wife and children, brothers and sisters, yes,
> and even life itself cannot be my disciple. Whoever does not
> carry the cross and follow me cannot be my disciple. . . . None
> of you can become my disciple if you do not give up all your
> possessions. Salt is good; but if salt has lost its taste, how can its
> saltiness be restored? It is fit neither for the soil nor for the ma-
> nure pile; they throw it away. Let anyone with ears to hear lis-
> ten! (14:26-27, 33-35)

In using the metaphor of salt losing its taste, Jesus explains the key
aspect of discipleship: true loyalty and commitment must remain
strong if they are to flavor the world. In light of the radical nature of
discipleship, the English writer G. K. Chesterton once remarked that
Christianity has not been tried and found wanting, it has been found
difficult and so not tried. In light of the demands Jesus makes on his
followers, we naturally wonder what it would be like to follow Jesus so
completely—to give up everything and hit the road with only a tunic,
sandals, and a staff to proclaim the good news.

To help answer this question, the gospels provide us with the story
of a rich young man who refused to give up his possessions to follow
Christ. As Mark tells the story (10:17-22), the rich young man knelt before Jesus and asked "What must I do to inherit eternal life?" When
Jesus listed the commandments, the man proudly said, "Teacher, I have
kept all these since my youth." Jesus, looking at him, loved him and
said, "You lack one thing; go, sell what you own, and give the money to
the poor, and you will have treasure in heaven; then come, follow me."
When the man heard this, he was shocked and went away grieving, for
he had many possessions.

What is most striking about the story is that even though Jesus looked upon the rich young man with love and directly invited him to be a disciple, the man decided instead to hang onto his possessions. This is the only story in scripture in which someone rejects Jesus' direct invitation to discipleship. And while we may wonder what it would be like to give up our possessions and follow Jesus, we know from the story that clinging to our possessions leaves us grieving and alone.

Responding to Christ's call to service is never easy. We are busy, we have our own needs to worry about, we fear those who are not like us. But Christ never promised us that service would be easy. In fact, he taught us that to be a disciple is to pay a price. From the teacher who takes a small salary and puts in long hours to the Peace Corps volunteer who lives in abject poverty for at least two years to the martyr who dies fighting against an unjust government, there is a cost to discipleship.

Without making too great a leap from everyday examples of discipleship, it is worth reflecting on the nature of discipleship with the Lutheran martyr-theologian Dietrich Bonhoeffer, who died at age thirty-nine in 1945 at the hands of the Gestapo in the concentration camp at Flossenbürg. In his now-famous book *The Cost of Discipleship*, Bonhoeffer explains that the greatest enemy of discipleship is "cheap grace," that is, the kind of grace that showers blessings without asking questions, fixing limits, or requiring action; the kind of grace that means the justification of sin without the justification of the sinner, baptism without church discipline, communion without confession, absolution without contrition, discipleship without the cross. Cheap grace is grace without Jesus Christ, living and incarnate.[1]

True discipleship, Bonhoeffer explains, is a costly grace—*costly* because it calls us to follow, *grace* because it calls us to follow Jesus Christ. It is costly because it costs a person her life, and it is grace because it gives her true life. It is costly because it condemns sin, and grace because it justifies the sinner. Above all, it is *costly* because it cost God the life of his Son, and what has cost God so much cannot be cheap for us. Above all, it is *grace* because God did not reckon his Son too dear a price to pay for our life, but delivered him up for us. Costly grace is the Incarnation of God.

And if we truly believe that the Incarnation does not end with Jesus on the cross but carries on in the work of our hands, then we will come to know the cost of discipleship in our world. Jesuit peace activist John Dear sums it up very well in his book *Jesus the Rebel: Bearer of God's Peace and Justice:*

Following Jesus today in a land of nuclear weapons, rampant racism, and widespread economic injustice means actively going against our culture of violence. As the culture promotes violence, we promote Jesus' nonviolence. As the culture calls for war, we call for Jesus' peace. As the culture supports racism, sexism, and classism, we demand Jesus' vision of equality, community, and reconciliation. As the culture summons us to be successful, to make money, to have a career, to get to the top, and to be number one, we race in the opposite direction and go with Jesus into voluntary poverty, powerlessness, humility, suffering and death.

Discipleship to Jesus, according to the gospel, requires that we love our enemies, demand justice for the poor, seek liberation for the oppressed, visit the sick and the imprisoned, topple the idols of death, resist militarism, reject consumerism, dismantle racism, create community, beat swords into plowshares, and worship the God of peace. If we try to engage in these social practices, we will feel the sting of discipleship and the gospel will come alive.[2]

The essence of discipleship, then, is that in following Christ we obey the call to follow and fix our eyes on the Word that works through us. The reward for those who respond to the call and remain loyal and committed is simply stated by Jesus in all four gospels: "Whoever listens to you listens to me, and whoever rejects you, rejects me, and whoever rejects me rejects the one who sent me" (Lk 10:16; cf. Mk 9:41; Mt 10:40-42; Jn 13:20). Jesus also makes a profound statement and asks an equally profound question: "Those who want to save their life will lose it, and those who lose their life for my sake will save it. What does it profit them if they gain the whole world, but lose or forfeit themselves?" (Lk 9:24-25).

The reward of discipleship, then, is that we die to the self that we have created and find the self that exists as a living, breathing image of the divine. We let go of the possessions that weigh us down and we become free to live more fully. We find our truest selves, and in turn, we help others find theirs in everyday life and in extraordinary ways.

18

Community and the Common Good

Two of the strongest claims scripture and tradition make upon us as disciples are that we are to form community and serve the common good. In our consumer culture, it is easy to worry more and more about ourselves, to become individualistic, to use others as a means of personal gain. But the Christian call is to move out beyond ourselves, to give and receive love, to form a community that works for a better world.

Our generation places great emphasis on friendships and community. In our diversity we are open-minded and accepting of people of different backgrounds and lifestyles. The Christian community we are talking about here does not limit us nor is it an isolated, elite cult of "the saved" that stands above or outside society at large.

Quite the contrary. Christian community is a form of the *communion* that Saint Paul spoke of when he said that through the Holy Spirit Christians enjoy fellowship with the triune God, other baptized Christians, and the world at large. Like Jesus, we work with and serve everyone—women and men, poor and rich, young and old, established and disenfranchised, believers and nonbelievers, healthy and lame, free and incarcerated, those with sight and the blind. We work in the world. We witness to the fact that through Jesus the reign of God is at hand, here and now, at this very moment. And, as a result, we nurture the common good of all people, whom we believe are "created and destined for that reign of love and mercy, where our beloved God dwells."[1]

When Jesus commissions the seventy (or, according to some texts, seventy-two) in the Gospel of Luke, he moves out beyond the mission of the twelve apostles. He sends his followers into every town and place where he himself will go. He tells them, "The harvest is plentiful, but

170

the laborers are few; pray therefore the Lord of the harvest to send out laborers into his harvest." He sends them on their way with the radical instructions to carry no purse, no bag, no sandals; to salute no one on the road; and not to shop around for the best hospitality but to eat and drink only what is laid before them in the houses that will accept them. The seventy, who represent all of us who wish to follow Christ, are to be equipped only with trust in God as they go to the towns to heal and to proclaim that "the kingdom of God has come near to you." Whether received or rejected, their message is the same. The responsibility for its effectiveness relies upon the hearers and doers of the Word.

It is uncomfortable for most of us to imagine traveling with nothing but trust in the Lord and to run around proclaiming that the kingdom of God has come near. But if we listen carefully to Jesus' words, his point is that we, like the seventy, will be going to many different cities and towns in our day-to-day lives. And, as believers, it is our challenge to go to these places with something to offer. Jesus is not necessarily asking us to change our routines—he is asking us to change our hearts, to transform the places where we will go, to bring light where there is darkness, peace where there is strife, acceptance where there is rejection, kindness where there is injury. Each time we head to our jobs, the grocery store, the bank, the gym, the movies, we are to bring life with us.

The way Catholic Christians love as community stems from how we come together as Church in our worship, liturgy, sacraments, Eucharist, virtues, prayer, and actions. And it flows out into the world when we serve the common good by honoring all people, upholding and fighting for their rights, and loving them.

In his landmark book *Bowling Alone: The Collapse and Revival of American Community*, Harvard Professor Robert Putnam explains that over the past twenty-five years we Americans have become increasingly disconnected from family, friends, neighbors, and social structures. The result, he says, is not only that we have a creeping suspicion that the country is morally and civically off-track, but also that we are, quite simply, less happy.

In our consumer-driven culture, we are led to believe that money really can buy us love, acceptance, security, and happiness. Daily we are tempted to purchase faddish clothing and cutting-edge gadgets so that we "fit in"; trade meaningful careers for the highest-paying jobs; look the other way when faced with moral challenges that could compromise personal gain; swap slogans of "get involved" for "get it while you can"; replace communal religion and genuine spirituality with self-help quick fixes; and build walls between us and our neighbors.

When we buy into such individualism, we sell out.

This is why the Christian tradition, rooted in Trinitarian love, can seem so countercultural. At base, Christianity calls us to befriend God and each other, to join hands, and to work together for the mutual benefit of all. It teaches that the Trinity—one God in three, coequal persons of the Father, Son, and Holy Spirit—is pure relationship. As the central mystery of our faith, the Trinity reveals that God—simultaneously Creator (Father), Redeemer (Son), and Sanctifier (Holy Spirit)—is a living community whose actions reveal God's inmost being *and* ongoing love for creation.

As God's relationships reveal who God is, so too do our relationships and actions reveal who we are. The way we interact with family, friends, co-workers, children, leaders, people on the street, and the poor shows how we regard ourselves and others. As part of God's ongoing creation, we are meant to experience oneness, wholeness, happiness, forgiveness, healing, salvation. We are meant to offer these things to others. We are meant for love.

Jesus, the incarnate Son of God, tells us, "For where two or three are gathered in my name, I am there among them" (Mt 18:20). Being gathered in God's name means being gathered in love. And loving means taking seriously first that we are created in God's image and unconditionally offered God's friendship, and second that we are in solidarity with others as friends.

Jesus' own friendships teach us what it means to love, heal, forgive, include, magnify, revive, and even resurrect.

As a young boy already teaching in the temple, Jesus came to know his earthly family not so much as superiors but as friends. When he chose his disciples, in essence his co-workers, he treated them, women and men, with respect and he tirelessly drew out the best each had to offer. When he hung out with the marginalized and dispossessed, his friendship healed. When he taught his friends how to pray, he used the word *Abba* and made possible a new kind of intimacy with the Father.

In his most trying times, Jesus' lessons on love became most clear. When he learned that his friend Lazarus had died, Jesus wept and then journeyed to the tomb and brought Lazarus back to life (Jn 11:43-44). When Peter, for fear of his life, denied knowing him, Jesus forgave his friend. When he was condemned to death and hung on a cross, he cried out, "Father, forgive them; for they do not know what they are doing" (Lk 23:34). And when, upon being raised from the dead, he appeared to his friends only to be doubted by Thomas, Jesus lovingly said, "Put your finger here and see my hands. Reach out your hand and put it in my side. Do not doubt but believe" (Jn 20:27).

A key message of scripture and the Christian tradition is "Do not doubt but believe in the power of community and friendship." In the giving and taking of friendship, we connect with others not for reward but for love. We call each other from our self-made graves. We acknowledge that we cannot go it alone and are set free to accept God's gracious friendship and share it with the world.

During every presidential race we get barraged with lofty promises of a "better America" in which families, neighborhoods, schools, civic institutions, and society at large can flourish. Candidates vow to uphold the timeless American ideal of securing for individuals their God-given rights to life, liberty, and the pursuit of happiness *in the context of* building stronger communities and serving the common good.

Yet in many ways, it is becoming increasingly harder for politicians —let alone parents, employers, teachers, or leaders—to honor the two-fold promise of a better life for individuals and society as a whole. America is consumed by a consumerism that seduces individuals into a get-while-the-getting-is-good mentality. Rather than being a nation of citizens accountable to one another and the common good, we are in many ways a nation of consumers accountable to our personal desires and wants. With the breakdown of the family, of loyalty between employers and employees, of the welfare and social security systems, of safe schools, of accessible health care, individualism reigns free: "Life is tough enough," we argue. "Why not get what we can and guard it at all costs?" And when we are left feeling isolated and empty at the end of the day, statistics show that we consume more alcohol, drugs, and anti-depressants than at any other time in our country's history.

The truth is, there can be no community, no common good, until we reassess our values and learn to reach out beyond ourselves, join with others, and commit ourselves to serving one another and those less fortunate.

Throughout recent presidential races the candidates have acknowledged the difficulty in encouraging and empowering people and subsequently have referenced the importance of faith and religious institutions in the battle against isolation for the sake of community. It goes without saying that religious institutions are not perfect; in fact, they are far from it. But there is something instructive here: faith really matters, faith really makes a difference.

One of the primary keys to understanding the Catholic Christian tradition is recognizing that it is a religion of discipleship and community. Catholicism calls people to follow Jesus, which means being open to letting go of those things that get in the way of our forming a relationship with God, being integrated and whole people, living in solidarity with others and all of creation, and receiving and giving hope and joy and love. The *Catechism of the Catholic Church*, itself a national bestseller upon its release in 1994, offers a helpful explanation: "The human person needs to live in society. Society is not an extraneous addition but a requirement of human nature. Through the exchange with others, mutual service and dialogue...humans develop their potential [and] thus respond to their vocation [to show forth the image of God]."[2]

Rooted in revelation and scripture, Catholicism is a call to love.

It sounds easy, doesn't it? But we know that love is one of the most difficult things we can do. Whereas cynicism, negativity, hatred, prejudice, apathy, and selfishness close us in on ourselves, love pushes us outward and challenges us to see the sacred that lies deep within everyone and everything. Jesus himself well understood how hard it is for people to love, so he showed us what it looks like to live a life of love and he commanded his disciples to follow his example: "I give you a new commandment, that you love one another. Just as I have loved you, you also should love one another. By this everyone will know that you are my disciples, if you have love for one another" (Jn 13:34-35). Where the Golden Rule challenges us to love our neighbors as ourselves, Jesus challenges us to go further and love others as he loves us.

A crucial component of the Catholic tradition, then, is its emphasis on social justice. James teaches us that "faith without works is dead" (2:26). And the Church teaches us that the work of love is respecting the dignity of the human person, serving the common good, honoring and defending people's right to live quality lives, putting the needs of the poor first, doing our work to the best of our ability while making an honest living, and building community that empowers people to attain their full human potential.

None of these aspects of church teaching are easy. But—no matter what age we are—if we work to close the gap between "us" and "them";

if we strive to love our families, our co-workers, the people we encounter everyday, and the marginalized and dispossessed we see and do not see; and if we tap into the spiritual richness of our tradition, then we move away from being isolated individuals and toward being part of a community of citizens who serve the common good and bear witness as disciples who truly love one another and the world.

19

Catholic Social Teaching
The Church's "Best Kept Secret"

According to recent surveys, when we young adult Catholics talk about what we see as the core of our faith tradition, we list the sacraments, devotion to Mary, and charitable efforts toward helping the poor.[1] Yet, many of us are unaware of the Church's teachings in these areas, especially when it comes to the progressive tradition of Catholic social justice.

For all the twists and turns my own journey of faith has taken, I have never questioned the call of the Bible and Christian tradition to love and serve others. The times when I help another in need or receive someone else's care in my need are the times faith most makes sense, when it is relevant, when it lives and breathes. The more I have mined the Catholic tradition for its pearls of wisdom, models of faith, integrated approach to spirituality, and testaments to the power of love, the more I have been surprised and energized by its emphasis on social justice.

In recent years the rich heritage of Catholic social teaching has been referred to as the Church's "best kept secret." There are several reasons the Church's social teachings are not very well known. First, the key documents rarely make their way into the hands of everyday believers. Starting with Pope Leo XIII's 1891 encyclical *Rerum Novarum* (The Condition of Labor) through the Second Vatican Council's 1965 *Gaudium et Spes* (Pastoral Constitution on the Church in the Modern World) to John Paul II's 1991 encyclical *Centesimus Annus* (On the Hundredth Anniversary of *Rerum Novarum*), the Church's major documents of social teaching have not been very well disseminated to lay people, and in some cases even to clergy, pastors, and lay leaders. Second, even when we do come across these documents through our parishes or the Vatican website, we find them long, abstract, and even boring. Third, some have even commented that the documents are too challenging and idealistic in the way they call Christians to analyze and critique every economic, political, and social structure in light of the gospels. Fourth, long before Catholics, especially immigrants, held positions of prominence in our culture, they focused on assimilating into the American way of life. Not wanting to appear too tied to Rome or the pope's authority, immigrants bought into the American dream of pulling themselves up by their bootstraps and becoming successful. As Catholics gained prominence in our culture, they did not have a strong sense of the social tradition that, in many cases, had helped them reach their goals.

The point is that we often know the fruit of the Church's labors without recognizing the Church as the laborer acting on behalf of the good of all. Many of our modern social institutions and practices that promote the common good of society, for example, have become so commonplace that we simply overlook their religious roots. But it is true that hospitals, health care providers, labor unions, group insurance policies, schools, social service agencies, and nursing sprang from the work of the churches in previous centuries. And the Church continues to have a significant impact on the shape of these activities and professions as well as various social movements for justice, civil rights, and a more humane world.[2] Though many people across the world are recognizing the rich tradition of Catholic social teaching, part of the mission of Catholics today is to learn and share the "secret" as well as to find new ways of serving the common good of humanity.

Like the call of discipleship, the foundation for social justice is rooted in scripture. The Book of Genesis, for example, affirms that (1) God made all people in his image and likeness and in seeing creation as good gave us all equal dignity and rights; (2) the earth and everything in it belong equally to everyone as gifts that we are to care for and preserve for new generations; (3) all human beings, equally, are co-responsible with God in helping to protect the dignity of everybody and everything; and (4) the physical earth itself must be respected in and of itself and not just as a stage for human activity. These affirmations are the basis for all subsequent moral teaching regarding the social order.[3]

The scriptures also make it clear that if we wish to find God, we must seek among the poor. Jesus takes this one step further and says that our very salvation depends on how we treat the least among us:

When the Son of Man comes in his glory, and all the angels with him, then he will sit on the throne of his glory. All the nations will be gathered before him, and he will separate people one from another as a shepherd separates the sheep from the goats, and he will put the sheep at his right hand and the goats at the left. Then the king will say to those at his right hand, "Come, you that are blessed by my Father, inherit the kingdom prepared for you from the foundation of the world; for I was hungry and you gave me food, I was thirsty and you gave me something to drink, I was a stranger and you welcomed me, I was naked and you gave me clothing, I was sick and you took care of me, I was in prison and you visited me." Then the righteous will answer him, "Lord, when was it that we saw you hungry and gave you food, or thirsty and gave you something to drink? And when was it that we saw you a stranger and welcomed you, or naked and gave you clothing? And when was it that we saw you sick or in prison and visited you?" And the king will answer them, "Truly I tell you, just as you did it to one of the least of these who are members of my family, you did it to me." (Mt 25:31-40)

But knowing what the scriptures teach us and acting on them are two entirely different things. The tradition of Catholic social teaching, therefore, provides a framework for action among people who seek to connect love of neighbor with love of God. At the same time, it also welcomes opportunities to involve people of other faiths and no faith at all in the common mission of serving those in need.

At its base, Catholic social teaching works to both inspire individuals to charity and promote justice at a systemic level. While the church of the past emphasized the need for believers to help those in need, the contemporary church works to align social structures such as civil law and governmental budget priorities with the needs of the people. Through the work of the National Conference of Catholic Bishops (NCCB) in Washington, D.C., for example, the Church lobbies members of Congress and the executive branch of government. Through the Catholic Campaign for Human Development (CCHD), the Church has served education and self-help programs since 1969. And through scores of other institutions such as Catholic Charities, the Saint Vincent DePaul Society, Catholic Relief Services, Caritas International, the Jesuit Volunteer Corps, and Holy Cross Associates, the Church seeks to help wherever there is a need.

The modern church, then, is committed to both charity and justice through individuals and institutions. While it does not control the social order, the Church offers a vision of an ideal world where virtues, love, and compassion reign. Through the tenets and actions of Catholic social teaching, the Church negotiates a delicate balance between "the hope that lies in human history and the hope that lies in the Kingdom of God."[4] By navigating between an exclusively other-worldly approach and an exclusively this-worldly approach, the Church works to make life on earth more humane while keeping its eye on the promise of heaven.

Over the past century or so Catholic social teaching has come a long way primarily through papal encyclicals, statements of Vatican offices and commissions, church councils, and episcopal conferences of bishops. It has also been developed through the work of lay women and men who interpret the scriptures and tradition in their daily lives. People such as Mother Teresa, Dorothy Day, Cesar Chavez, Daniel and Philip Berrigan, John Dear, Oscar Romero, Sister Helen Prejean, and many others show us what it looks like to serve the cause of peace and justice in the world and have both drawn from and challenged the wider tradition of social service.

While it is beyond the scope of this book to offer a comprehensive examination of the development and essence of Catholic social teaching, it may be useful to offer a brief overview of the tradition to help reveal the secret and, hopefully, spark new ways of relating to the Church and serving the world for our generation. In his book *Living Justice: Catholic Social Teaching in Action*, Catholic ethicist Thomas Massaro, S.J., has identified the following nine key themes as essential elements of Catholic social teaching:

1. The dignity of every person and human rights. Because scripture teaches that all human beings are created in the image and likeness of God, the Church upholds the sanctity, equality, and infinite value of every life and opposes all threats to human dignity, including abortion, euthanasia, and capital punishment. The late Cardinal Joseph Bernardin called for "a consistent ethic of life" that respects the sanctity of life at every moment of its duration, from conception to natural death.

2. Solidarity, common good, and participation. Because humans are social in nature, the Church places rights in the context of solidarity and concern for the well-being of the wider community. In other words, rights come with duties: "All things that persons have rightful claims to are necessarily matched with the things these same persons are expected to give back to others who depend upon them."[5] When we serve the common good through mutual participation in the ideals, values, and actions of justice, we work not only for our personal benefit, but for the benefit of all.

3. Family life. The family is a microcosm of society at large; it is where people teach and learn about love, human dignity, rights, and duty. Church documents sometimes refer to the family as the "domestic church" because it is where young people first encounter God, form their consciences, and learn moral virtues. For these reasons, Catholic social teaching works to protect and nurture families through the people who comprise them and the societies in which they dwell.

4. Subsidiarity and the proper role of government. *Subsidiarity* comes from the Latin word for "assistance" and refers to "the way various levels of society should relate to each other and assist one another in bringing about the best outcomes for all people."[6] Generally speaking, Catholic social teaching instructs people to rely as much as possible on those solutions that are closest to them and permit the maximum participation of citizens in shaping their own societies. But, for example, it also recognizes that local and federal government are needed to help solve certain problems.

5. Property ownership in modern society: rights and responsibilities. In light of its teachings about the common good, Catholic social teaching recognizes the benefits of individual ownership—which not only encourages the most efficient and the most orderly manner of property arrangement but also gives people an incentive to be productive and to care for the good that God has created—while putting limits on the acquisition of goods. In essence, we cannot disregard the needs of the less fortunate, use our property in ways that harm them, or exclude them from full participation in society.

6. The dignity of work, rights of workers, and support for labor unions. In Catholic social teaching, labor is portrayed as "neither a necessary evil nor merely a means to the end of supporting family life; rather, labor is presented as something that is intrinsically good for us.

In our work, we can discover rich meaning and develop our potential"[7] such as using our talents and collaborating with others. Theologically speaking, work invites us to become co-creators with God of the material world, which is why workers have rights and, through such organization as labor unions, must protect themselves from being undervalued, abused, or taken for granted.

7. Colonialism and economic development. One of the major topics of Catholic social teaching in the past fifty years has been the legacy of colonialism (where countries maintain foreign colonies, especially for economic exploitation) and the challenge of economic development in the poorest parts of the world. The Church repeatedly reminds us that we have a moral obligation to address world poverty, as all people are part of the human family. It also challenges us to work toward alleviating poverty and underdevelopment through our own behaviors (such as limiting what we buy, not purchasing products produced by child labor) as well as through advocating for government actions (such as international economic aid, health care and education aid, and redistribution of food and tools). The slogan "Think globally, act locally" applies here.

8. Peace and disarmament. While the just war theory that in certain circumstances force is an appropriate response to unjust aggressors has prevailed, there has been much talk about active nonviolence. The gospel message of peace prompts us all to join people like Dorothy Day and the Catholic Worker movement as well as the Berrigan brothers and the Plowshares movement in not only refusing to bear arms but also working toward global disarmament and peace.

9. Option for the poor and vulnerable. Not until recently have papal encyclicals referred to the "preferential option for the poor," but the idea has been a longstanding component of Catholic social teaching. At base, Catholics maintain that we must place the concerns of the most vulnerable members of society among our top priorities, thus making a conscious decision to tend to the material and spiritual needs of the less fortunate.

While these briefly stated themes of Catholic social teaching hardly do justice to the tradition, they do tie in with our generation's hunger to do good in the world. Like other generations, ours seeks individuals and institutions who move beyond idle rhetoric and provide authentic witness to the power of love, solidarity, and the common good. Catholic social teaching helps us imagine a world dedicated to peace and justice. There is no question that, as an institution itself, the Church has to face its own internal issues of equality and justice. But that does not prevent the Church from providing a context and structure for inspiring and helping us use our gifts and energies to help those in need. If we remember that *we* are the Church, then we see more clearly that it is up to us to create a healthy, vibrant witness to the power of love, solidarity, and the common good.

And when we doubt what we as individuals can do, it is helpful to remember the words of Nelson Mandela:

> Our deepest fear is not that we are inadequate. Our deepest fear is that we are powerful beyond measure. It is our light, not our darkness, that frightens us.... We are all meant to shine. ...It's not just some of us: it's in everyone. And as we let our own light shine, we unconsciously give other people permission to do the same. As we are liberated from our own fear, our presence automatically liberates others.

Now imagine what a community of such empowered individuals can accomplish! At its best, the Church is such a community.

Ten years ago, my father and stepmother adopted a biracial baby boy, whom they named Trevor. Three years later they adopted a biracial baby girl, whom they named Emily. From the moment each of these beautiful children entered our family, there has been no question that they are loved equally if not more than any of the rest of us. Though we have long since made our own way in the world and are many years older than Trevor and Emily, Josh and I embrace them as our siblings and revel in showing our love as they grow into their own fine people.

When Trevor first came into our lives I was a sophomore in college and Josh was a senior in high school. We could not have been more surprised, or more delighted. The feelings doubled when Emily was adopted. For years we had heard my father talk about his desire to move out to the country so that Jill could run her publishing company and he could write, teach, and enjoy the peace. Now, it seemed that any move to the country would be anything but idyllic.

In 1991 my dad and Jill finally did purchase a sixteen-acre farm just south of South Bend—only they had modified their original vision to include building onto the hundred-year-old farmhouse and raising Trevor and Emily. At the time, one of the books my dad was teaching in a course at Notre Dame was *There Are No Children Here: The Story of Two Boys Growing Up in the Other America,* by Alex Kotlowitz. The haunting account of the life of a family in one of Chicago's housing projects got its name from a mother who told Kotlowitz that there were no children there because they had lost their innocence, security, safety and playfulness even before they had a chance to know these basic rights of childhood. The book touched my dad so deeply, especially in light of adopting Trevor and Emily and coming into contact with other adoptive and foster parents, teachers, therapists, and programs dedicated to helping kids in need, that he shared it with Jill. Together they decided to change their plans even more radically. They decided to found a program for disadvantaged kids.

Because of Kotlowitz's book, they named the program "There *Are* Children Here." Without pretending that they had, or have, all the answers to the problems outlined in the book and in the increasingly alarming statistics about child poverty and abuse today, they pledged to give kids a place to be kids. In one particularly striking scene in the book, Kotlowitz follows Pharoah, the younger of the two brothers featured, to a small island of grass amidst the sea of cement in the projects. As he watches Pharoah—a small, scared kid who stutters, struggles in school, and gets picked on by just about everybody—he notices that the child looks relaxed and is singing flawlessly to himself. When he asks Pharoah why he goes to the small patch of grass, the boy responds that it is the only place he feels free. My dad and Jill believed then as they do today that their land would provide inner-city kids with their own patches of grass to explore the world and themselves free from gunfire, drug dealing, violence, crime, and oppression.

There Are Children Here works primarily with disadvantaged children from the ages of four to eleven who come from agencies in Indiana and Chicago. But it also works with parents and some older kids. Its budget is based on grants and donations and its staff is almost entirely volunteers from colleges. What began as a seasonal camp has evolved over the past six years into a year-round program that features nine wooded acres with trails, a fire pit for storytelling, and ample stealth locations for hide-and-go-seek, a full-scale baseball field ("If you build it, they will come!"), a basketball court, a volleyball court, slides, jungle gyms, sandboxes, bike trails, picnic tables and grills, and hay and sleigh rides. It also has a clubhouse—with a huge fireplace—for telling stories, eating birthday cake, finger painting, playing computer games, watching movies, and napping. Recently, with the help of generous donors, the camp has added a new auditorium for blossoming perform- ing artists and a van to help transport kids who otherwise would not be able to play there. My dad's new favorite job is bus driver.

Last summer my dad went out in the van to get a group of kids for the day. When he pulled up to the camp, the children were so eager to hit the ground running that they barely waited for the van to stop. That is, all the children but one little girl. As the kids raced from the van with the energy only kids have, this little girl moped her way across the field. Jill had been observing the little girl and silently decided to dedi- cate herself to getting a smile from her. As it turned out, the child came from an abusive home and, though she undoubtedly enjoyed moments of freedom, she dreaded the end of the day when she would be sub- jected to the trauma of abuse.

As the kids got a hot game of kickball going, the little girl seemed less than interested. But she took her turn at the plate, kicked the ball, and made it to first. As she stopped on the plate she noticed that Jill was clapping and cheering. She looked around, as if to say, "You couldn't possibly be cheering for me. Nobody cheers for me." But it suddenly dawned on her that Jill was, indeed, cheering her on.

Jill's cheering and subtle gestures of love lasted throughout the day. And bit by bit the little girl seemed to perk up until she eventually smiled.

At the end of the day, in a moment Jill says she will never forget, the little girl said something that the greatest theologians and mystics have struggled to say for centuries. As the children got into the van the little girl ran over to Jill and asked her to take off the sunglasses she had been wearing throughout that bright, sunny day.

"Why?" Jill asked.

"Because," the girl said, "I want to see your eyes so that I can know you and remember you."

Jill took off her sunglasses and the tears welled up in her eyes as she and this little girl met eye to eye, soul to soul. After a hug, the little girl ran away and boarded the van. A fleeting moment of unsolicited love became a God moment that will last a lifetime for a little girl, a grown woman, and all who hear the story.

For who among us does not want to peer into another's eyes and know the bond of love? Who among us does not want to be surprised by someone's care, or surprise another with our care? And who among us does not want, one day, to enjoy the beatific vision of staring directly into God's eyes only to discover that we have been staring into them all along?

CONCLUSION

The Road to Emmaus:
A Challenge to Our Generation
and Those Who Minister to Us

Now on that same day two of them were going to a village called Emmaus, about seven miles from Jerusalem, and talking with each other about all these things that had happened. While they were talking and discussing, Jesus himself came near and went with them, but their eyes were kept from recognizing him. And he said to them, "What are you discussing with each other while you walk along?" They stood still, looking sad. Then one of them, whose name was Cleopas, answered him, "Are you the only stranger in Jerusalem who does not know the things that have taken place there in these days?" He asked them, "What things?" They replied, "The things about Jesus of Nazareth, who was a prophet mighty in deed and word before God and all the people, and how our chief priests and leaders handed him over to be condemned to death and crucified him. But we had hoped that he was the one to redeem Israel. Yes, and besides all this, it is now the third day since these things took place. Moreover, some women of our group astounded us. They were at the tomb early this morning, and when they did not find his body there, they came back and told us that they had indeed seen a vision of angels who said that he was alive. Some of those who were with us went to the tomb and found it just as the women had said; but they did not see him." Then he said to them, "Oh, how foolish you are, and how slow of heart to believe all that the prophets have declared! Was it not necessary that the Messiah should suffer these things and then enter into his glory?" Then beginning with Moses and all the prophets, he interpreted to them the things about himself in all the scriptures.

As they came near the village to which they were going, he walked ahead as if he were going on. But they urged him strongly, saying, "Stay with us, because it is almost evening and the day is now nearly over." So he went in to stay with them. When he was at the table with them, he took bread, blessed and broke it, and gave it to them. Then their eyes were opened, and they recognized him; and he vanished from their sight. They said to each other, "Were not our hearts burning within us while he was talking to us on the road, while he was opening the scriptures to us?" That same hour they got up and returned to Jerusalem; and they found the eleven and their companions gathered together. They were saying, "The Lord has risen indeed, and he has appeared to Simon!" Then they told what had happened on the road, and how he had been made known to them in the breaking of the bread. (Lk 24:13-35)

Throughout my faith journey I have wandered on and off the Catholic path only to return to it in my late twenties through conscious choice and God's grace. Though I have worked in Catholic publishing since graduating from college, it was not until I found a community of fellow seekers in an exciting parish that I felt energized enough by Catholicism to embrace it more fully. Now, as a graduate student in theology and as a young adult minister, I enjoy exploring both the Catholic tradition and the hearts and minds of a broad cross-section of our generation who hunger for spiritual wisdom. As more and more is being said *about* our generation, I grow increasingly interested in speaking *with* and *to* our peers and those who minister to us. My hope is to invite all to come and see the God moments that make life so special and meaningful and to realize that the Catholic tradition is a powerful lens through which to see God at work in our lives.

Many in our generation ask, "Does the Church have anything to offer me? If so, isn't it the case that if I don't buy into *everything* the Church teaches, I shouldn't even consider it?" At the same time, ministers often ask, "How can the Church, how can I, best reach young adults, especially those who do not seem to care about the Church?" In addition to what I have already said in this book, I have found Luke's story of Jesus' resurrection appearance to the two disciples on the road to Emmaus extremely helpful for me as both a young Catholic seeker and as a minister working with my peers.

At a time when I was doing a great deal of research and thinking about Luke's resurrection account, I attended a retreat in Chicago with forty of my peers. The speaker we brought in was Lou Nanni, a thirty-something young adult who, after graduating from Notre Dame, had spent ten years working as executive director of the Center for the Homeless in South Bend, Indiana. Among his many accomplishments as a leader in social work, Lou had helped found and develop the Center into a nationally recognized organization that is setting the standard for addressing the problems of homelessness on many levels. Throughout his presentation on the call of young people to be leaders and to make a positive difference in the world, Lou referred to the lessons of Luke's Emmaus story. I owe Lou a deep debt of gratitude for his insights during that retreat and for helping me to shape my thinking around applying the Emmaus story to the dialogue between young adults in search of belief and Catholic ministers in search of sharing the faith.

Above all, Luke's story shows us that faith and ministry are part of a process, a journey. Jesus joins the dejected disciples as they walk away from Jerusalem and gradually helps them understand the scriptures, recognize him, and begin their own evangelization. For those in the so-called Generation X—especially the lapsed, marginal, or disillusioned—and those who minister to us, Jesus teaches us five actions that lead to fuller faith and more effective ministry: walking with, listening to, talking with, breaking bread with, and empowering.

Walking With

We young adults are very much like the disciples in Luke's story. We walk and talk with each other about our lives, our struggles, and our quests for meaning, but we do not always see just how near to us God really is. And, like the disciples who turn their backs on Jerusalem and walk toward what many scholars believe is an imaginary town called Emmaus, we sometimes turn away from what we do not understand and walk out on the road to nowhere.

A disillusioned peer once said to me, "I have trouble with the Church. It seems ministers believe it's their way or the highway, or they just don't know how to reach us." Around that time, a frustrated priest said to me, "I just don't get young people today. I don't know who they are or what they want. And I refuse to pander to them. The gospel and the tradition speak for themselves, and sooner or later people have to realize that faith is not like ordering coffee at Starbucks—you can't have any flavor you want!" Another time a lay minister shared with me her failed attempts at reaching young adults: "I browse through the Internet and watch some of the popular television shows and movies, but on the rare occasions when I am around young people, I don't seem to connect, especially when it comes to faith and the Church."

These snippets of conversation miss something essential: it is crucial for young adults and ministers to walk with each other, even if we do so as silent strangers. Jesus did not presume anything about the two Emmaus disciples or rush to tell them who he was. Instead, he put himself in their midst and experienced what they experienced, all the way down to the dirt beneath their feet. At the same time, the disciples did not reject the stranger who joined them at the worst time in their lives. They simply kept walking and talking.

Listening To

Mark Twain once remarked that we have two ears and one mouth and should use them in proportion. Primary among the challenges of being a discerning young adult and a good minister is being a good listener— one who truly *hears*, one who is skilled enough to read and interpret what people are expressing verbally and nonverbally.

The good news is that our generation is willing, even hungry, to talk—so much so that we often make use of the acronym TMI ("too much information") when our peers tell us more about their personal lives than we want to know.

Like the dejected disciples walking toward Emmaus, many of us are trying to make sense of our fractured lives. Some of us even stop dead in our tracks out of sadness and despair.

Like Jesus, ministers have the tremendous obligation and opportunity to share God's love.

In his beautiful book *Becoming Human*, Jean Vanier, the founder of l'Arche community that serves the mentally challenged, relates how years of experience have taught him that true listening is a profound act of love. Listening tells another, "*You* are important. Your whole being, your experiences, your opinions, and your observations matter." Listening begins and ends in being present to another in mind, body, and spirit. It is the launching pad for dialogue, bonding, learning, community, and growth.

Listening is crucial in the interplay between those who seek and those who have found. To transform blindness into sight, despair into hope, confusion into commitment, young adults and ministers must listen as Jesus did—eagerly, patiently.

Talking With

Living amidst rapid social, moral, religious, and cultural changes, our generation is quite comfortable with pluralism and relativism.

Given that by and large we lack a religious vocabulary, we do not communicate our deeper yearnings the same way previous generations did. The good news for ministers is that, like the Emmaus disciples, we welcome meeting "strangers" from whom we can learn. Watching the movie *City of Angels*, our generation resonated with the love story of an angel (played by Nicolas Cage) and a human (played by Meg Ryan). Lyrics from the Goo Goo Dolls' single "Iris" off the soundtrack gave voice to our cry for encounters with deeper, transcendent meaning: "When everything's made to be broken, I just want you to know who I am" and "When everything feels like the movies, yeah, you bleed just to know you're alive."

Like Jesus, ministers must be true to themselves and offer authentic witness. Jesus does not worry that his words might offend or alienate but bluntly exclaims: "O foolish men, and slow of heart to believe all that the prophets have spoken!" Then he explains that scripture and faith find their meaning and fulfillment in an incarnate Messiah who suffers and is raised from the dead. The disciples still do not recognize the risen Jesus and his truth, but neither do they reject him for being piercingly honest.

As an undergraduate at Notre Dame, I became good friends with the rector of my dorm, Rev. Stephen Newton, C.S.C. Besides being a terrific preacher and celebrant at dorm Masses, Steve was a true friend, counselor, and spiritual director to many of the men in the dorm. While I remember several life-defining conversations with Steve during those days, none was more important than the night I told him that I had lost my faith in God after my friend Jay died.

In anger I told Steve that, to me, faith was an all-or-nothing proposition, and I had so many doubts because of Jay's death that I was opting for nothing. I had not gone to Mass in a long time and had stopped praying, and I had no intention of doing either ever again.

Steve paused a moment and said, "That's ridiculous and you know it! Faith is not 'all-or-nothing'; it's a *process*. Right now you've hit a wall and faith makes no sense because you are suffering a loss. And perhaps you don't go to Mass or pray regularly right now. That does not exclude you from the Church, and certainly not from God's love."

If anyone else had said these brutally honest words to me, I would have rejected them. But Steve had walked with and listened to me during that crucial time in my young life. He had earned my trust and allowed me to earn his. Never before had he been so blunt. And never before had I heard him so clearly.

Breaking Bread With

One of my favorite cookbooks opens with the line: "Nothing brings people together like a good meal."

Our generation understands this. When we move out on our own, even on slim budgets and in cramped studio apartments, we love to host parties. We might not have the right table, chairs, or dinnerware, but preparing a meal is a rite of passage. And we know that the food and ambiance are not as important as what they give rise to: people talking, laughing, and enjoying each other's company.

Like the Emmaus disciples, we young adults are open to table fellowship with those we do not yet know. We revel in diversity, and welcoming the stranger—often a friend of a friend—to the table is a chance to meet someone new, hear fresh stories, and widen familiar circles. And though it may not be explicit or comfortable, we sense the sacredness of the meal and even God's presence in the table fellowship.

At a recent party of twenty-somethings, an agnostic friend paused before the meal and said half-jokingly, "Isn't anyone going to say a prayer before we eat?" Everyone laughed. Then there was a moment of silence as if the idea were not half bad. We put my friend on the spot, and rather earnestly he offered: "Hello God, it's me, Rob. It's been a long time since you last heard from me, but I just wanted to say thanks for bringing us all together and for the food we are about to eat. Well, until next time..."

Jesus treated every meal as a sacred event. For the Emmaus disciples, the meal provided a pivotal moment: it allowed them the chance to
welcome and come to know the stranger. At the meal Jesus the guest becomes Jesus the host, blessing and breaking the bread. And it is in the
breaking of the bread that the disciples finally recognize the risen Christ.

James Gingerich, a doctor from the University of Chicago, tells a
story about the power of table fellowship. Dr. Gingerich once had as a
patient a young pregnant Mexican woman. With her husband and two
children, she had entered the United States illegally. When she needed
medical care to properly deliver her baby, Dr. Gingerich worked hard
to get her emergency Medicaid.

Shortly thereafter, the woman developed gallbladder trouble and
needed surgery. But she and her husband, who worked two part-time
jobs, were barely able to feed and clothe their children. They had no insurance. Eventually she was admitted to the hospital as an emergency
case.

Following successful surgery the woman was faced with bills she
could not pay. Dr. Gingerich wrote to each of the doctors involved—
the surgeon, radiologist, and anesthesiologist—to ask if they could help
the family pay off its debt. One doctor offered to give $10 in credit for
every dollar paid; the others simply canceled their bills.

To express their gratitude, the family saved their money for weeks
and invited the hospital administrators and their spouses to a Mexican
feast held at Dr. Gingerich's center. The family spent days preparing,
and then hosted their high-paid, well-educated guests. As the feast went
on, the lines between doctors and patient, donor and recipient disappeared, and all that remained were people, speaking in English and
Spanish, enjoying a meal together. In Dr. Gingerich's words, "It was a
foretaste of the Great Banquet to which we are all invited."

Empowering

In his August 1999 *Atlantic Monthly* cover story, "A Politics for Generation X," Ted Halstead, thirty and the president and CEO of New
America Foundation, summarizes the alarming findings of recent surveys about our generation: we are less politically engaged, exhibit less
social trust or confidence in government, have a weaker allegiance to
our country or to political parties, and are more materialistic than our
predecessors.

Some blame television, others the government-bashing of the Reagan-Bush eras, still others the breakdown of the traditional family. But could it be the case, Halstead asks, that we Generation Xers are merely reacting to our world as we perceive it? Coming of age at a time of falling wages, shrinking benefits, downsizing, environmental crises, loss of civility, and growing economic inequality combined with what we see as a lack of leadership on issues that most affect our generation has left us jaded and disengaged.

The big question now is, Will there come a time when we tire of griping and band together to make a difference?

It has been well documented that we are tired of rhetoric and are committed to service. The *New York Times* reported on July 11, 1999, for example, that "despite low prestige and pay," the number of young adults interested in teaching is at a thirty-year high. Young people, the article explains, seek meaningful work, are concerned about the plight of at-risk children, and want to improve the overall quality of education. We turn out in droves to help build homes, clean up neighborhoods, serve food to the poor, tutor inner-city children.

Following Jesus' example, community leaders, politicians, and ministers can reach out and empower young people to make a difference. Jesus subtly let the disciples take the initiative to invite him to stay with them; after he revealed himself, he vanished and left them to make up their minds as to how they would handle the good news. And they wasted no time in racing back to Jerusalem to tell the others what had happened.

As I have said, one of the most transformative experiences in my life was working closely with Cardinal Bernardin on his book *The Gift of Peace* in the final months of his life. This holy and gifted man shaped my understanding of what it means to be empowered and to empower. In working with him, I felt myself bloom professionally, personally, and spiritually. His trust and confidence challenged me to work harder and more efficiently than I ever had before. His witness and faith made me nurture my relationship with God. His service to those in need opened my eyes to what it means to be an instrument in God's hands. His humility helped me understand how better to close the gap between who I am and who God calls me to be.

When the Cardinal died on November 14, 1996, I wished I had had more time to know him, to ask him questions, to talk about faith and peace and justice. I miss him. But throughout our brief friendship, Cardinal Bernardin prepared me, indeed empowered me, to continue developing my relationship with God, to make a difference in the world, and to empower others—especially my peers.

The interaction between our generation and the Church is its own special relationship. But by following Jesus' example, we—young adults and those who minister to us—become more open to one another and the larger quest for meaning, freedom, peace, and happiness. The teaching church becomes the listening church made up of people of all ages from all generations and backgrounds. The truth is that we, today's young adults, are the Church, here and now. We are also the leaders who will pass on the faith to the generations that follow us as well as to our own children.

My hope and prayer is that we will all come to see that Jesus walks as closely with us as he did with the disciples on the road to Emmaus. By walking with, listening to, talking with, breaking bread with, and empowering each other we catch God moments as they happen and realize why and how faith really matters. We let go of what is not essential and embrace what is essential. And we walk farther along the path that leads to peace, freedom, happiness, and love.[1]

ACKNOWLEDGMENTS

Writing this book has been an extended God moment. In many ways, I have been creating it my whole life. But it was not until the past five years when I began speaking to audiences of young adults, working in young adult ministry, and writing articles here and there that my own faith and the contents herein took shape. Having this opportunity to capture something of the journey of being a young adult Catholic and the gift of the God moments that have happened along the way set my mind afire. As I snuck away for long weekends, stayed up until my eyes ached, used my shower and exercise and drive time to think, and jotted down thoughts on scraps of paper in between all else, I experienced God moments as I wrote about them. A writer friend of mine wisely remarked, "The reward is in the writing, not in the having written." I could not agree more. And so I offer you these words not so much as a finished book but as thoughts in motion, as God moments.

This being a book about community, I would like to thank some of the key people whose friendship, love, encouragement, challenges, and insights have taught me and helped me on my pilgrim way.

Deep thanks to Liz, who has journeyed with me through thick and thin for four years, helped me immeasurably in writing this book (especially the sections on social justice), and who said yes to my proposal of marriage as this book was being finished—giving me the greatest of all God moments and the promise of many more to come! And to my family, Margaret, Jim, Jill, Josh, Trevor, and Emily for their love, faith, support, humor, and understanding.

To Cardinal Joseph Bernardin for his gifts of trust, faith, and peace, and to his close friends who have deeply touched my life, especially Monsignor Kenneth Velo and Bishop Raymond Goedert. A special thanks to John H. White, the "picture man," and Al Spilly, C.PP.S. (and mother Spilly) for being such true friends and wonderful collaborators, and to the Bernardin Center at Catholic Theological Union, especially Bob Schreiter, C.PP.S., Barbara Bowe, R.S.C.J., John Pawlikowski, O.S.M., and Don Senior, C.P.

To Fr. John Cusick, Kate DeVries and the fine staff of the Young Adult Ministry Office of the Archdiocese of Chicago; Al Gustafson and staff and board of The Crossroad Center for Faith and Work; Bob Condor, Mary Beth Sammons, Robyn Johnson, and the staff of *The Works* magazine; Fr. Jack Wall and the young leaders of Old Saint Patrick's Church; and Fr. Pat Brennan and the Journeys ministry at Holy Family for teaching me and allowing me to teach.

To Mike Leach, one of the best in religious publishing, for believing in me and for inviting me to write this book in the first place. To Robert Ellsberg, who, with Mike, treated me with a care, grace, and honesty I will never forget and who dramatically improved this text. And to Kathy Kikkert for her beautiful cover design and the Orbis staff for copyediting, producing, and promoting this book.

To my colleagues at Sheed & Ward for their professionalism and friendship—Steve Hrycyniak, Kass Dotterweich, Chris Schmidt, Debbie Krejci, Nathan Bubenzer, Madonna Gauding, Judy and Scott Wannemuehler, Kathy Kikkert, and Robin Booth.

To Rev. Stephen Newton, C.S.C., who has been a close friend and mentor since we met during my sophomore year at Notre Dame when he became rector of our dorm, Sorin Hall. And to my Sorin brothers— especially, Andy Pauline, Terrence Murphy, Jay Kelly, Andy Cavallari, Dan Reidy, Pete Flemming, Mike Hudson, Bill Nichols, and Tom Gerth. Our friendships have made all the difference

To the Kelly family for welcoming me into their family; Bob Ludwig for his theological insights and friendship; Megan McKenna for her witness and wisdom; Tom Beaudoin for his work with Generation X, countless helpful conversations, and endless encouragement; Bill Cadigan for being such a good friend and for all the laughs and insights; and Michelle and Karl Clifton-Soderstrom and Dave Collins, S.J., for many rich discussions and fun times.

To Ed Schmidt, S.J., for always being there and for many journeys into far-away lands both geographical and metaphorical. And finally to James Martin, S.J., for introducing me to Liz and being such a good coach and friend.

NOTES

Prologue

1. This meditation originally appeared in "Odyssey of a Young Adult Catholic," *New Theology Review* 11, no. 1 (1998): 42–44.

PART ONE

1. *X* Marks What Spot?

1. Tom Beaudoin, *Virtual Faith: The Irreverent Spiritual Quest of Generation X* (San Francisco: Simon & Schuster, Jossey-Bass, 1998), 28.

2. Geoffrey T. Holtz, *Welcome to the Jungle: The Why Behind "Generation X"* (New York: St. Martin's Press, Griffen, 1995), 2.

3. Vann Wesson, *Generation X: Field Guide and Lexicon* (San Diego: Orion Media, 1997), iv.

4. Beaudoin, *Virtual Faith*, 27.

5. Douglas Coupland, *Generation X: Tales for an Accelerated Generation* (New York: St. Martin's Press, 1991).

6. Harvey Cox, foreword to *Virtual Faith*, by Beaudoin, ix.

7. Beaudoin, *Virtual Faith*, 27.

8. Melissa Shirk, *Sojourners* (November 1994), as cited in Robert Ludwig, *Reconstructing Catholicism for a New Generation* (New York: Crossroad, 1995), 16.

9. Margot Hornblower, "Great Xpectations," *Time* 149, no. 23 (June 9, 1997): 58.

2. Generation eX

1. William Strauss and Neil Howe, *The Fourth Turning: What the Cycles of History Tell Us About America's Next Rendezvous with Destiny* (New York: Bantam Doubleday Dell, Broadway Books, 1997), 146–47.

2. Ibid., 168.

3. Ibid., 190.

4. Ibid., 193.

5. David Brooks, *Bobos in Paradise: The New Upper Class and How They Got There* (New York: Simon & Schuster, 2000), 42.

6. Phyllis A. Tickle, *Re-Discovering the Sacred: Spirituality in America* (New York: Crossroad, 1995), 23.

7. Strauss and Howe, *The Fourth Turning*, 227.

8. Ibid., 224.

9. Ibid.

10. Holtz, *Welcome to the Jungle*, 2.

11. Ibid., 4.

12. Ibid., 26.

13. Ibid., 27.

14. Walter Kirn, "Should You Stay Together for the Sake of the Kids?" *Time* 156, no. 13 (September 25, 2000): 77.

15. Holtz, *Welcome to the Jungle*, 29.

16. Kirn, "Should You Stay Together," 76–78.

17. In Holtz, *Welcome to the Jungle*, 45.

18. From 1973 to 1982 appropriations to the poor were smaller and the number of poor children receiving them declined. In 1981 President Ronald Reagan slashed $1 billion off a total budget of $7 billion for assistance programs for impoverished families with dependent children. Over a six-year span benefits for children and families were slashed by more than $50 billion, meaning that over a million people lost their food stamps and 2 million kids were dropped from school lunch programs. From the early seventies to the early eighties other federal programs were cut back. For example, health care for the poor was decreased while those eligible for it increased. Federal housing support dropped from $32 billion to less than $10 billion, meaning that only one in three renting households below the poverty line were receiving housing aid by the early eighties. Even middle-income families faced increases in taxes, while the taxes for childless families remained steady through the seventies and eighties (ibid., 47–48).

19. As eXers entered high school, financing for schools across the country fell by more than 20 percent, which became obvious by 1983 when schools were literally falling apart and an estimated $25 billion was needed to help repair them (ibid., 110). And while teachers' salaries were being cut and the overall academic achievement of young students was slipping, the costs of going to college were soaring. As students had to work harder to afford college, it took them longer and therefore cost them more money to complete their degrees. By 1990 the average college undergraduate was taking more than six years to earn a degree (fewer than half graduated after four years of study) and spending 50 percent more than the already high price for education. Graduate studies take even more time and money (ibid., 124). Of course, college serves as preparation for getting a job. Yet, as eXers have entered the job market, there are far fewer jobs than were available to their predecessors at the same age. "Downsizing" has become such a bad word that corporations call layoffs and job freezes "right sizing." The net effect is the same, fewer jobs and less job security. The greatest casualties have been those without a college education who have faced a sharp decline in the manufacturing job market and have little or no prospect of winning a job over a college-educated worker (ibid., 149–50).

Generation eXers also face a divorce from the American dream of getting the most out of their peak earning years, becoming homeowners, and enjoying health care and Social Security benefits. According to Geoffrey Holtz, "It is an often quoted statistic that incomes have stagnated in the United States over the last two decades. What the statistics usually don't show, however, is that while *on average* incomes have been flat, this phenomenon has not affected all age groups equally. In the last two decades, the median household income of young adults has fallen more than 27 percent to a level lower than has been seen in more than thirty years. But over this period the incomes of all other age groups have *risen*—considerably, in the cases of the oldest Boomers and the elderly" (ibid., 158). While eXers' salaries and savings have not kept up with those of their predecessors, the cost of houses has skyrocketed. In 1940, 43.2 percent of all married couples lived in their own homes. By 1980 that figure had risen to 79 percent. But in that same year the trend started moving downward and has ever since. In the eighties the median age of first-time homebuyers rose from twenty-seven to thirty-five, due in part to the rising costs of houses and in part to the steep requirements for down payments. Given lower wages and higher taxes, nearly a quarter of those buying their first homes have needed financial assistance from parents or other relatives (ibid., 167–68). Many eXers who have been able to buy a home feel tied down by their investment as they work harder to meet their mortgage payments. And some projections indicate that in the long run they will not realize the same gains in equity that previous generations experienced. Since most Boomers have already bought their homes, the demand for houses is lower and therefore over the next twenty years the value of houses will decline, making it somewhat easier to buy a home but taking away much of the investment value (ibid., 170–71). Also, the financial safety nets their elders have come to count on in the form of Social Security may not exist by the time eXers are old enough to receive it. More eXers believe in UFOs than in Social Security.

3. Life at the Speed of Time

1. Daniel J. Boorstin, *The Discoverers: A History of Man's Search to Know His World and Himself* (New York: Random House, Vintage Books, 1985), 26–72.
2. Beaudoin, *Virtual Faith*, 22.
3. James Gleick, *Faster: The Acceleration of Just About Everything* (Random House, Pantheon, 1999), 9–10.

4. Our Spiritual Hungers

1. Harvey Cox, foreword to *Virtual Faith*, by Beaudoin, ix.
2. National Conference of Catholic Bishops Committee on the Laity, *Sons and Daughters of the Light* (Washington, D.C.: United States Catholic Conference, 1997), 7–15.
3. Beaudoin, *Virtual Faith*, 41–42.

PART TWO

5. The Art of Seeking

1. For a full discussion of the Galileo affair, see Jerome J. Langford, *Galileo, Science and the Church*, 3rd edition (Ann Arbor: University of Michigan Press, 1998).
2. Christopher F. Mooney, S.J., *Theology and Scientific Knowledge: Changing Models of God's Presence in the World* (Notre Dame: University of Notre Dame Press, 1996), 1.

7. "Spiritual but Not Religious"

1. Robert Barron, *And Now I See...A Theology of Transformation* (New York: Crossroad, 1998), 12–13.

2. Lawrence S. Cunningham and Keith J. Egan, *Christian Spirituality: Themes from the Tradition* (Mahwah, New Jersey: Paulist Press, 1996), 5.

3. Ibid., 6.

4. Ronald Rolheiser, *The Holy Longing: The Search for a Christian Spirituality* (New York: Doubleday, 1999), 6–7.

5. Ibid.

6. Cunningham and Egan, *Christian Spirituality*, 6.

7. Rolheiser, *The Holy Longing*, 21.

8. Ibid., 78

9. Ibid., 53.

10. Interview in *Publishers Weekly*, March 13, 1995.

11. Rolheiser, *The Holy Longing*, 134–140.

12. C. S. Lewis, *Mere Christianity* (New York: Macmillan, Collier Books, 1943), 11–12.

8. Catholicism: A Tradition of Seekers, Sacraments, and Imagination

1. Augustine, *Confessions* (I,1), translated by R. S. Pine-Coffin (New York: Penguin, 1961), 21.

2. Timothy Barton, "Celtic Revived: The Artistry of Thomas O'Shaughnessy," in *At the Crossroads: Old Saint Patrick's and the Chicago Irish*, edited by Ellen Skerrett (Chicago: Wild Onion Books, Loyola Press, 1997), 85–101.

3. Andrew Greeley, *The Catholic Imagination* (Berkeley: University of California Press, 2000), 1.

4. Andre Dubus, "Sacraments," in *Meditations from a Movable Chair* (New York: Random House, Knopf, 1998), 85–90.

5. Ibid.

9. Seeking the God Who Seeks Us

1. C. S. Lewis, *God in the Dock: Essays on Theology and Ethics*, edited by Walter Hooper (Grand Rapids, Michigan: William B. Eerdmans, 1970), 244.

2. James Martin, ed., *How Can I Find God? The Famous and the Not-So-Famous Consider the Quintessential Question* (Liguori, Missouri: Triumph Books, 1997), 5–7.

3. Ibid., 68–72.

4. Ibid., 151–152.

5. Ibid., 95–96.

6. Francis Thompson, *I Fled Him Down the Nights and Down the Days*, edited by John F. Quinn (Chicago: Loyola Press, 1970), 119.

10. Six Rules for the Road

1. Blaise Pascal, *Pensées* (199, H9), translated by A. J. Krailsheimer (New York: Penguin, 1966), 88.

2. Harrison Birtwhistle, "Composing Music to Seize Moments in Time," interview by Paul Griffiths, *New York Times*, 31 December 1997, B3.

3. C. S. Lewis, *The Four Loves* (New York: Harcourt Brace Jovanovich, Harvest, 1960), 92.

4. Lewis, *Mere Christianity*, 43.

5. *Catechism of the Catholic Church* (Vatican City: Libreria Editrice Vaticana, 1994), #1830–32.

6. As cited in Michael O'Neill McGrath, *Journey with Thérèse of Lisieux: Celebrating the Artist in Us All* (Franklin, Wisconsin: Sheed & Ward, 2001), 20.

7. Ibid., 16.

8. Ibid., 50.

PART THREE

Introduction

1. Mark Twain, *Life on the Mississippi* (New York: Oxford University Press, 1990), 38.

2. Ibid., 59.

3. Ibid., 63–64.

4. Lewis, *Mere Christianity*, 75.

11. The Great Invitation of Christianity

1. Barron, *And Now I See*, 1.

12. What Does It Mean to See?

1. Robert Ellsberg, *All Saints* (New York: Crossroad, 1997), 343.

2. Barron, *And Now I See*, 2.

3. Ibid., 3.

4. Ibid., 8–9.

14. Walking the Tightrope over the Abyss

1. William Shakespeare, *Macbeth* (V.v.15–28) in *The Riverside Shakespeare* (Boston: Houghton Mifflin, 1974), 1337.

2. Friedrich Nietzsche, *The Gay Science* (III, 125), translated by Walter Kaufman (New York: Random House, Vintage, 1974), 181.

3. Ibid.

4. Friedrich Nietzsche, *Thus Spoke Zarathustra*, translated by Walter Kaufman (New York: Penguin, 1954), 14–15.

5. Terry Anderson, *Den of Lions: Memoirs of Seven Years* (New York: Random House, Ballantine Books, 1993), 68.

6. Ibid., 88–89.

7. Ibid., 116–117.

8. Ibid., 117–118.

15. The Courage to Be . . . Fully Alive

1. Paul Tillich, *The Courage to Be* (New Haven, Connecticut: Yale, 1952), 156.
2. Ibid., 173.
3. Ibid., 166–167.
4. Ibid., 190.
5. Ibid., 188.
6. This meditation appeared in slightly different form as "The Courage to Be," *The Works* 2, no. 2 (winter 2000): 22.

16. Accepting God's Gift of Peace

1. Joseph Cardinal Bernardin, *The Gift of Peace* (Chicago: Loyola Press, 1997), 20.
2. Ibid., 29.
3. Ibid., 133.
4. John H. White, *The Final Journey of Joseph Cardinal Bernardin* (Chicago: Loyola Press, 1997), 19.
5. Ibid.
6. Bernardin, *Gift of Peace*, 152.
7. Joseph Cardinal Bernardin, *The Journey to Peace: Reflections on Faith, Embracing Suffering, and Finding New Life*, edited by Alphonse P. Spilly, C.PP.S., and Jeremy Langford (New York: Doubleday, 2001), 135.
8. Portions of "Accepting the Gift of Peace" originally appeared in *The Works* 1, no. 1 (fall 1999): 23–25.

Part Four

Introduction

1. Michele Mitchell, *A New Kind of Party Animal: How the Young Are Tearing Up the American Political Landscape* (New York: Simon & Schuster, 1998), 11–23.
2. Meredith Bagby, *Rational Exuberance: The Influence of Generation X on the New American Economy* (New York: Penguin, Dutton, 1998), xii.
3. Ibid., 55–58.
4. Ibid., 3.

17. The Call and Cost of Discipleship

1. Dietrich Bonhoeffer, *Dietrich Bonhoeffer: Witness to Jesus Christ*, edited by John de Gruchy (Minneapolis: Fortress Press, 1991), 158.
2. John Dear, *Jesus the Rebel: Bearer of God's Peace and Justice* (Franklin, Wisconsin: Sheed & Ward, 2000), 29.

18. Community and the Common Good

1. Dear, *Jesus the Rebel*, 193.
2. *Catechism*, #1878.

19. Catholic Social Teaching

1. William Dinges, et al., "A Faith Loosely Held: The Institutional Allegiance of Young Catholics," *Commonweal* (July 17, 1998): 13–18.

2. Thomas Massaro, *Living Justice: Catholic Social Teaching in Action* (Franklin, Wisconsin: Sheed & Ward, 2000), 14–15.

3. Rolheiser, *The Holy Longing*, 175.

4. Massaro, *Living Justice*, 46.

5. Ibid., 120.

6. Ibid., 128.

7. Ibid., 141.

Conclusion

1. "The Road to Emmaus: A Challenge to Our Generation and Those Who Minister to Us" originally appeared in slightly different form as "Ministering to Gen-X Catholics, Jesus Style," *America* 182, no. 14 (April 22, 2000): 6–10.

BIBLIOGRAPHY

Anderson, Terry. *Den of Lions: Memoirs of Seven Years*. New York: Random House, Ballantine Books, 1993.

Augustine. *Confessions*, trans. R. S. Pine-Coffin. New York: Penguin, 1961.

Bagby, Meredith. *Rational Exuberance: The Influence of Generation X on the New American Economy*. New York: Penguin, Dutton, 1998.

Barron, Robert. *And Now I See...A Theology of Transformation*. New York: Crossroad, 1998.

Barton, Timothy. "Celtic Revived: The Artistry of Thomas O'Shaughnessy." In *At the Crossroads: Old Saint Patrick's and the Chicago Irish*, ed. Ellen Skerrett. Chicago: Loyola Press, Wild Onion Books, 1997.

Beaudoin, Tom. *Virtual Faith: The Irreverent Spiritual Quest of Generation X*. San Francisco: Simon & Schuster, Jossey-Bass Publishers, 1998.

Bernardin, Joseph. *The Gift of Peace*. Chicago: Loyola Press, 1997.

———. *The Journey to Peace: Reflections on Faith, Embracing Suffering, and Finding New Life*, ed. Alphonse P. Spilly, C.PP.S., and Jeremy Langford. New York: Doubleday, 2001.

Bonhoeffer, Dietrich. *Dietrich Bonhoeffer: Witness to Jesus Christ*, ed. John de Gruchy. Minneapolis: Fortress Press, 1991.

Boorstin, Daniel J. *The Discoverers: A History of Man's Search to Know His World and Himself*. New York: Random House, Vintage Books, 1985.

———. *The Creators: A History of Heroes of the Imagination*. New York: Random House, Vintage Books, 1992.

———. *The Seekers: The Story of Man's Continuing Quest to Understand His World*. New York: Random House, Vintage Books, 1998.

Brooks, David. *Bobos in Paradise: The New Upper Class and How They Got There*. New York: Simon & Schuster, 2000.

Coupland, Douglas. *Generation X: Tales for an Accelerated Culture*. New York: St. Martin's Press, 1991.

———. *Life After God*. New York: Simon & Schuster, Pocket Books, 1994.

Cunningham, Lawrence S., and Keith J. Egan. *Christian Spirituality: Themes from the Tradition*. Mahwah, New Jersey: Paulist Press, 1996.

Dear, John. *Jesus the Rebel: Bearer of God's Peace and Justice*. Franklin, Wisconsin: Sheed & Ward, 2000.

Dubus, Andre. *Meditations from a Movable Chair*. New York: Random House, Knopf, 1998.

Eliot, T. S. *Four Quartets*. The Centenary Edition: 1888–1988. New York: Harvest/Harcourt Brace Jovanovich Publishers, 1988.

Frum, David. *How We Got Here, The 70's: The Decade That Brought You Modern Life—For Better or Worse*. New York: Basic Books, 2000.

Gleick, James. *Faster: The Acceleration of Just About Everything*. New York: Random House, Pantheon Books, 1999.

Greeley, Andrew. *The Catholic Imagination*. Berkeley: University of California Press, 2000.

Holtz, Geoffrey T. *Welcome to the Jungle: The Why Behind "Generation X."* New York: St. Martin's Press, Griffen, 1995.

Holy See. *Catechism of the Catholic Church*. Vatican City: Libreria Editrice Vaticana, 1994.

Hornblower, Margot. "Great Xpectations." *Time* 149, no. 23 (June 9, 1997): 58–63.

Kirn, Walter. "Should You Stay Together for the Sake of the Kids?" *Time* 156, no. 13 (September 25, 2000): 74–88.

Langford, Jeremy. "Odyssey of a Young Adult Catholic." *New Theology Review* 11, no. 1 (1998): 41–52.

———. "Welcome Generation X!?!" *Church* 14, no. 4 (1998): 13–18.

———. "Accepting the Gift of Peace." *The Works* 1, no. 1 (fall 1999): 23–25.

———. "The Courage to Be." *The Works* 2, no. 2 (winter 2000): 22.

———. "Ministering to Gen-X Catholics, Jesus Style." *America* 182, no. 14 (April 22, 2000): 6–10.

———. "Buying into Citizenship." *The Works* 2, no. 4 (summer 2000): 34–35.

———. "The Gospel of Friendship." *The Works* 2, no. 5 (fall 2000): 25.

———. "Faith-Filled Transitions." *The Works* 3, no. 1 (winter 2001): 23.

Langford, Jerome J. *Happy Are They: Living the Beatitudes in America*. Liguori, Missouri: Triumph Books, 1997.

———. *Galileo, Science and the Church*, 3rd edition. Ann Arbor: University of Michigan Press, 1998.

Lewis, C. S. *Mere Christianity*. New York: Macmillan, Collier Books, 1943.

———. *The Four Loves*. New York: Harcourt Brace Jovanovich, Harvest, 1960.

———. *God in the Dock: Essays on Theology and Ethics*, ed. Walter Hooper. Grand Rapids, Michigan: William B. Eerdmans Publishing Company, 1970.

Ludwig, Robert A. *Reconstructing Catholicism for a New Generation*. New York: Crossroad, 1995.

Martin, James, ed. *How Can I Find God? The Famous and the Not-So-Famous Consider the Quintessential Question*. Liguori, Missouri: Triumph Books, 1997.

Massaro, Thomas. *Living Justice: Catholic Social Teaching in Action*. Franklin, Wisconsin: Sheed & Ward, 2000.

McGrath, Michael O'Neill. *Journey with Thérèse of Lisieux: Celebrating the Artist in Us All*. Franklin, Wisconsin: Sheed & Ward, 2001.

Mitchell, Michele. *A New Kind of Party Animal: How the Young Are Tearing Up the American Political Landscape*. New York: Simon & Schuster, 1998.

Mooney, Christopher F. *Theology and Scientific Knowledge: Changing Models of God's Presence in the World*. Notre Dame: University of Notre Dame Press, 1996.

National Conference of Catholic Bishops Committee on the Laity. *Sons and Daughters of the Light*. Washington, D.C.: United States Catholic Conference, 1997.

Nietzsche, Friedrich. *Thus Spoke Zarathustra*, trans. Walter Kaufmann. New York: Penguin, 1954.

———. *The Gay Science*, trans. Walter Kaufmann. New York: Random House, Vintage, 1974.

Owen, Rob. *Gen X TV: The Brady Bunch to Melrose Place*. Syracuse, New York: Syracuse University Press, 1997.

Pascal, Blaise. *Pensées*, trans. A. J. Krailsheimer. New York: Penguin, 1966.

Peck, M. Scott. *The Road Less Traveled: A New Psychology of Love, Traditional Values and Spiritual Growth*. New York: Simon & Schuster, A Touchstone Book, 1978.

Putnam, Robert D. *Bowling Alone: The Collapse and Revival of American Community*. New York: Simon & Schuster, 2000.

Rilke, Rainer Maria. *Stories of God*, trans. M.D. Herter Norton. New York: W.W. Norton & Company, 1963.

Rolheiser, Ronald. *The Holy Longing: The Search for a Christian Spirituality*. New York: Doubleday, 1999.

Ryder, Andrew. *Following Christ: Models of Discipleship in the New Testament*. Franklin, Wisconsin: Sheed & Ward, 1999.

Strauss, William, and Neil Howe. *The Fourth Turning: What the Cycles of History Tell Us About America's Next Rendezvous with Destiny*. New York: Bantam Doubleday Dell Publishing Group, Broadway Books, 1997.

Thompson, Francis. *I Fled Him Down the Nights and Down the Days*, ed. John F. Quinn. Chicago: Loyola Press, 1970.

Tickle, Phyllis A. *Re-Discovering the Sacred: Spirituality in America*. New York: Crossroad, 1995.

———. *God-Talk in America*. New York: Crossroad, 1997.

Tillich, Paul. *The Courage to Be*. New Haven, Connecticut: Yale University Press, 1980.

Twain, Mark. *Life on the Mississippi*. The World's Classics. New York: Oxford University Press, 1990.

Vanier, Jean. *Becoming Human*. Mahwah, New Jersey: Paulist Press, 1998.

Wesson, Vann. *Generation X: Field Guide and Lexicon*. San Diego: Orion Media, 1997.

White, John H. *This Man Bernardin*. Chicago: Loyola Press, 1996.

———. *The Final Journey of Joseph Cardinal Bernardin*. Chicago: Loyola Press, 1997.

OF RELATED INTEREST

Winging It
Meditations of a Young Adult
Therese Johnson Borchard
ISBN, 1-57075-357-1, paperback
"Therese Borchard's fresh and original voice will resonate not only in the minds and hearts of other 'twenty-somethings' but in spiritual seekers of all ages."
— Teresa Rhodes McGee, author of *Ordinary Mysteries*

Why Not Be a Missioner?
Young Maryknollers Tell Their Stories
Michael Leach and Susan Perry, Editors
ISBN, 1-57075-391-1, paperback
Inspiring first person accounts of young men and women in their twenties and thirties who are serving God and neighbor in every corner of the earth.

The Basic Guide to Young Adult Ministry
John C. Cusick and Katherine DeVries, Editors
ISBN, 1-57075-392-X
Everything pastors and parish leaders need to know to attract those between twenty and thirty into the active life of the church.

Please support your local bookstore, or call 1-800-258-5838

For a free catalog, please write us at
Orbis Books, Box 308
Maryknoll, NY 10545-0308
or visit our website at www.orbisbooks.com

Thank you for reading *God Moments*. We hope you enjoyed it.